EXAM CRAM™

GRE®

Steven W. Dulan

Advantage Education

Que®

CERTIFICATION

GRE Exam Cram

Copyright © 2006 by Que Publishing

International Standard Book Number: 0-7897-3413-3

Library of Congress Catalog Card Number: 2005905948

Printed in the United States of America

First Printing: November 2005

08 07 06 05   4 3 2 1

Trademarks

All terms mentioned in this book that are known to be trademarks or service marks have been appropriately capitalized. Que Publishing cannot attest to the accuracy of this information. Use of a term in this book should not be regarded as affecting the validity of any trademark or service mark.

Warning and Disclaimer

Bulk Sales

Que Publishing offers excellent discounts on this book when ordered in quantity for bulk purchases or special sales. For more information, please contact

U.S. Corporate and Government Sales
1-800-382-3419
corpsales@pearsontechgroup.com

For sales outside the U.S., please contact

International Sales
international@pearsoned.com

Publisher
Paul Boger

Executive Editor
Jeff Riley

Acquisitions Editor
Carol Ackerman

Development Editor
Steve Rowe

Managing Editor
Charlotte Clapp

Project Editor
Mandie Frank

Copy Editor
Karen Annett

Indexer
Ken Johnson

Proofreader
Linda Seifert

Technical Editor
Michael Bellomo

Publishing Coordinator
Vanessa Evans

Multimedia Developer
Dan Scherf

Designer
Gary Adair

Page Layout
Toi Davis

About the Author

Steve Dulan has been involved with GRE preparation since 1989, when, as a former U.S. Army Infantry Sergeant, and undergraduate student at Michigan State University, Steve became a GRE instructor. He has been helping students to prepare for success on the GRE and other standardized exams ever since. Steve scored in the 99th percentile on every standardized test he has ever taken. After graduating from Michigan State, Steve attended The Thomas M. Cooley Law School on a full Honors Scholarship. While attending law school, Steve continued to teach standardized test prep classes (including ACT, SAT, PSAT, GRE, GMAT, and LSAT) an average of 30 hours each week, and tutored some of his fellow law students in a variety of subjects and in essay exam writing techniques. Professor Dulan has also served as an instructor at Baker University, Cleary University, Lansing Community College, The Ohio State University-Real Estate Institute, and The Thomas M. Cooley Law School. Guest lecturer credits include Michigan State University, University of Michigan, Detroit College of Law, Marquette University, Texas Technical University, University of Miami, and Wright State University.

Thousands of students have benefited from Steve's instruction, coaching, and admissions consulting, and have entered the graduate programs of their choice. Steve's students have gained admission to some of the most prestigious institutions of higher learning in the world, and have received numerous scholarships and fellowships of their own.

Since 1997, Steve has served as the president of Advantage Education (www.study-smart.com), a company dedicated to providing effective and affordable test prep education in a variety of settings, including one-on-one tutoring via the Internet worldwide using its Personal Distance Learning^{SM} system. The information and techniques included in this book are the result of Steve's experiences with test preparation students at all levels over the years.

About the Technical Editor

Michael Bellomo holds an MBA from UC Irvine, a Juris Doctor in Law from the University of California, San Francisco, and a Black Belt certification in Six Sigma project management.

He currently works with ARES Corporation, a project and risk management firm that works with the Department of Defense, NASA, and the Department of Energy. Since starting at ARES, he has worked on projects relating to the International Space Station and has been featured as the narrator for a multimedia presentation sent to Congress on the development of NASA's Orbital Space Plane.

Michael has written 15 books in various nonfiction fields, including technology, business operations, and graduate school prep.

Acknowledgments

I would like to acknowledge the contribution of the faculty and staff of Advantage Education. You are not only the smartest, but also the best. Special thanks to: Jennifer Kostamo, a quiet genius who almost always keeps her composure no matter how often she is rudely interrupted by me, and Pamela Chamberlain, our brilliant, versatile, and hard-working contributor/editor.

Thanks to Carol Ackerman of Que Publishing for her help throughout this project. Her good nature and positive attitude were greatly appreciated.

Most importantly, I would like to acknowledge the single biggest contributor to this work: my wife, colleague, co-author, editor, typist, employee, boss, and friend: Amy Dulan. None of this would have been possible without your hard work and dedication.

Contents at a Glance

Table of Contents

We Want to Hear from You!

As the reader of this book, *you* are our most important critic and commentator. We value your opinion and want to know what we're doing right, what we could do better, what areas you'd like to see us publish in, and any other words of wisdom you're willing to pass our way.

As an executive editor for Que Publishing, I welcome your comments. You can email or write me directly to let me know what you did or didn't like about this book—as well as what we can do to make our books better.

Please note that I cannot help you with technical problems related to the topic of this book. We do have a User Services group, however, where I will forward specific technical questions related to the book.

When you write, please be sure to include this book's title and author as well as your name, email address, and phone number. I will carefully review your comments and share them with the author and editors who worked on the book.

Email: feedback@quepublishing.com

Mail: Jeff Riley
            Executive Editor
            Que Publishing
            800 East 96th Street
            Indianapolis, IN 46240 USA

For more information about this book or another Que Certification title, visit our website at www.examcram2.com. Type the ISBN (excluding hyphens) or the title of a book in the Search field to find the page you're looking for.

Introduction: Getting Started

This book includes general information about the GRE General Test and chapters with specific information on each of the test sections, as well as paper versions of two simulated tests.

In an ideal situation, you will be reading this at least 3 to 4 weeks before you take the actual GRE General Test. If that is not the case, even just a few hours of study and practice can have a positive impact on your GRE score.

The practice exams found in this book are reasonably accurate simulations written by GRE experts. They contain basically the same mix of question types as a real GRE. If you work through all the material provided, you can rest assured that there won't be any surprises on test day. The biggest difference between these exams and your real GRE is the fact that these are paper exams and you will take your GRE using a computer. We've tried to mimic the computer exam as much as possible. But, you should definitely plan to do some practicing with POWERPREP®, the free software from the author of the GRE that is made available at www.gre.org. Generally, students tend to score a little better on each successive practice exam. But, GRE tests are sensitive to individual conditions, such as fatigue and stress. Therefore, the time of day that you take your practice exams, your environment, and other things that might be going on in your life can have an impact on your scores. Don't get worried if you see some score fluctuation because of a bad day or because the practice exam reveals weaknesses in your knowledge or skills. Simply use this information to help you improve.

In our experience, the students who see the largest increases in their scores are those who put in consistent effort over several weeks. Try to keep your frustration to a minimum if you are struggling. In addition, try to keep from becoming overconfident when everything is going your way.

What This Book Will Not Do

This book will not prepare you for the GRE Subject Tests. This book is not a substitute for regular textbooks or course work. It will not teach you everything you need to know about the subject matter tested on the GRE General Test. Although the GRE is primarily considered a skills-based test, you will be required to have a basic understanding of certain mathematical concepts and standard written English. This book introduces you to some of those concepts, but it does not provide an in-depth review.

The focus of this book is on helping you to maximize your GRE General Test score. Each chapter includes specific test-taking strategies, some content area review, and practice questions.

About the GRE General Test

The GRE General Test is required by most institutions and programs granting Masters or Doctorate degrees (Ph.D.). It is not required by all programs. More competitive programs generally have higher score requirements. Some programs also require Subject Tests, which are beyond the scope of this volume. The GRE General Test is a computer-based test in four sections, including an experimental section, called the "pretest" section, which will be mixed in with the other sections as you take your test. It will appear as either a Verbal or Quantitative section. There might also be a "research" section, which will always be the final section presented if you have one included in your test. The answers on the pretest and research sections will not count toward your GRE score. The questions are meant to help ETS (Educational Testing Service) refine their methods and try out new material that may be included in future GRE tests. The pretest is not identified. It will seem like just another test section as you work through it. So, you have to do your best on all sections. The research section, if you have one on your test, will be identified as such.

The whole testing process will take at least $3\frac{1}{2}$ hours, and might be a bit longer if you have a research section. The first section is always the Analytical Writing Section, which consists of two tasks: the Issue task and the Argument task. On the Issue task, you get to choose one of two topics on which to write. On the Argument task, you do not get a choice. There is only one argument presented and you must respond to it in writing using the word processor that is built in to the GRE software.

The basic time breakdown is as follows (note that all sections after Analytical Writing can appear in any order on your test):

Analytical Writing: Issue Task—45 minutes

                            Argument Task—30 minutes

Verbal Section: 30 Questions—30 minutes

Quantitative (Math) Section: 28 Questions—45 minutes

Pretest (experimental Verbal or Quantitative): Time and number of questions vary, but you will be told both as you begin the section.

Research: Time and number of questions vary. Your GRE might not include this section.

 Your GRE may include questions that are the same or similar to released GRE questions that appear on POWERPREP® or in official GRE publications, such as *Practicing to Take the General Test, 10th Edition* (ETS, 2002). Be very careful when responding to these questions because they might be slightly different from the questions that you may remember. There might be different facts in the stimuli and there might be different answer choices.

The GRE is a Computer Adaptive Test (CAT). The software starts you off with a medium-difficulty question and then adapts to you for the second and all subsequent questions. Essentially, the exam chooses an easier question, which is worth fewer points, if you get the first question wrong. If you get the first one right, the second question will be harder and worth more points, and so on. If you keep answering questions correctly, the software will continue to present questions that are in the more difficult range and your score will reflect that fact.

Because the computer program chooses questions based on your previous responses, you have to answer each question as it is presented before you are allowed to move on. You cannot skip around through the section, or change answers after you have left a question.

The questions are very well documented, in terms of their difficulty level, before they are included in your test. For this reason, GRE feels confident in assigning scores to students that can be compared to one another even though the students answered different questions on their respective tests. In fact, ETS reports that scores for students taking the computer-based test and the paper-based test are comparable to one another.

Our experience has shown that test takers need a bit of time to get used to answering the questions in order. Many test takers are used to other standardized tests, such as the ACT and SAT, which allow the test taker to skip around and come back to answer more difficult questions if time allows. As mentioned previously, the GRE General Test requires that you answer a question before you are allowed to move on to the next question. Therefore, we strongly recommend practicing with POWERPREP® before taking your actual GRE.

Although there is still a paper-based GRE test, it is generally not available to students within the United States. If you are going to be taking the GRE General Test outside the United States, visit the GRE website at www.gre.org for detailed information on test dates and locations.

Registering for the GRE General Test

You can register to take the GRE on the World Wide Web, by telephone, or by U.S. mail. You will schedule your GRE test on a first-come, first-served basis at a testing location near you. The test is offered throughout the year at many locations around the United States. The GRE is also given in many countries. The full list, and other registration details, can be found online at www.gre.org. You can register via telephone by calling 1-800-GRE-CALL (1-800-473-2255). Registrations sent by mail can take up to four weeks to process and can only be done by sending the appropriate forms, either printed from the GRE website or found in the GRE Bulletin. The latter is available at many college counseling offices.

After you register you will receive detailed information about your testing center and you will receive free test prep materials, including the POWER-PREP® software mentioned previously.

There is a limit of one GRE per calendar month and a maximum of five tests within any 12-month period. When you send your GRE scores to schools, they see all scores from all GREs you have taken within the past five years. You cannot choose to only reveal scores from a certain test date.

Scoring the GRE General Test

The process for scoring the CAT version of the GRE is similar to the process for scoring the traditional paper-based GRE: The number of questions answered correctly is adjusted according to the difficulty level of the questions on each particular test. However, with adaptive testing, the scoring process incorporates the statistical properties of the questions, the test taker's performance on the questions, and the number of questions that are answered. Depending on how you progress through the exam, you might be presented with fewer questions than another test taker might be presented with.

You can select up to four institutions to receive your score report. Score reports will be sent to you and the institutions selected within 10 to 15 days after you complete the test.

A Note on Scoring the Practice Exams

Because actual GRE tests are scored with scales that are unique to each test form, we have not included specific scoring information for the simulated practice tests in this book. After you work through this book, we suggest that you take additional practice exams with the official POWERPREP® software. It contains the same scoring "engine" as the real GRE exam and can give you a very good idea of how you should expect to do on test day. At this stage, and throughout most of your practice, you should not get overly worried about your test scores; your goal should be to learn something from every practice experience and to get used to the format and types of questions on the GRE.

The General Test Analytical Writing Section

Each essay receives a score from two highly trained readers using a six-point holistic scale. This means that the readers are trained to assign a score based on the overall quality of an essay in response to a specific task. If the two scores differ by more than one point on the scale, a third reader steps in to resolve the discrepancy. In this case, the first two scores are dropped and the score given by the third reader is used. Otherwise, the scores from the two readers are averaged so that a single score from 0 to 6 (in half-point increments) is reported. If no essay response is given, a No Score (NS) is reported for this section. If an essay response is provided for one of the two writing tasks, the task for which no response is written receives a score of zero. Scoring guides are available at www.gre.org.

The General Test Verbal and Quantitative Sections

These scores will depend on your specific performance on the questions given as well as the number of questions answered in the allotted time. The Verbal and Quantitative scores are reported on a 200–800 score scale, in 10-point increments. Each section receives a separate score. If you answer no questions at all in either section, a No Score (NS) is reported.

Preparing for the GRE

When using this book for GRE preparation, the Self-Assessment should be your first step. It will help you to focus on areas of strength and weakness in your knowledge base and skill set. Using what you learned from your initial self-assessment, you should then work through each chapter noting the examples and answering all practice questions you encounter.

There is a detailed explanation for each of the practice questions in this book. You will probably not need to read each and every one of them. Sometimes, when you look back over a practice exam that you took, you can tell right away why you got a particular question wrong. We have heard many students call these errors "stupid mistakes." We suggest that you refer to these errors as "concentration errors." Everyone makes them from time to time, and you should not get overly upset or concerned when they occur. There is a good chance that your focus will be much better on the real test as long as you train yourself properly using this book.

Pay close attention to any questions that you get wrong because of a lack of understanding or holes in your knowledge base. If you have the time, it is probably worth reading the explanations for any of these questions you got wrong due to a lack of understanding. In fact, it is worth your time to read the explanation to any questions that were at all difficult for you—even questions you might have answered correctly. Sometimes students get questions correct but for the wrong reasons, or because they simply guessed correctly. While you are practicing, you should mark any questions that you want to recheck and be sure to read the explanations for those questions.

Key Test-taking Strategies

The following sections contain important information that should help you to approach the GRE with confidence. Additional chapters in the book include strategies and techniques specific to each of the GRE General Test sections.

KSA

Cognitive psychologists, those who study learning and thinking, use the letters **K-S-A** to refer to the basic parts of human performance in all activities, ranging from academics to athletics, playing music to playing games. The letters stand for **K**nowledge, **S**kills, and **A**bilities.

The human brain stores and retrieves factual knowledge a little bit differently from the way it acquires and executes skills. Knowledge can generally be learned fairly quickly and is fairly durable, even when you are under stress. You learn factual information by studying, and you acquire skills through practice. There is some overlap between these actions and, hopefully, you will do some learning while you practice, and vice versa. In fact, research shows that repetition is important for both information storage and skills acquisition. Later in this book, we'll go into great detail about the facts that make up the "knowledge base" that is essential for GRE success. First, we need to tell you about the skills and strategies.

There is a large difference between knowledge and skills: Knowing about a skill, or understanding how the skill should be executed, is not the same as actually *having* that skill. For instance, you might be told all about a skill such as driving a car with a standard (stick shift) transmission, or playing the piano, or typing on a computer keyboard. You could have a great teacher, have wonderful learning tools, and pay attention very carefully. You might *understand* everything perfectly. But, the first few times that you actually attempt the skill, you will probably make some mistakes. In fact, you will probably experience some frustration because of the gap between your *understanding* of the skill and your actual ability to *perform* the skill.

Perfecting skills takes practice. You need repetition to create the pathways in your brain that control your skills. Therefore, you shouldn't be satisfied with simply reading this book and then saying to yourself, "I get it." You will not reach your full GRE scoring potential unless you put in sufficient time practicing as well as understanding and learning.

As mentioned previously, the GRE General Test measures certain predictable areas of knowledge, and it measures a specific set of skills. We suggest that you do sufficient practice so that you will develop your test-taking skills, and, specifically, good GRE-taking skills. Thousands and thousands of students have successfully raised their GRE scores through study and practice. While you practice, you should distinguish between practice that is meant to serve as a learning experience and practice that is meant to be a realistic simulation of your actual GRE.

During practice that is meant for learning, it is okay to "cheat." What we mean is that you should feel free to disregard the time limits and just think about how the questions are put together and even stop to look up information in textbooks, on the Internet, or look at the explanations in the back of the book. It is even okay to talk to others about what you are learning during your "learning practice." But, you also need to do some simulated testing practice, where you time yourself carefully and try to control as many variables in your environment as you can. Some research shows that you will have an easier time executing your skills and remembering information when the environment that you are testing in is similar to the environment where you studied and practiced. It is important to note that you should not attempt any timed practice tests when you are mentally or physically exhausted. This will only add additional unwanted stress to an already stressful situation.

Manage Stress

In graduate school, there will be stress that arises from sources such as family expectations, fear of failure, heavy workload, competition, and difficult subjects. The GRE tries to create similar stresses. The *psychometricians* (specialized psychologists who study the measurement of the mind), who contribute to the design of standardized tests, use *artificial stressors* to test how you will respond to the stress of graduate school.

The main *stressor* is the time limit. The time limits are set on the GRE so that some students cannot finish all the questions in the time allowed. So, you will have to get used to the idea that you might not have time to finish each section on test day. You should try to answer as many questions as you can accurately because the GRE is an adaptive test and actually awards more points for tougher questions.

Another stressor is the fact that you cannot skip around in the sections. You must answer the questions in order, as they appear. Try not to worry about whether the question you are working on is harder or easier than the one that came before. Just focus on doing your best on each question. The computer will keep track of your time, so note your progress every few questions and stay on pace to avoid any rushing after the computer gives you the five-minute "warning."

Relax to Succeed

Probably the worst thing that can happen to a test taker is to panic. Research shows that there are very predictable results when a person panics. To panic is to have a specific set of easily recognizable symptoms: sweating, shortness of breath, muscle tension, increased pulse rate, tunnel vision, nausea, light-headedness, and, in rare cases, even loss of consciousness. These symptoms are the results of chemical changes in the brain brought on by some stimulus. The stimulus does not even have to be external. Therefore, we can panic ourselves just by thinking about certain things.

The stress chemical in your body called *epinephrine*, more commonly known as *adrenalin*, brings on these symptoms. Adrenalin changes the priorities in your brain activity. It moves blood and electrical energy away from some parts of the brain and to others. Specifically, it increases brain activity in the areas that control your body and away from the parts of your brain that are involved in complex thinking. Therefore, panic makes a person stronger and faster, and also less able to perform the type of thinking that is important on a GRE test.

It is not a bad thing to have a small amount of adrenalin in your bloodstream because of a healthy amount of excitement about your test. But, you should be careful not to panic before or during a test. You can control your adrenalin levels by minimizing the unknown factors in the GRE testing process. The biggest stress-inducing questions are: "What do the GRE writers expect?" "Am I ready?" "How will I do on test day?" If you spend time and energy studying and practicing under realistic conditions before your test day, you'll have a much better chance of controlling your adrenalin levels and handling the test with no panic. The goals of your preparation should be to learn about the test, acquire the knowledge and skills that are being measured by the test, and learn about yourself and how you respond to the different parts of the test.

You should also consider which question types you will try on test day and which ones you will just make an educated guess on. You need to be familiar with the material that is tested on each section of your test. As you work through this book, make an assessment of the best use of your time and energy. Concentrate on the areas that will give you the highest score in the amount of time that you have until the test. This will result in a feeling of confidence on test day even when you are facing very challenging questions.

Specific Relaxation Techniques

The following sections offer you some useful information on how to be as relaxed and confident as possible on test day.

Be Prepared

The more prepared you feel, the less likely it is that you'll be stressed on test day. Study and practice consistently during the time between now and your test day. Be organized. Have your supplies and lucky testing clothes ready in advance. Make a practice trip to the test center before your test day.

Know Yourself

Get to know your strengths and weaknesses on the GRE and the things that help you to relax. Some test takers like to have a slightly anxious feeling to help them focus. Others do best when they are so relaxed that they are almost asleep. You will learn about yourself through practice.

Rest

The better rested you are, the better things seem. As you get fatigued, you are more likely to look on the dark side of things and worry more, which hurts your test scores.

Eat Well

Sugar is bad for stress and brain function in general. Consuming refined sugar creates biological stress that has an impact on your brain chemistry. Keep it to a minimum for several days before your test. If you are actually addicted to caffeine, (you can tell that you are if you get headaches when you skip a day), get your normal amount. Don't forget to eat regularly while you're preparing for the GRE. It's not a good idea to skip meals simply because you are experiencing some additional stress. It is also important to eat something before you take the GRE. An empty stomach might be distracting and uncomfortable on test day.

Breathe

If you feel yourself tensing up, slow down and take deeper breaths. This will relax you and get more oxygen to your brain so that you can think more clearly.

Take Breaks

You cannot stay sharply focused on your GRE for the whole time in the testing center. You are certainly going to have distracting thoughts, or times when you just can't process all the information. When this happens, you should close your eyes, clear your mind, and then start back on your test. This process should take only a minute or so. You could pray, meditate, or just picture a place or person that helps you to relax. Try thinking of something fun that you have planned for right after your GRE.

Have a Plan of Attack

Know how you are going to work through each part of the test. There is no time to make up a plan of attack on test day. Hopefully, you will do enough practice that you internalize the skills you need to do your best on each section, and you won't have to stop to think about what to do next.

Be Aware of Time

You should time yourself on test day. You should time yourself on some of your practice exams. We suggest that you use an analog (dial face) watch. You can turn the hands on your watch back from noon to allow enough time for the section that you are working on. Remember, all that matters during the test is your test. All of life's other issues will have to be dealt with after your test is finished. You might find this attitude easier to attain if you lose track of what time it is in the "outside world."

What to Expect on Test Day

If you work through the material in this book and do some additional practice using the POWERPREP® software, you should be more than adequately prepared for the GRE General Test. The following sections contain further suggestions to help the entire testing process go smoothly.

Do a Dry Run

Make sure that you know how long it will take to get to the testing center and where you will park, alternative routes, and so on. If you are testing in a place that is new to you, try to get into the building between now and test day so that you can absorb the sounds and smells, find out where the bathrooms and snack machines are, and so on.

Wake Up Early

We recommend scheduling your GRE for as early in the morning as you can. This way you are likely to be rested and not as distracted as you might be if you have already had things going on in your day before you sit down to take your GRE.

Dress for Success

Wear loose, comfortable, clothes in layers so that you can adjust to the temperature. Remember your watch. There might not be a clock in your testing room.

Fuel Up

Eat something without too much sugar in it on the morning of your test. Get your normal dose of caffeine, if any. (Test day is not the time to "try coffee" for the first time!)

Bring Supplies

Bring your driver's license (or passport) and your admission ticket. If you need them, bring your glasses or contact lenses. You won't be able to eat or drink while the GRE is in progress, but you can bring a snack for the break time if you want.

Warm Up Your Brain

Read a newspaper or something similar, or review some practice material so that the GRE isn't the first thing you read on test day.

Plan a Mini-vacation

Most students find it easier to concentrate on their test preparation and on their GRE if they have a plan for some fun right after the test. Plan something that you can look forward to as a reward for all the hard work and energy that you're putting in. Then, when it gets hard to concentrate, you can say, "If I do my work now, I'll have tons of fun right after the test!"

Test Takers with Disabilities

GRE General Test takers with documented disabilities are eligible for special accommodations. If you have a previous diagnosis and require accommodations, contact Disability Services at ETS immediately to allow for extra processing time (up to 6 weeks) so that arrangements can be made.

Contact information:

Telephone:	1-866-387-8602
TTY:	1-609-771-7714
Fax:	1-609-771-7165
E-mail:	stassd@ets.org
U.S. Mail:	ETS
	Disability Services
	P.O. Box 6054
	Princeton, NJ 08541-6054

Some examples of accommodations that can be made for those who qualify are:

➤ Additional testing time

➤ Extended or additional rest breaks

➤ An assistant to read/write/record answers on your behalf

➤ Sign language interpreter

➤ Specialized computer equipment/settings

➤ Enlarged print

➤ Braille

➤ Audio recording of test material

Documentation of your disability must meet ETS requirements. Among the requirements are:

➤ Must be on official letterhead of the professional rendering the diagnosis

➤ Must be current (within the last five years for learning disabilities, within the last six months for psychiatric disorders, within the last three years for ADHD)

➤ Must request specific accommodations

➤ Must clearly state the diagnosis and limitations that result from your condition

Moving on from Here

The remaining chapters in this book cover the specific sections on the GRE General Test. There are additional strategies and practice questions in each chapter. The full-length practice exams can be found directly following these content-area chapters. Plan to take one full-length test about one week prior to the actual GRE. Read the explanations for the questions that you missed, and review the content-area chapters as necessary. Remember, practice as much as you can under realistic testing conditions to maximize your GRE score.

A Final Note

ETS, the folks who write and administer the GRE, are considering significant changes to the GRE General Test beginning in October 2006. Planned changes include the following:

➤ **Verbal**—Greater emphasis will be placed on higher cognitive skills, and vocabulary skills will take a back seat. More text-based reading passages drawn from expanded sources will be included. In addition, complex reasoning skills will be tested, and the computer-enabled tasks inherent to the CAT will be augmented.

➤ **Quantitative**—Quantitative reasoning skills that are more closely related to skills used in graduate school will be tested. Geometry questions will be decreased, while the proportion of questions involving "real-world" scenarios will be increased. In addition, technology improvements, such as an on-screen calculator, will be seen.

➤ **Analytical Writing**—The essay prompts will be updated and will be more focused. Also, each task (Issue and Argument) will be 30 minutes in length.

Visit the GRE website often for further information and updates regarding the new GRE General Test.

Self-Assessment

This section will assist you in evaluating your current readiness for the GRE. Sample questions representing each section of the GRE are included to help you pinpoint areas of strength and weakness in your knowledge base and your skill set. Make an honest effort to answer each question, and then review the explanation that follows. Don't worry if you are unable to answer many or most of the questions at this point. The rest of the book contains information and resources to help you maximize your GRE score.

Even if you already know that your strength is either verbal or math, attempt all the questions. Now is a good time to become familiar with the types of questions that will appear on the GRE.

Analytical Writing

This section of the GRE requires you to write two essays: The first essay is a discussion of a relevant issue, and the second essay is an analysis of an argument. Your essays will be considered "first drafts," but should still be the best possible examples of your writing that you can produce under test conditions. The following are sample essay prompts for each of the two required essays on the GRE. It is recommended that you write essays based on these prompts, and then refer to Chapter 1, "Verbal Section: Analytical Writing," for a thorough discussion of GRE essay-writing techniques.

The GRE Program has developed a pool of topics from which the test topics will be selected. This topic pool can be viewed at www.gre.org/issuetop.html and www.gre.org/argutop.html. You should practice writing additional essays based on these topics.

➤ **Issue task**—Discuss your perspective on the following issue: "National governments should devote more money to assist small businesses than to social service programs."

➤ **Argument task**—Analyze and critique the following argument: "Certain states have enacted laws that require all drivers to reach the age of 18 before they are allowed to drive a car carrying more than one passenger. Other states have opted not to support this type of legislation, because citizens believe that such laws punish all teen drivers for the mistakes of a few irresponsible, unsafe drivers. Studies have shown that thousands of high school students die each year in accidents involving a single car with several teenagers as passengers and a teenage driver. Therefore, laws requiring a minimum age for drivers are simply commonsense safety measures, and should be mandatory in all states."

Verbal Assessment

This portion of the GRE tests your ability to effectively understand and use standard written English. It also assesses your critical thinking skills as well as your vocabulary. Following are sample questions, similar to those that may appear on the GRE.

Verbal Section—Antonyms

Select the word or phrase that is opposite in meaning to the word in capital letters.

1. AMIABLE:
   (A) lengthy
   (B) unfriendly
   (C) fertile
   (D) unwilling
   (E) garrulous

2. GRATUITOUS:

  (A) lacking spirit

  (B) highly unlikely

  (C) necessary

  (D) very familiar

  (E) important

3. FORTITUDE:

  (A) cowardice

  (B) persistence

  (C) valor

  (D) courage

  (E) tenacity

4. SURFEIT:

  (A) concession

  (B) brine

  (C) exigency

  (D) abundance

  (E) deficit

5. TIMOROUS:

  (A) eccentric

  (B) pernicious

  (C) repulsive

  (D) valiant

  (E) benevolent

Verbal Section—Antonyms—Answer Key and Explanations

   1. The best answer is B. "Amiable" comes from the Latin word "amicabilis," which is also the root for the word "amicable," and means "friendly and sociable." Therefore, "unfriendly" is an antonym of "amiable." Answer choices A, C, D, and E are not antonyms of "amiable."

   2. The best answer is C. "Gratuitous" comes from the Latin word "gratuitus" and means "unnecessary or unearned." Therefore, "necessary" is an antonym of "gratuitous." Answer choices A, B, D, and E are not antonyms of "gratuitous."

3. **The best answer is A.** "Fortitude" comes from the Latin word "forti-tuo," from "fortis," which means "strong." "Fortitude," then, refers to strength, specifically strength of character. "Cowardice" is an antonym of "fortitude." Answer choices B, C, D, and E are not antonyms of "fortitude."

4. **The best answer is E.** "Surfeit" comes from the prefix "super-" plus the Latin word "facere," which means to "overdo." Specifically, "surfeit" means "surplus or excess." "Deficit" refers to "inadequacy or insufficiency," and is, therefore, an antonym of "surfeit." Answer choices A, B, C, and D are not antonyms of "surfeit."

5. **The best answer is D.** "Timorous" comes from the Latin word "timere," which means "to fear," and is also the root of "timid." Therefore, "valiant," which means "brave," is an antonym of "timorous." Answer choices A, B, C, and E are not antonyms of "timorous."

Verbal Section—Analogies

Select the answer choice that contains the pair of words that best expresses a relationship similar to that expressed in the capitalized pair of words.

1. CORDIAL : GREETING ::
    (A) antisocial : neighbor
    (B) hostile : environment
    (C) earnest : apology
    (D) benign : tumor
    (E) aggressive : utterance

2. BURGEONING : WEALTH ::
    (A) waning : fortune
    (B) escalating : fame
    (C) fermenting : cache
    (D) convalescing : patient
    (E) demeaning : narrative

3. POLITE : SOLICITOUS ::
    (A) affable : contrary
    (B) vehement : apathetic
    (C) ingratiating : repulsive
    (D) disdainful : inconsiderate
    (E) urbane : quarrelsome

4. ONEROUS : JOURNEY ::

(A) somnolent : campaign

(B) mitigating : circumstance

(C) formidable : opponent

(D) magnanimous : spirit

(E) facile : trek

5. REMEDIATION : DEFICIENCY ::

(A) reparation : misfortune

(B) discrimination : poverty

(C) repudiation : duty

(D) speculation : evidence

(E) liquidation : investment

Verbal Section—Analogies—Answer Key and Explanations

1. The best answer is C. The relationship that exists between "cordial" and "greeting" can be expressed with the following sentence: Jane offered a cordial greeting. "Cordial" means "friendly or sincere," so a cordial greeting is a friendly or sincere greeting. "Earnest" means "sincere," so an earnest apology is a sincere apology. This relationship can be expressed in a similar sentence: Jane offered an earnest apology.

An "antisocial" neighbor would probably not be friendly, a "hostile" environment would not be a "friendly" environment, and an "aggressive" utterance would probably not be a "friendly" utterance, so answer choices A, B, and D do not best express the same relationship as that expressed in the question. Although "benign" is similar in meaning to "cordial," the relationship between "benign" and "tumor" is not the same as the relationship that exists between "cordial" and "greeting." You do not offer a "tumor."

2. The best answer is B. "Burgeoning" means "growing or flourishing," so burgeoning wealth is growing wealth. "Escalating" means "increasing," so escalating fame means increasing fame. The same relationship exists between "burgeoning wealth" and "escalating fame."

"Waning" means "decreasing." Even though "fortune" in answer choice A is a synonym for "wealth," the same relationship does not exist between "burgeoning wealth" and "waning fortune." Answer choices C, D, and E do not best express the same relationship as that expressed in the question.

3. **The best answer is D.** The relationship that exists between "polite" and "sincere" can be expressed with the following sentence: A polite person is solicitous. "Polite" means "considerate," and "solicitous" can mean "eager to please or thoughtful."

An "affable" person is generally not "contrary," so answer choice A is incorrect. "Affable" means "friendly or agreeable." A "vehement" person is not "apathetic," so answer choice B is incorrect. "Vehement" means "forceful or strong," and "apathetic" means "indifferent." An "ingratiating" person is not "repulsive." "Ingratiating" means "pleasing or agreeable," and "repulsive" means "disgusting or repellant." A "disdainful" person is "inconsiderate," so this choice best expresses the relationship that exists between the words in the question. An "urbane" person is generally not "quarrelsome." "Urbane" means "polite and refined." Therefore, answer choices A, B, C, and E do not best express the same relationship as that expressed in the question.

4. **The best answer is C.** "Onerous" means "troublesome or oppressive," so an onerous journey could be described as being very difficult to complete. "Formidable" can mean "difficult to defeat," so a formidable opponent could be described as being very difficult to defeat.

"Somnolent" means "inducing sleep," so the relationship between "somnolent" and "campaign" is not the same as the relationship between "onerous" and "journey." "Mitigating" means "helping or alleviating," so a mitigating circumstance could not be described as being very difficult. "Magnanimous" means "generous or unselfish," so the relationship between "magnanimous" and "spirit" is not the same as the relationship between "onerous" and "journey." Although "trek" is a synonym for "journey," "facile" means "easy," so the relationship between "facile" and "trek" is not the same as the relationship between "onerous" and "journey." Therefore, answer choices A, B, D, and E do not best express the same relationship as that expressed in the question.

5. **The best answer is A.** The relationship that exists between "remediation" and "deficiency" can be expressed with the following sentence: A deficiency can be corrected through remediation. "Remediation" means "the act of correcting a fault or deficiency." A "misfortune" can be corrected through "reparation," which means "the act or process of making amends," so this choice best expresses the relationship that exists between the words in the question.

"Poverty" cannot be corrected through "discrimination," "duty" is not corrected through "repudiation," "evidence" is not corrected through "speculation," and "investment" is not corrected through "liquidation," so answer choices B, C, D, and E do not best express the same relationship as that expressed in the question.

Verbal Section—Sentence Completions

Select the best word or words to complete the following sentences.

1. Despite the pressure of _____ his good grades, Josh _____ academically during his tenure at a major university.
   (A) achieving..declined
   (B) deducing..transcended
   (C) maintaining..excelled
   (D) perpetuating..failed
   (E) squandering..triumphed

2. To guarantee the mandatory adherence to all new company policies, there must be constant _____ between upper management and the development teams.
   (A) autonomy
   (B) collaboration
   (C) distinction
   (D) controversy
   (E) animosity

3. As an erudite scholar, the professor's lectures were typically somewhat _____ for the average student, but today's lecture was surprisingly _____.
   (A) inscrutable..ambiguous
   (B) terse..subtle
   (C) technical..comprehensive
   (D) inane..superficial
   (E) esoteric..comprehensible

4. Although the description of fifteenth-century Europe that was included in the textbook was relatively meticulous, some _____ details were apparently excluded in an effort to abridge the chapter.

(A) crucial
(B) irrelevant
(C) laconic
(D) extraneous
(E) trivial

5. The common notion that all children of very wealthy families lead _____ lives is false; indeed, most live reasonably modest and normal lives.

(A) humble
(B) ostentatious
(C) unpretentious
(D) indolent
(E) obsequious

Verbal Section—Sentence Completions—Answer Key and Explanations

1. **The best answer is C.** The word "despite" indicates that the second part of the sentence is somehow contradictory to the first part of the sentence. The implication is that, even though Josh felt pressure to "maintain" good grades, he still managed to "excel" while in college. Answer choices A, B, D, and E are not consistent with the context of the sentence.

2. **The best answer is B.** In this sentence, the information following the blank defines the relationship that must exist between upper management and the development team. The sentence indicates that adherence to the new policy is mandatory; therefore, the blank should be filled with a word that suggests cooperation. "Collaboration" means "to work together or cooperate," so it is the best selection. "Autonomy" means "the condition of being independent," and "distinction" means "the condition of being different," neither of which fit the context of the sentence. Eliminate answer choices A and C. Both "controversy" and "animosity" suggest a lack of cooperation, so eliminate answer choices D and E.

3. **The best answer is E.** The first part of the sentence provides a description of the professor that should shed some light on the type of lectures she is likely to give. "Erudite" means "having profound scholarly knowledge." Therefore, to the average student, the professor's lectures may be

difficult to understand. The first blank should be filled with a word that means "difficult to understand" or "unclear." Both "inscrutable" in answer choice A, and "esoteric" in answer choice E could be inserted into the first blank. The word "surprisingly" directly preceding the second blank suggests a contrast between a typical lecture, and today's lecture. Therefore, the second blank should be filled with a word that means "understandable," which makes answer choice E the best choice.

4. **The best answer is A.** The word "although" indicates that the second part of the sentence, where the blank appears, will include some information that contradicts the first part of the sentence. "Meticulous" means "precise and attentive to detail"; therefore, a "meticulous" description would most likely include as many "crucial" or important details as possible. The sentence implies that, although the book was relatively precise, some important information was left out to shorten, or "abridge" the chapter. "Irrelevant," "extraneous," and "trivial" refer to details that are either unimportant or unnecessary; therefore, answer choices B, D, and E are incorrect. "Laconic" means "using few words," which doesn't fit the context of the sentence, so answer choice C is incorrect.

5. **The best answer is B.** According to the context of the sentence, the "common notion" stated in the sentence is false. Therefore, the word to be inserted in the blank must be opposite in meaning to the information that follows the semicolon. "Ostentatious" means "pretentious, or showy," which directly contradicts the statement that most children of wealthy families live reasonably modest and normal lives. "Humble," "unpretentious," and "obsequious" have meanings that are opposite to that of "ostentatious," so answer choices A, C, and E are incorrect. "Indolent" means lazy, which is not supported by the context of the sentence; therefore, answer choice D is incorrect.

Verbal Section—Reading Comprehension

Select the best answers to the questions that follow the passage.

A conscientious automotive engineer has to evaluate the specific characteristics, distinctive design, and unique purpose of an automobile or vehicle part. It is here that he faces a quandary. An engineer must distinguish between the creative elements of the design that require a subjective response and the scientific fundamentals necessary for its utility. Although an engineer is responsible for producing the most efficient result possible, he must not be prejudiced against the artistic additions that the designers deemed necessary. An engineer's preferences are not necessarily an accurate reflection of the desires and demands of the consumer. The design team is far better equipped to envisage what will make a product or vehicle attractive to the general public. Therefore, it is essential that an engineer focus his attention on the rudiments of the merchandise rather than the aesthetics. On the other hand, if an element in the design greatly affects the product's efficiency or productivity, an engineer has the responsibility of collaborating with the design team to alter the existing drawing. The engineer's familiarity and education prepare him to view objects pragmatically. For instance, an automotive engineer might focus on creating an engine part that is light and durable. A designer, on the other hand, is trained to view her work as an inspired creation. Tensions may arise when the more rational plans of the engineer interfere with the designer's creative ideas.

1. According to the author, a conscientious automotive engineer should avoid
   (A) discussing alternatives with designers when conflicts occur
   (B) concentrating on efficiency to produce artistic creations
   (C) discovering what will attract the consumer
   (D) allowing personal artistic preferences to influence his decisions
   (E) limiting the creativity of the designers to produce the highest-quality product

2. The author implies that an engineer should respect the work of a design team because
   (A) an engineer is completely unable to envision what will attract a consumer
   (B) productivity and efficiency do not influence a consumer's decision to purchase a product
   (C) an engineer may not fully be aware of creative or artistic additions that should be included
   (D) design teams never suggest additions or features that decrease the product's value
   (E) engineers are unable to incorporate creativity or innovation in their work

3. The passage suggests that the author would be most likely to agree with which of the following statements?

   (A) It is the designer, rather than the engineer, who ensures that a quality product is made.

   (B) An engineer should be able to separate art and expression from science and technology.

   (C) If a product is efficient and productive, no other elements are needed to make it marketable.

   (D) Engineers are known for being prejudiced against creativity and artistic expression.

   (E) An engineer's concerns should always trump the artistic desires of the design team.

4. The author's argument is developed primarily by the use of

   (A) an attack on engineers

   (B) an example of successful collaboration between designers and engineers

   (C) a critique of engineers' training

   (D) a warning against choosing aesthetics over utility

   (E) an explanation about how and why designers and engineers should interact with each other

Verbal Section—Reading Comprehension—Answer Key and Explanations

1. The best answer is D. The passage states, "Although an engineer is responsible for producing the most efficient result possible, he must not be prejudiced against the artistic additions that the designers deemed necessary. An engineer's preferences are not necessarily an accurate reflection of the desires and demands of the consumer." Answer choice E may have appeared to be correct. However, the passage states, "On the other hand, if an element in the design is greatly affecting the product's efficiency or productivity, an engineer has the responsibility of collaborating with the design team to alter the existing drawing."

2. The best answer is C. The passages states, "An engineer's preferences are not necessarily an accurate reflection of the desires and demands of the consumer. The design team is far better equipped to envisage what will make a product or vehicle attractive to the general public." Answer choice A may have appeared to be correct. However, the author's main point in the passage is that both designers and engineers are needed to create a quality product. Productivity and efficiency may be factors that attract consumers.

3. **The best answer is B.** The passage states, "An engineer must distinguish between the creative elements of the design that require a subjective response and the scientific fundamentals necessary for its utility." Answer choice E may have appeared to be correct. However, the passage states that engineers should collaborate with the design team if the engineers have concerns. This does not imply that the engineers' concerns trump those of the design team automatically.

4. **The best answer is E.** The passage discusses the importance of both positions and what they contribute to a team effort. As stated, "Although an engineer is responsible for producing the most efficient result possible, he must not be prejudiced against the artistic additions that the designers deemed necessary." The passage also gives instruction about how the two positions should interact with each other. Answer choice B may have appeared to be correct. However, the author does not show a real example of a successful collaboration.

 You should now have a good idea of the types of questions found on the different Verbal sections of the GRE. If this is your weak area, refer specifically to the chapters in this book that focus on strengthening your verbal skills.

Quantitative Assessment

This portion of the GRE tests your ability to effectively apply mathematical concepts, including Arithmetic, Algebra, Geometry, and Data Analysis. It also assesses your critical thinking skills. Following are sample questions, similar to those that may appear on the GRE.

Quantitative Comparison

Compare the quantity in Column A with the quantity in Column B. If the quantity in Column A is greater, select answer choice A; if the quantity in Column B is greater, select answer choice B; if the quantities are equal, select answer choice C; if the relationship cannot be determined from the information given, select answer choice D. Note that answer choice E is never a correct answer in this section. Use the information in the box to assist you in determining the relationship between the two quantities.

Column A	Column B

$$x^2 + y^2 = 1$$

1. x y

Column A	Column B

The area of circle C is 16π.

2.   The circumference of 4π
circle C.

Column A	Column B

$$\frac{m - 9n}{3n - m} = 1$$

3. m $6n$

Column A	Column B

At constant rates, copy machine A can print x copies in 15 minutes and copy machine B can print x copies in 20 minutes.

4.   The copies produced by   The copies produced by
machine A in 2 hours.   machine B in 3 hours.

Column A	Column B

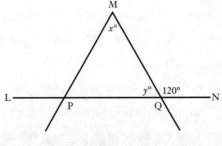

MQ=PQ

5. x y

Quantitative Comparison—Answer Key and Explanations

1. **The correct answer is D.** It is not possible to determine a relationship between x and y from the information given. If, for example, you set y equal to 0, then x could be either 1 or –1, which means that x could be either greater than or less than y. Alternatively, if you set x equal to 0, then y could be either 1 or –1, which means that y could be either greater than or less than x.

2. **The correct answer is A.** The formula for the area of a circle is $A=\pi r^2$. The problem states that the area of circle C is 16π, which means that $r^2 = 16$, and $r = 4$. The formula for the circumference of a circle is $2\pi r$, so the quantity in Column A is equivalent to 8π. This quantity is greater than the quantity in Column B (4π), so the correct answer is A.

3. **The correct answer is C.** The first step in solving this problem is to first solve the equation in the box for m in terms of n.

   ➤ $\dfrac{m - 9n}{3n - m} = 1$

   ➤ $m - 9n = 1(3n - m)$

   ➤ $m = 3n - m + 9n$

   ➤ $m = 12n - m$

   ➤ $2m = 12n$

   Simplify by dividing both sides by 2 to get $m = 6n$. Therefore, the correct answer is C; the quantities are equal.

4. **The correct answer is B.** To solve this problem, first calculate the number of copies produced by machine A in 2 hours. The problem states that copy machine A can print x copies in 15 minutes. Two hours is equivalent to 120 minutes. Therefore, copy machine A can produce $\dfrac{120}{15}$, or $8x$ copies in 2 hours. Now, calculate the number of copies produced by machine B in 3 hours. The problem states that copy machine B can print x copies in 20 minutes. Three hours is equivalent to 180 minutes. Therefore, copy machine B can produce $\dfrac{180}{20}$, or $9x$ copies in 3 hours. The number of copies produced by copy machine B in 3 hours ($9x$) is greater than the number of copies produced by copy machine A in 2 hours, ($8x$), so B is the correct answer.

5. **The correct answer is C.** The first step in solving this problem is to determine the value of angle y. Because there are 180° in a straight line, and the angle supplementary to angle y is 120°, angle y must equal 180° – 120°, or 60°. You are given that MQ = PQ, which means that the measure of the angles opposite those sides is also equal. Therefore, the measure of angle x is equal to the measure of the unmarked angle. The sum of the interior angles of a triangle is 180°. Because angle y equals 60°, the sum of the other two interior angles (angle x and the unmarked angle) must be 180° – 60°, or 120°. And, because these two angles are equal, they must each measure 60°; therefore, the measure of angle x is 60°. The quantity in Column A, (x), is equal to the quantity in Column B, (y), and the correct answer is C.

Problem Solving—Discrete Quantitative Questions

Select the best answer from the choices given.

1. Which of the following is equal to $\dfrac{n^2(n^4)^3}{n^3(n^2)^2}$, if $n \neq 0$?
   - (A) n
   - (B) n^2
   - (C) n^3
   - (D) n^4
   - (E) n^5

2. Jeremy delivered $k + 3$ newspapers on Wednesday, four times as many newspapers on Thursday as on Wednesday, and nine more newspapers on Friday than on Wednesday. What is the average (arithmetic mean) number of newspapers he delivered per day over the three days?
   - (A) $2k + 9$
   - (B) $2k + 27$
   - (C) $3k + 12$
   - (D) $6k + 9$
   - (E) $36k + 3$

3. In the following figure, the radius of the circle with center P is 6.5. What is the area of triangle *RST*?

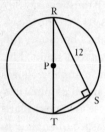

(A) 30
(B) 36
(C) 48
(D) 60
(E) 78

4. If $5x^2 - 118 = -38$, which of the following is equal to $3x^2 - 14x + 5$?
(A) 109
(B) 68
(C) 13
(D) –3
(E) –16

5. If 25 percent of 80 percent of a positive number is equal to 10 percent of *m* percent of the same number, what is the value of *m*?
(A) 20
(B) 40
(C) 80
(D) 100
(E) 200

Discrete Quantitative Questions—Answer Key and Explanations

1. **The correct answer is B.** To solve this problem, simplify both the numerator and the denominator. Apply the rules of exponents, as follows:

    ➤ Numerator: $n^2(n^4)^3 = n^2(n^{12})$

    ➤ $n^2(n^{12}) = n^{14}$

    ➤ Denominator: $n^3(n^2)^2 = n^3(n^4)$

    ➤ $n^3(n^4) = n^7$

    ➤ $\dfrac{n^{14}}{n^7} = n^7$

    The other answer choices could have been arrived at if the rules of exponents had not been accurately followed.

2. **The correct answer is A.** On Wednesday, Jeremy delivered $k + 3$ newspapers. On Thursday, Jeremy delivered $4(k + 3)$ newspapers. On Friday, Jeremy delivered $(k + 3) + 9$ newspapers. Calculate the total number of newspapers that Jeremy delivered as follows:

    ➤ $(k + 3) + 4(k +3) + (k + 12)$

    ➤ $(k + 3) + (4k +12) + (k + 12)$

    ➤ $(k + 4k + k) + 3 + 12 + 12$

    ➤ $(6k) + 27$

    Calculate the average by dividing the total number of newspapers delivered $(6k + 27)$, by the number of days (3).

    ➤ $(6k + 27) \div 3 = 2k + 9$, answer choice A.

    If you multiplied 9 by 4 and incorrectly combined the product (36) with the number of newspapers delivered on the first day, you would arrive at answer choice E. If you neglected to account for all of the newspapers, you could arrive at the other answer choices.

3. **The correct answer is A.** The formula for the area of a triangle is $A = \dfrac{1}{2}(bh)$, where b is the length of the base, and h is the height. According to the figure, the height is 12 (side RS). The problem states that the radius of the circle is 6.5, which means that the diameter is 2(6.5), or 13. The length of side RT of the triangle is equivalent to the diameter, as

shown in the figure. Side *RT* is also the hypotenuse of triangle *RST*. To calculate the length of the base (side *TS*), apply the Pythagorean Theorem, $a^2 + b^2 = c^2$.

➤ $a^2 + 12^2 = 13^2$

➤ $a^2 = 169 - 144$

➤ $a^2 = 25$

➤ $a = 5$

The length of the base is 5. Plug the value for the height (12) and the value for the base (5) into the formula for the area of a triangle.

➤ $A = \dfrac{1}{2}(bh)$

➤ $A = \dfrac{1}{2}(12 \times 5)$

➤ $A = \dfrac{1}{2}(60) = 30$

If you simply multiplied the length of the given side (12) by 3, you would get answer choice B, which is incorrect. If you forgot to multiply (bh) by $\dfrac{1}{2}$, you would get answer choice D, which is incorrect.

4. **The correct answer is D.** To solve this problem, first solve for x in the first equation.

➤ $5x^2 - 118 = -38$

➤ $5x^2 = -38 + 118$

➤ $5x^2 = 80$

➤ $x^2 = 16$

➤ $x = 4$

Now, substitute 4 for x in the second equation.

➤ $3x^2 - 14x + 5 =$

➤ $3(4)^2 - 14(4) + 5 =$

➤ $3(16) - 56 + 5 =$

➤ $48 - 56 + 5 = -3$

If you added 56 instead of subtracting it in the final equation, you would arrive at answer choice A.

5. The correct answer is E. To solve this problem, let x be the "mystery" number. Convert the percentages to decimals, and plug them into the given information. The problem states that 25% of 80% of some "mystery" number equals 10% of m% of the "mystery" number. This can be expressed mathematically as follows:

➤ $(0.25)(0.80)(x) = (0.1)(m)(x)$

➤ $0.2x = 0.1mx$

➤ Divide both sides by x to get $0.2 = 0.1m$

➤ Divide both sides by 0.1 to get $m = 2.0$

2.0 is equivalent to 200%, so answer choice E is correct.

Problem Solving—Data Interpretation Questions

Select the best answer from the choices given. The questions refer to the figures shown.

AGES OF PRIVATE PRACTICE ATTORNEYS (2002)

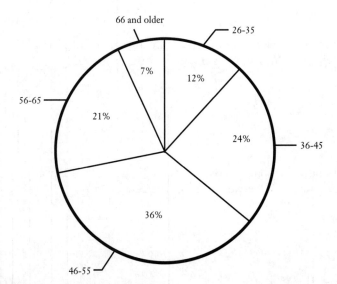

NUMBER OF U.S. ATTORNEYS IN SELECT CAREERS (2002)

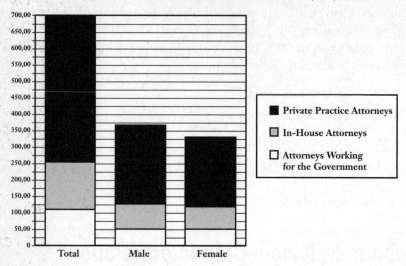

1. According to the graph, approximately what percent of attorneys in the United States in 2002 were females working in Private Practice?

   (A) 18%

   (B) 29%

   (C) 36%

   (D) 46%

   (E) 57%

2. According to the graph, what was the approximate ratio of In-House Attorneys to Attorneys Working for the Government in 2002?

   (A) 10:1

   (B) 4:1

   (C) 5:4

   (D) 1:1

   (E) 5:6

3. According to the graph, what was the approximate number of Private Practice Attorneys in 2002 between the ages of 26 and 35?

   (A) 24,000

   (B) 30,000

   (C) 54,000

   (D) 84,000

   (E) 108,000

4. Which of the following statements can be inferred from the graphs?

   I. Most female attorneys in Private Practice in 2002 were between the ages of 46 and 55.

   II. In 2002, the number of male attorneys Working for the Government was approximately equal to the number of female attorneys Working for the Government.

   III. There was approximately the same number of male attorneys between the ages of 26 and 45 as there was male attorneys between the ages of 46 and 55 in 2002.

   (A) I only

   (B) II only

   (C) I and II only

   (D) II and III only

   (E) I, II, and III

5. In 2003, the number of female In-House Attorneys increased by 7.5%, the number of female Private Practice Attorneys increased by 3%, and the number of female Attorneys Working for the Government remained constant. According to the graph, what was the approximate total number of female attorneys in 2003?

   (A) 11,625

   (B) 55,250

   (C) 286,625

   (D) 325,000

   (E) 336,625

Data Interpretation Questions—Answer Key and Explanations

1. **The best answer is B.** To answer this question, you must first calculate the number of female attorneys in private practice in 2002, based on the information given in the graph. According to the graph, Private Practice Attorneys are indicated by the dark gray bars. Because the question asks only about female attorneys, look at the bar directly above "Female" on the x-axis. The dark gray bar extends from approximately 125,000 to 325,000, which means that there were approximately 325,000 – 125,000, or 200,000 female attorneys in private practice in 2002. The question asks for the percent of the total number of attorneys, which, according to the graph was 700,000. To calculate the percent, divide the number of female attorneys in private practice in 2002 (200,000) by the total number of attorneys in 2002 (700,000) and multiply the result by 100.

   ➤ 200,000 ÷ 700,000 = .2857

   ➤ .2857 × 100 = 28.57

   Apply standard rounding rules to arrive at approximately 29%, answer choice B. If you mistakenly used the number of female attorneys working in other select careers, you may have arrived at the other answer choices.

2. **The best answer is D.** To answer this question, you must first calculate the number of "in-house" attorneys and the number of attorneys working for the government. Look at the bar directly above "Total" on the x-axis. According to the graph, "in-house" attorneys are indicated by the medium gray bar, and attorneys working for the government are indicated by the light gray bar. The medium gray bar extends from approximately 125,000 to approximately 250,000. Therefore, there were approximately 250,000 – 125,000, or 125,000 "in-house" attorneys in 2002. The light gray bar extends from 0 to approximately 125,000. Therefore, there were approximately 125,000 attorneys working for the government in 2002. Because the numbers are the same, the ratio is 1:1. If you mistakenly used the number of attorneys working in other select careers, you may have arrived at the other answer choices.

3. **The best answer is C.** To answer this question, you must first calculate the number of attorneys in private practice in 2002. Look at the bar directly above "Total" on the x-axis. Attorneys in private practice are indicated by the dark gray bar, which extends from approximately 250,000 to 700,000. Therefore, the number of attorneys in private practice in 2002 was approximately 700,000 – 250,000, or 450,000. The pie graph indicates the distribution of ages of attorneys in private practice

in 2002. According to the pie graph, 12% of attorneys in private practice in 2002 were between the ages of 26 and 35. Convert 12% to .12, its decimal equivalent, and multiply by 450,000, as shown next.

➤ .12 × 450,000 = 54,000

If you mistakenly used the number of attorneys working in other select careers, or used different percentages, you may have arrived at the other answer choices.

4. **The best answer is B.** The best approach to this problem is to identify whether each of the Roman numerals is a true statement, based on the information provided in the graphs.

➤ Roman numeral I is not a true statement because the pie graph does not differentiate between male and female attorneys. Therefore, it is not possible to reach a conclusion about the ages of female attorneys, only about the ages of attorneys in general. Eliminate answer choices A, C, and E because they include Roman numeral I.

➤ Roman numeral II is a true statement. According to the graph, the number of male attorneys working for the government was approximately 50,000, and the number of female attorneys working for the government was approximately 50,000.

➤ Roman numeral III is not a true statement because the pie chart only indicates the ages of attorneys in general. Therefore, it is not possible to reach a conclusion about the ages of male attorneys specifically. Eliminate answer choice D.

5. **The best answer is E.** To answer this question, you must first calculate the number of female "in-house" attorneys in 2002, the number of female attorneys in private practice in 2002, and the number of female attorneys working for the government in 2002.

➤ **In-House**—The number of female "in-house" attorneys in 2002 is represented by the medium gray bar on the graph. This bar extends from approximately 50,000 to 125,000, which means that there were approximately 125,000 − 50,000, or 75,000 female "in-house" attorneys in 2002.

➤ **Private Practice**—The number of female attorneys in private practice in 2002 is represented by the dark gray bar on the graph. This bar extends from approximately 125,000 to 325,000, which means that there were approximately 325,000 − 125,000, or 200,000 female attorneys in private practice in 2002.

➤ **Government**—The number of female attorneys working for the government in 2002 is represented by the light gray bar on the graph. This bar extends from approximately 0 to 50,000, which means that there were approximately 50,000 female attorneys working for the government in 2002.

Next, calculate the percent increase from 2002 to 2003 in each area.

➤ **In-House**—The percent increase was 7.5%. Multiply 75,000 by 1.075 to account for the increase. 75,000 × 1.075 = 80,625; there were approximately 80,625 female "in-house" attorneys in 2003.

➤ **Private Practice**—The percent increase was 3%. Multiply 200,000 by 1.03 to account for the increase. 200,000 × 1.03 = 206,000; there were approximately 206,000 female attorneys in private practice in 2003.

➤ **Government**—The percent increase was 0%, which means that the approximate number of female attorneys working for the government in 2003 was 50,000.

Now find the approximate total number of female attorneys in 2003: 80,625 + 206,000 + 50,000 = 336,625, answer choice E. Answer choice A is incorrect because it is the difference between the number of female attorneys in 2002 and the number of female attorneys in 2003. Answer choice D is incorrect because it is the total number of female attorneys in 2002. If you did not account for each group, you may have mistakenly arrived at either answer choice B or C.

You should now have a good idea of the types of questions found on the different Quantitative, or Math sections of the GRE. If this is your weak area, refer specifically to the chapters in this book that focus on strengthening your math skills.

Now that you've assessed your readiness for GRE, you can begin to work on the remaining sections of this book. Focus first on the areas in which you need the most improvement, and apply the strategies and techniques provided. The old adage "practice makes perfect" really holds true here, so be sure to try all the practice questions included in the chapters, as well as the two full-length practice tests at the end of the book.

GRE Analytical Writing Section

The Analytical Writing portion of the GRE is purely a skills test. This means that you are not tested on any knowledge whatsoever. Instead, you are given an opportunity to demonstrate your ability to reason clearly and write coherently and concisely.

There are two separate tasks within this section: "Present Your Perspective on an Issue," (which we'll call the Issue task) and "Analyze an Argument," (which we'll call the Argument task). You are allowed 45 minutes for the Issue task, and 30 minutes for the Argument task, including reading and prewriting.

The Issue task allows you to choose one of the two given issues, and then write a short essay supporting your position on that issue. Although you cannot be certain what the issue choices will be in advance, some examples are provided later in this chapter so that you can get an idea of the type of issue that is likely to appear. The GRE Power Prep® software also includes sample Issue tasks.

On the Argument task, you are only given one argument, which you must respond to in the time allowed, using the somewhat primitive word processor that is built in to the GRE software. Be sure to practice using GRE PowerPrep® to become familiar with the features of the software.

On this task, you are expected to respond to an argument and discuss how well its evidence supports its conclusion. Essentially, you must critique the argument in detail as opposed to creating your own argument as you must do on the Issue task.

Each essay is scored on a scale of 0–6 by two carefully trained people (usually college faculty members) using a "rubric" or scoring guide. The process contains a number of safeguards to ensure fairness. For instance, the essays are randomly assigned to the readers, who have no way of learning the identity of the writer. Two readers grade each essay. The scores of the two readers are then averaged. If the two scores given to a single essay differ by more than one point, a third, senior reader is called in to assign the final grade.

The essays are scored holistically, which means that a reader evaluates the whole essay and simply assigns a single number grade to the essay. Although many factors may enter into the reader's decision, the most important factors are critical thinking (logic) and analytical writing (also, logic). Logic is far more important than mechanics such as spelling and grammar. However, we suggest that you not take any chances with mechanics. For example, if you aren't absolutely certain how to use a semicolon properly, just replace it with a period and a capital letter. (By the way, that is exactly how you will know that you have used it correctly: If you can replace your semicolon with a period and a capital letter, you have two independent clauses that are closely related and have, therefore, used the semicolon correctly.)

Here is a description of how essays are scored at each level on both tasks. Essays that receive the following scores exhibit one or more of the characteristics listed:

➤ **0**—Response does not address the assigned task, or is in a foreign language, or is indecipherable or contains no text (not attempted).

➤ **.5–1**—Fundamentally deficient. The essay is extremely confusing and/or mostly irrelevant. There is little or no development of ideas. Contains severe and pervasive errors.

➤ **1.5–2**—Seriously weak. Contains frequent problems in sentence structure and/or use of language. Errors obscure meaning. Lacks analysis or development of ideas.

➤ **2.5–3**—Shows some competence. Contains little analysis or development of ideas. Limited organization with flawed control or sentence structure and/or language. Essay is vague and lacks clarity.

➤ **3.5–4**—Competent. Main ideas are supported with relevant evidence and examples. Shows adequate organization and is reasonably clear. There is adequate control of sentences and language but the essay may include some errors that reduce overall clarity.

➤ **4.5–5**—Generally thoughtful analysis of complex ideas. Sound reasons and well-chosen examples support conclusions. Well organized and focused. Uses sentences of varying length and complexity. Any errors are minor and do not affect the meaning of the essay.

➤ **5.5–6**—Insightful, in-depth analysis of complex ideas. Compelling logic and very persuasive examples. Essay is well organized and focused and displays skill in structuring sentences; vocabulary is precise and relevant. If there are any errors, they do not affect the logic or meaning of the essay.

Now that you have an idea of what the graders are looking for, review the following sections for a discussion of the specifics of the tasks.

Issue Task

The topics presented are usually of general public interest. You are expected to think clearly and critically about them and then create a thoughtful, well-reasoned essay supporting your position. There is never a "correct" answer. Your task is simply to write a good essay from whatever perspective you choose on whichever of the two topics you choose.

Read the topics carefully and choose the one that seems the most interesting to you. Don't spend too much time choosing. The overall time limit starts running from the moment that the issues are revealed to you on the computer screen. You will be given some scratch paper. It will probably be helpful to make a few notes about the pluses and minuses of various sides to the issue. You will definitely earn points if, in your essay, you reveal an ability to anticipate counterarguments to your position and deal with them effectively.

There are many possible responses to any Issue prompt. You might agree or disagree in part, or in whole. You may attack the underlying assumptions in the statement that is given. You may decide to discuss the fact that the statement you are writing about has only limited applicability in certain situations. You should certainly use at least one example to support your position. You may choose to use more than one example, and that is fine as long as the examples you select are relevant and you stay focused on your main idea.

The issues are carefully chosen so that they aren't biased toward any one college major or profession. However, luck is a bit of a factor on this section of the GRE. If you happen to be presented with an issue that you know something about, you will probably feel more comfortable in writing about it. However, be careful to respond to the issue presented. Don't answer a question that wasn't asked just because you happen to know something about the subject matter.

Sample Essay Prompt: Present Your Perspective on an Issue

Directions: Plan and compose a response that represents your perspective on the following topic. Support your views with reasons and examples drawn from personal experience, reading, observations, or academic studies. Take a few minutes to think about the issue and plan a response. Organize and fully develop your ideas; be sure to leave time to evaluate your response and revise as necessary.

> "Political matters are an unnecessary distraction from the more important matters in society, which are deeper and more weighty than politics."

➤ *The following essay received a score of 6 because it is well organized and focused, uses the language effectively, and provides an insightful in-depth analysis of a complex issue.*

Since in any complex society there are many aspects and spheres to be considered, political and otherwise, it is an over-simplification and a mistake to label political issues as a mere "distraction." In fact, politics is a supremely important field, in problems ranging in importance from the possibility of nuclear war, to the price of a postage stamp. However, it is true that there may be matters at least as important as politics, or even more important at times. Therefore, one must work for a balanced appreciation of both the political and the non-political.

First, a reiteration: politics are vital. Without a government to coordinate the various functions of society, life would be chaos. Private groups would likely work only for their own selfish purposes, and we would all suffer. Elected bodies, while not perfect, often do excellent work in regulating private life through the law, while representing their constituents, thus accomplishing great things.

Then again, one thing often considered more important than politics is religion. The Bible says, "What is it to gain the whole world, if you lose your soul for eternity?" Perhaps meditating on that phrase would have given powerful politicians (and dictators) like Adolf Hitler some pause in their maniacal campaigns to rule the whole world. Even on a less intense scale than "world domination," though, is the idea that one's personal life, one's loves, family relations, etc., are more important than the government or the thorny thicket of laws, tax forms, road signs, and other state machinery which politicians often inflict upon us.

However, while most of us would agree that our personal lives are more important than political entanglements, one must note that religion itself is not free of politics. Moreover, some religious leaders also double as political leaders, such as the late Ayatollah Khomeini in Iran. So, a factor making it hard to pronounce simplistically that politics unnecessarily distract from more crucial matters, is that politics intermingles frequently with many of those other matters.

Despite this, it is sometimes legitimate to say that politics is a distraction. There may be some legitimate business buried in all the hot air, such as consideration of how much money will be spent on a certain bill. However, with all the wasted time spent word-slinging, not to mention the salaries paid to the politicians, an observer may wonder if society could have just let private individuals arrange matters among themselves, rather than having politicians manage those matters instead. Thus, all the red tape and self-serving political wrangling distracts from the more important issues at hand.

And politics may not only have distractions within itself, such as the time-wasting just mentioned; it can itself serve as a "distraction" to the public, by taking up endless hours on television and newspapers, that would be better spent otherwise.

Evidently, then, while politics is pervasive and important, it can also take our attention away from other important aspects of life. What deeper general conclusion can we draw from this? For help, we may call upon the spirit of Winston Churchill's quip "Democracy is the worst political system of all, except for all the other systems," and pronounce, "Life with politics is the worst kind of life, except for life without politics." In seeking the "balanced appreciation of the political and the non-political" that was mentioned at the beginning of this essay, we note that while it is often difficult to live with politics and its distractions and trivialities, it may be more difficult to live without its benefits. We should not elevate politics above everything else, but we are hardly in the position to scorn it, either.

➤ *The following essay received a score of 4 because, although the ideas were supported with relevant examples, the essay lacks focus and includes errors that reduce its overall clarity.*

There is nothing as distracting as politics sometimes. It is painful to see how much of societys effort goes down the tubes in pursuit of politics, when so much else is available to focus on. Society will only become better when we are less obsessed with politics and politicians.

If we are interested in entertainment, sports are a better and healthier thing. Baseball, football, and soccer are good for the participants in term of exercise. By contrast, the entertainment that politics provides is not really very healthy. Maybe marching around a rally for a couple of hours? And just to see some guy with shiny teeth telling you his campaign promises.

Imagine a politician's day. First, he gets up in the morning and has his staff tell him what to say, even though he didn't think of it himself. Then he goes to a bunch of meetings with "fat cats" and butters them up, even if he doesn't really mean it, so that they'll donate money to his campaign. Then maybe he will work on a TV appearance where he spews out a bunch of rhetoric that does not help solve a problem. So there's a whole bunch of distraction, as we can see.

Business is more important than politics too. Our economics have billions and billions of dollars floating around. Do the politicians really help with this? When is the last time this writer saw a politician doing any real work, like driving around a cement truck and boosting the economy? Not ever, really. Politicians may pass some laws, but business is a lot more important than politics. We would all starve unless the economy were providing us food, and we'd have no houses unless business enterprises were building them.

We have to consider that maybe other things can be distracting too. If somebody is addicted to drugs, that is even a worse distraction than politics are. Or computers. People waste many days on the internet fooling around. But even if these things are worse than politics, politics is still a considerable distraction in the lives of American people.

Now how can we get rid of politics, or at least get rid of the distracting part? A person can just make up his mind to spend less time on it. All the flyers that campaigns send to your house don't have to be read after all; they can just go right in the trash. You can't put all the politicians in jail, but at least you can put their paper waste in a plastic bag and put it by the curb for the garbagemen to pick up.

Of course, this is not to sound ungrateful to all politicians. Some were good, like Teddy Roosevelt, who provided real leadership to the country. He was a hero in the Spanish-American War, and a tough warrior. If more politicians could be like that, then politics would not be so much of a mere distraction.

In conclusion, we must have some politicians to greet foreign leaders and do other "meet and greet" functions. And we need some laws to keep criminals in jail, However, politics is mostly a big distraction, even if not bad as drugs or computer games. Hopefully individuals can work together to keep the politics out of their lives more and more, so they have more time to live their own lives without all the nonsense that politics brings.

➤ *The following essay received a score of 2 because it lacks any serious development of the stimulus, and contains frequent errors that either distract from or obscure the author's intended meaning.*

Politics is a very important matter for all of us. It can be quite distracting. They are always on television, after all. This makes political matter overly time consuming.

There is nothing more important than politics though. The President decides if we will have a war, and who we will invade or bomb. And millions of people could be killed. So political matter are a crucial thing to consider. That is a reason there are so many different political bodies in the United Staes of America. The Senate, and the House of Representatives, and the Supreme Court too. They all have their place and their job to perform.

Other important things are the economy, envyronment, and safety. They are important like politics. But politics are more important, because the President and other big leaders make so many huge decisions about our lives. Sometimes about the economy too, and the other factors as well.

Argument Task

You should read the prompt in the Argument task even more carefully than you read the prompts in the Issue task. You are being asked to critique an argument, not to present your own views on the subject. You should look for any potential flaws in the structure of the argument. This means that you must examine the relationship between the evidence that is stated, any assumptions (unstated evidence) that are made, and the conclusion of the argument. You should also give some thought to the implications of the argument. That is, what will probably follow if the conclusion of the argument is accepted at face value?

Pay special attention to the structural signal words that indicate evidence (since, because, and so on), conclusion (therefore, thus, and so on), contrast (but, however, on the other hand, and so on), and continuation (similarly, next, and so on). These terms usually just sort of blend into the background as we read. However, in this case, the structure is what you are analyzing and critiquing. So, you need to pay careful attention to the building blocks of the argument; these signals are the signposts that point out the function of each sentence within the argument.

Sample Essay Prompt: Analyze an Argument

<u>Directions:</u> Plan and write a critique of the argument presented. Analyze the line of reasoning in the argument and consider any questionable assumptions that underlie the thinking. Discuss the evidence provided and whether or not there might be evidence that strengthens or weakens the argument, as well as what changes would make the argument more logically sound. You are NOT being asked to present your views on the subject.

> The following appeared on an educational website.
>
> "Education is a factor that always helps the income-earning power of the person who is educated. This assertion is supported by a comprehensive study done over a 2-year period by the American Educational Foundation, which polled and studied over 1000 different wage-earners, finding that those with a higher degree of education earned more than those who were less well-educated."

➤ *The following essay received a score of 6 because it correctly identifies and supports the argument, and contains compelling logic and persuasive examples. Any errors are minor and do not affect the logic of the essay.*

Although one looks for sense and structure in the claims of the American Educational Foundation regarding education and earning power, there is remarkably little. Common sense may tell us that education can be a powerful impetus in the ability to earn income, but reasoning would be a nice supplement to common sense in the assertion we are given.

The most glaring problem may be the word "always." Outside of mathematics, where 2 and 2 always equal 4, there may be a few 100% correlations in daily life, at least in complex situations. (A simple situation may be, e.g., "Women can bear children, men cannot." Here we seem to have a 100% correlation, although of course, some women may be unable to bear children.) It is highly doubtful that in every single case, a better-educated person will earn more than a less-educated one. For example, high-school dropouts who become rock stars may become millionaires.

Methodologically, there also seem to be problems with the purportedly "comprehensive" study itself. The polling, for example: how, precisely, was that done, and with what sorts of questions? And could those polled give inaccurate answers, perhaps ones which either overly credited or under-credited the role of education in improving their income? (A poll might be more useful in a study of whether people THINK "education is a factor that always helps... income-earning power", than in a study of whether or not education really IS such a factor.)

Moreover, the study may not even know what it is studying. Where is "education" defined? We may assume it is formal education of the grade-school-high school-university sort, but we are not allowed to know. In fact, we don't know if the study itself even bothered to define education at all.

And even if there were an adequate definition of "education"   which would give us a logical basis for understanding just what helped income-earners   and even if there were more information about polling, and about exactly what studies the "studying" of the 1000+ wage-earners comprised, there is still the issue of correlation. That is, there may be other reasons for the high performance of the well-educated, such as socioeconomic, racial, or other factors which might privilege those who also happen to be well-educated. Without a serious discussion of these other factors, it is difficult to take the American Educational Foundation's purported study seriously.

To sum up: the argument we are presented may be a classic example of a massive overgeneralization, supported by bad, if "institutional," evidence. In fact, this example shows us how "institutions" themselves are sometimes overrated in their ability to conduct meaningful research about society: an unfortunate tendency about which we deserve to be educated, indeed.

➤ *The following essay received a score of 4 because it shows an adequate grasp of the argument and is reasonably clear. However, it includes some errors in logic and construction that reduce its overall clarity.*

This assertion does not make complete sense, as there are gaps in the reasoning, and unclear aspects.

First, "education" is not well defined. Could it be formal education, or the informal "school of hard knocks" and "street smarts" instead? So we do not even know what "education" is supposed to be precisely.

Second, "always" is a little general. If we knew that in 100% of the cases, the wage-earners made more money, then "always" would make a little more sense. However, the assertion overgeneralizes here.

Third, the better-educated wage-earners studied by the American Educational Foundation may have earned more for other reasons than their education. Say, maybe they came from richer families to start with. The Foundation is making a leap of logic here that may not be justified, so that the reasoning of the Foundation is poor. (Unless there are other factors in the study that we don't know about, e.g., an appendix which explains the role of other factors beside education)

In conclusion, the study is not that comprehensive really! It could have been done much better, or we should be given more information about the study so we can see if it is adequate or inadequate in explaining the role of education in people's earning capacity.

➤ *The following essay received a score of 2 because it lacks analysis of the argument, is vague, and contains pervasive structural and grammatical errors.*

It is important to recognize the value of Education. Since education evidently makes people earn more money, there must be no barriers to educational advancement, this is why the American Education Foundation study is necessary for all young people to consider.

You can even see a connection over the generations. The older income earners will have more income, that they can use to educate their offsprings with. Then their children themselves can earn more money, since they have been educated. By contrast, those with lower income can not educate their children well, leading to a poorer income. This is tragic.

Therefore, the lessons of the AEF study are profound for the American nation.

Strategies for Writing Well

As was noted earlier in this book, humans acquire skills through practice. Because the Analytical Writing section is a test of your writing skills, you should practice writing under testlike conditions in order to score better.

Specifically, you should practice the type of writing that is rewarded by the scoring rubric. The best way to make sure that you are on track is to have someone with experience in this area, someone you trust (such as a tutor), give you specific feedback on your practice essays. You can gain something by reading your own essays and comparing them to a rubric. But, writers tend to develop blind spots when it comes to areas that need improvement in their own essays. It is always a good idea to get a fresh set of eyes to review your work. It does not take long for an experienced grader to give feedback that can be immensely valuable.

If you will be critiquing your own essays, put them away for a week or so and then take them out for another spin. You might find errors and lapses in logic that were not evident to you as you were writing the essay.

Make sure that you understand the issue or argument that is presented before you begin writing. Remember that you will receive a score of zero if your response is off the topic.

Your essay should start out with a clear statement of your position on the issue. There should be no doubt in the reader's mind about which side you are on from the beginning of your essay. For the argument task, clearly identify important features of the argument. Use the scratch paper that is provided to outline the structure of your essay. Your outline does not have to include complete sentences. It does have to include the ideas that you will put into your final draft. You need to be sure that you have a clear picture of where you are going and how you will get there before you start to type your answer.

Too often, GRE test takers make broad, general statements in their essays without giving any specific support. Make sure that you provide clear, simple examples of the general statements that you make, and that your evaluations are logical and well supported. In your response to the argument task, be sure to include a cause-and-effect relationship between your evidence and your conclusion.

The practice tests included later in this book contain additional essay prompts. Use these as well as the prompts that can be found in the GRE topic pool (www.gre.org/pracmats.html) to write as much as possible between now and test day.

Putting It to Practice

Now that you've got a good feel for how to approach the different writing assignments found on the GRE, try some sample writing prompts in the

"Exam Prep Questions" section. Because grading the essay is subjective, we've chosen not to include any "graded" essays here. Your best bet is to have someone you trust, such as your personal tutor, read your essays and give you an honest critique. If you plan on grading your own essays, review the grading criteria and be as honest as possible regarding the structure, development, organization, technique, and appropriateness of your writing. Focus on your weak areas and continue to practice to improve your writing skills.

Exam Prep Questions

Issue Task

Directions: Plan and compose a response that represents your perspective on the following topic. Support your views with reasons and examples drawn from personal experience, reading, observations, or academic studies. Take a few minutes to think about the issue and plan a response. Organize and fully develop your ideas; be sure to leave time to evaluate your response and revise as necessary.

> "Planning is critical to success: No one should expect to succeed without creating a clear picture of his or her methods and goals beforehand."

Argument Task

Directions: Plan and write a critique of the argument presented. Analyze the line of reasoning in the argument and consider any questionable assumptions that underlie the thinking. Discuss the evidence provided and whether or not there might be evidence that strengthens or weakens the argument, as well as what changes would make the argument more logically sound. You are NOT being asked to present your views on the subject.

The following appeared in a memo from the quality control department of DeBergi Amplifier Company to the company president.

"In order to prevent manufacturing defects in our workplace, DeBergi Amplifier Company should require all its employees to attend workshops that teach the technique of 'peer checking,' a technique in which people ask one another for immediate confirmation of the accuracy of their work, and provide such confirmation for one another. This technique has clearly benefited Tap Record Company: Four years ago, three hundred recently hired Tap employees volunteered to participate in a one-day peer checking workshop. Four years later, only six percent of these employees had been disciplined for shoddy workmanship, whereas the company as a whole had an eleven percent discipline rate during that period."

GRE Verbal Section: Antonyms

Terms you'll need to know:

✓ Antonym
✓ Cognate
✓ Connotation
✓ Homonym
✓ Prefix
✓ Root
✓ Suffix
✓ Synonym

Concepts you'll need to master:

✓ Creating precise definitions
✓ Identifying slight variations in meaning
✓ Identifying multiple definitions for single words
✓ Defining unfamiliar words

The Antonym questions on the GRE Verbal section are designed not only to test the strength of your vocabulary, but also your ability to reason from one concept to an opposite concept. You should be able to answer many questions with only a general knowledge of a vocabulary word; however, some challenging questions might require you to make distinctions between more subtle meanings. Refer to Appendix A for a list of words commonly found on the GRE General Test.

Answering GRE Antonym Questions

Questions in this section will include a word in all capital letters, followed by five answer choices. You will be required to determine the answer choice that is the *antonym* of, or is most nearly opposite to, the definition of the given word. Following is an example of an antonym question similar to those found on the GRE General Test, along with a detailed explanation:

CREDULOUS :

  (A) skeptical

  (B) naive

  (C) spontaneous

  (D) sensitive

  (E) discrete

Because "credulous" means "gullible or believing too readily," the correct answer will be a word that is opposite in meaning. "Skeptical" means "marked by or prone to doubt," which is most nearly opposite to "credulous." "Naïve" is a synonym of "credulous," so answer choice B is incorrect. "Spontaneous" means "arising without apparent external cause"; "sensitive" means "responsive or receptive to stimuli"; "discrete" means "separate or distinct." None of these words are antonyms of "credulous," so answer choices C, D, and E are incorrect.

 In general, the words that appear in the antonym questions are limited to nouns, adjectives, or verbs. Answer choices will be either a single word or a short phrase. Some of the answer choices may be very similar to one another. Your job is to select the best choice from the five options.

There are several strategies that will help you to correctly answer GRE antonym questions. Following is a description of those strategies that we have found most helpful:

➤ Clearly define the given word

   ➤ Use the correct part of speech

   ➤ Beware of homonyms

   ➤ Use prefixes, suffixes, roots, and cognates

   ➤ Use connotations

➤ Use the given word in a sentence

➤ Predict an answer choice

➤ Use the process of elimination

Clearly Define the Given Word

Because you are looking for an antonym of the given word, it's important that you first determine the meaning of the given word. If you are only somewhat familiar with the given word, it might help to use the word in a sentence or recall a quotation that includes the word. In addition, pay attention to the following suggestions to help you correctly and clearly define the given word.

Use the Correct Part of Speech

Make sure that you recognize whether the word is a noun, adjective, or verb. The answer choices might help you to make this determination. If all of the answer choices are adjectives, for example, the given word will also be used as an adjective.

It is important to remember that a single word can often be used interchangeably as a verb and a noun, or a noun and an adjective, or might simply have multiple definitions.

For example, the word "bore" can be:

➤ A verb, as in "to cause a loss of interest"

➤ A verb, as in "to drill a hole"

➤ A verb, as in the past tense of "to bear," which means to "support," "carry," or "have" something

➤ A noun, as in "a dull or boring person or thing"

The key to successfully answering a GRE antonym question will often be your ability to quickly switch between possible meanings and select a correct answer based upon your reactions to the answer choices.

Keep in mind that GRE test writers rarely use exact opposites. In fact, you should not expect to find a perfect antonym among the answer choices. Remind yourself to look for the word that is "most nearly opposite."

Beware of Homonyms

Generally, *homonyms* are words that are pronounced the same, but have different spellings and different meanings. Be sure that you are defining the correct word. For example, the words "course" and "coarse" are pronounced exactly the same, but have very different meanings. If you mistakenly define "course" as "common or rough," you will have a hard time finding an antonym among the answer choices. Consider the following example of a question similar to those found on the GRE:

ASSENT:

(A) indifference

(B) disagreement

(C) carelessness

(D) stability

(E) significance

The word "assent" refers to "agreement," so the correct answer is B, "disagreement." If you had defined "assent" as "the act of climbing," (*ascent*), you would most likely have struggled to find an antonym.

It might help to study a list of common homonyms; a search on the Internet will yield many websites devoted to this topic.

Use Prefixes, Suffixes, Roots, and Cognates

If you have never seen the word before, use your knowledge of *prefixes*, *suffixes*, and *roots* to help you determine the meaning of the word.

Prefix refers to a letter or letters attached to the front of a word to produce a derivative of that word. For example, the prefix "multi-" means "many," as in "multilingual," which means "many languages."

A suffix, on the other hand, is a letter or series of letters added to the end of a word, serving to form a new word or functioning as an inflectional ending. For example, the suffix "-less" means "without," as in "careless."

Learn to recognize roots, or stems, that some words have in common. The root provides the basis from which certain words are derived. For example, the Latin root "gen" means "birth, class, or kin," as in "congenital," which refers to a condition that is present at birth.

In addition, look for *cognates* from French, Spanish, or Italian (the modern versions of Latin) if you recognize them. A *cognate* is a word that means the same or nearly the same thing in more than one language. For example, the word *amigo*, which means friend in Spanish, the word *ami*, which means friend in French, and the word *amicable*, which means friendly in English, all come from the Latin root word for friend, *amicus*. These words are considered cognates.

Following is an example of how to use a prefix to select the correct answer:

INVARIABLE:
- (A) overstated
- (B) sufficient
- (C) erratic
- (D) reasonable
- (E) intact

The prefix "in-" can mean "not, or without." Therefore, something that is "invariable" is "not variable." "Erratic" means "irregular, unpredictable, or subject to change," which is most nearly opposite to "invariable."

Use Connotations

Each word in the English language expresses two things: a *definition* and a *connotation*. A definition conveys the meaning of the word. A connotation is a positive, negative, or neutral feeling or emotion that is suggested by or associated with a word. For example, the noun "thrifty" implies a positive connotation, while "cheap" has a negative connotation. Using connotations may help you to determine the correct answer or at least eliminate a few wrong answers.

Here is an example of how to use a connotation to help you to select the correct answer:

FALLACY:
- (A) tentative disagreement
- (B) personal philosophy
- (C) simple hypothesis
- (D) legitimate claim
- (E) indirect statement

The word "fallacy" has a negative connotation because it relates to something that has errors, flaws, or is false. It comes from the Latin word "fallere," which means "to deceive." Therefore, the best answer will have an opposite, or positive connotation. Answer choice A is slightly negative, answer choice B is neutral, answer choice C is neutral, answer choice D is positive, and answer choice E is neutral but slightly negative. The connotations of the given word and the answer choices lead you to answer choice D, "legitimate claim."

Use the Given Word in a Sentence

Unfortunately, you cannot guess the meaning of an unfamiliar word from the context in GRE antonym questions. The good news is that you have probably seen or heard the unfamiliar word, or some version of it, at some point in your life. Create a sentence that uses the word in a familiar way, and use the sentence to help you establish the definition of the word. Substitute the answer choices for the word in the sentence; the choice that successfully reverses the meaning or tone of the sentence is the best choice. Consider the following example:

DORMANCY:

  (A) remaining active
  (B) creating confusion
  (C) lurking about
  (D) hibernation
  (E) opposition

You probably have heard the word "dormant," which means "inactive." "Dormancy," then, refers to the "state of being dormant, or inactive." Use the word in a sentence: "The bear awoke after several months of dormancy." Now, insert the answer choices; the one that changes the meaning of the sentence the most will be the correct answer. When you insert answer choice A, the sentence becomes "The bear awoke after several months of remaining active." Because the bear remained active for several months, it was *not* dormant during that period of time. Therefore, answer choice A is best. Answer choices B and C are nonsensical, answer choice D is a synonym of "dormancy," and answer choice E means "being in conflict," which is not an antonym of "dormancy."

Predict an Answer Choice

Before you look at the answer choices, try to predict an antonym on your own. Remember that experts create incorrect answers to distract you. If you predict an answer before you look at the answer choices, you can begin to eliminate words and are less likely to get caught up in these confusing, incorrect answers. If your antonym matches one of the answer choices, it is most likely correct. The following examples and detailed explanations show you how predicting an answer can help you to eliminate obviously incorrect answer choices:

LOCAL:

(A) clear

(B) anxious

(C) global

(D) unusual

(E) durable

Because "local" generally refers to a specific place on earth, an antonym would most likely involve the entire Earth. "Global" is a word that could easily be predicted and is the correct answer. You also could have easily eliminated most of the other answer choices by predicting an answer such as "nearby" or "in the same city."

RANDOM:

(A) hidden

(B) appropriate

(C) systematic

(D) deliberate

(E) genuine

You might have predicted "regular" or "orderly" as antonyms of "random." Both are correct, but neither appear as an answer choice. However, "systematic" is a synonym of both of your predicted answers, so answer choice C is correct. Answer choice D, "deliberate" might have been tempting, but "systematic" is more opposite because it implies a sense of order.

Be sure to look at all of the answer choices before you select a final answer, even if your predicted antonym is among the choices. Eliminate clearly incorrect answers as you work through the choices.

Use the Process of Elimination

This strategy is useful if you are unable to find the correct answer using any of the previously mentioned strategies. Look at each answer choice and determine whether you know something about each word or phrase, and use that information to eliminate answer choices that are clearly incorrect. For example, if you find answer choices that have similar meanings, those choices can usually be eliminated. The process of elimination can be time-consuming, so it should generally be saved for "last-ditch" efforts in selecting the correct answer. You will probably employ this strategy in conjunction with the others mentioned, eliminating answer choices that do not fit logically into the sentence that you created, for instance.

Putting It to Practice

The following section contains simulated GRE antonym questions. Read the directions carefully before you begin to answer the questions. Make guesses as necessary. Remember that on the actual computer adaptive exam, you will be required to select an answer before you can move on to the next question. Be sure to read the explanations to help you gain a better understanding of why the correct answer is correct.

Exam Prep Questions

Directions: Each question below contains a word in capital letters and five answer choices. Each answer choice contains a word or phrase. Select the word or phrase that best expresses a meaning *opposite* to the word in capital letters.

1. ABJECT:
   (A) hopeful
   (B) base
   (C) functional
   (D) pitiable
   (E) vile

2. CONFRONT:
   (A) advise
   (B) reconcile
   (C) correlate
   (D) ignore
   (E) reflect

3. OBLITERATE:

   (A) expunge

   (B) create

   (C) overwhelm

   (D) educate

   (E) restrict

4. PASSIVE:

   (A) belligerent

   (B) delayed

   (C) slovenly

   (D) resolute

   (E) appropriate

5. TORPID:

   (A) robust

   (B) tolerant

   (C) contrived

   (D) indolent

   (E) tractable

6. ARCANE:

   (A) increasingly apprehensive

   (B) highly valued

   (C) commonly understood

   (D) eminently qualified

   (E) moderately confident

7. LIMPID:

   (A) pleasant

   (B) radiant

   (C) contrite

   (D) opaque

   (E) sanguine

8. PLACATE:

   (A) exacerbate

   (B) alleviate

   (C) mitigate

   (D) insinuate

   (E) permeate

9. BUCOLIC:
   (A) enthusiastic
   (B) oblivious
   (C) provincial
   (D) permanent
   (E) metropolitan

10. IMPUDENCE:
   (A) indifference
   (B) humility
   (C) fortitude
   (D) treachery
   (E) stylishness

11. VINDICATE:
   (A) implicate
   (B) banish
   (C) penalize
   (D) liberate
   (E) validate

12. CIRCUITOUS:
   (A) unstable
   (B) direct
   (C) fundamental
   (D) devious
   (E) murky

13. WANING:
   (A) slowly expanding
   (B) gradually encroaching
   (C) noisily retreating
   (D) quickly increasing
   (E) silently advancing

14. DEROGATE:
   (A) pursue
   (B) broach
   (C) extol
   (D) eliminate
   (E) detain

15. EMBEZZLE:
    (A) portend
    (B) perform
    (C) obscure
    (D) reimburse
    (E) engender

16. OBDURATE:
    (A) apparently believable
    (B) greatly exaggerated
    (C) willing to comply
    (D) difficult to manage
    (E) thoroughly explained

17. COGNIZANT:
    (A) simplified
    (B) deferential
    (C) animated
    (D) forceful
    (E) oblivious

18. SPURIOUS:
    (A) relevant
    (B) indelible
    (C) effusive
    (D) concise
    (E) supportive

19. HEINOUS:
    (A) scandalous
    (B) admirable
    (C) ambiguous
    (D) lazy
    (E) critical

20. ENIGMATIC:
    (A) completely understood
    (B) lacking direction
    (C) intentionally neglectful
    (D) especially important
    (E) cautiously optimistic

Answers to Exam Prep Questions

1. **The best answer is A.** "Abject" means low in status or demeanor, or hopeless. "Hopeful" has the most nearly opposite meaning. Answer choice B is incorrect because "base," when used as an adjective, means lowest. "Functional" means relating to a function, and is not an antonym of "abject," so answer choice C is incorrect. Answer choice D is incorrect because "pitiable" means to be pitied, which is not opposite in meaning to "abject." Answer choice E is incorrect because "vile" means disgusting or unpleasant.

2. **The best answer is D.** To "confront" means to come face to face with. "Ignore" is the best choice because it has a meaning most opposite to that of "confront." "Advise" means to offer advice, so answer choice A is not correct. Answer choice B is not correct because "reconcile" means to settle or resolve, which is not opposite in meaning to "confront." Answer choice C is incorrect because to "correlate" means to establish a reciprocal relation. "Reflect" has several meanings, such as to bend light, or to make apparent, none of which are opposite in meaning to "confront," so answer choice E is incorrect.

3. **The best answer is B.** To "obliterate" means to do away with completely. "Create" is the best choice because it has a meaning opposite to that of "obliterate." Answer choice A is incorrect because "expunge" means to erase. Answer choices C and D are incorrect because neither "overwhelm" nor "educate" are opposite to "obliterate." "Restrict" means to confine within limits, which is not an antonym of "obliterate," so answer choice E is incorrect.

4. **The best answer is A.** "Passive" means inactive or submissive. "Belligerent" means rude or aggressive, which is nearly opposite in meaning to "passive." Answer choice B is incorrect because "delayed" is not the opposite of "passive." "Slovenly" means sloppy or lazy, which is not opposite in meaning to "passive," so answer choice C is incorrect. Answer choice D is incorrect because "resolute" means determined or unwavering. Answer choice E is incorrect because "appropriate" is not an antonym of "passive."

5. **The best answer is A.** "Torpid" means deprived of power, or inactive. "Robust" means vigorous and full of power, so it is the best choice. "Tolerant" is not an antonym for "torpid" so answer choice B is incorrect. "Contrived" means calculated or planned, so answer choice C is incorrect. "Indolent" means lazy, which has a similar meaning to "torpid," so answer choice D is incorrect. Answer choice E is incorrect because "tractable" means easily managed or controlled.

6. **The best answer is C.** "Arcane" means mysterious, or only understood by a few people. Therefore, "commonly understood" is the most opposite in meaning to "arcane." Something that is "arcane" could also be "highly valued"; however, this phrase is not an antonym of "arcane," so answer choice B is incorrect. Likewise, answer choices A, D, and E are not antonyms of "arcane."

7. **The best answer is D.** "Limpid" means transparent or clear. "Opaque" means impenetrable by light, or not transparent, so answer choice D is best. Answer choice A is incorrect, because "pleasant" is not an antonym of "limpid." "Radiant" means to emit light, or to glow, which is not opposite in meaning to "limpid," so answer choice B is incorrect. "Contrite" means regretful, which is not an antonym of "limpid," so answer choice C is incorrect. Answer choice E is incorrect because "sanguine" means either reddish in color, or optimistic.

8. **The best answer is A.** "Placate" means to make peace with, or appease. "Exacerbate" is the best choice because it means to aggravate, or to increase the severity of something. "Alleviate" means to make more bearable, and "mitigate" means to lessen, so answer choices B and C are incorrect. "Insinuate" means to introduce gradually, or to suggest, so answer choice D is incorrect. Answer choice E is incorrect because "permeate" means to spread throughout, which is not opposite in meaning to "placate."

9. **The best answer is E.** "Bucolic" means rustic, or relating to the country. "Metropolitan" means relating to the city, so it is most opposite in meaning to "bucolic." Neither "enthusiastic" nor "oblivious" are antonyms of "bucolic," so answer choices A and B are incorrect. "Provincial" means not fashionable or sophisticated, so answer choice C is incorrect. "Permanent" is not an antonym of "bucolic," so answer choice D is incorrect.

10. **The best answer is B.** "Impudence" means boldness or rudeness. "Humility" means the condition of being humble or modest, so it is the best choice. "Indifference" is not an antonym of "impudence," so answer choice A is incorrect. "Fortitude" means strength of mind or character, so answer choice C is incorrect. "Treachery" means willful betrayal, so answer choice D is incorrect. Answer choice E is incorrect because "stylishness" is not an antonym of "impudence."

11. **The best answer is A.** To "vindicate" means to clear of blame, or to justify. "Implicate" means to involve or to incriminate, so it is the best choice. "Banish" means to send away, so answer choice B is incorrect. "Penalize" means to punish, which is not quite the opposite of

"vindicate," so answer choice C is incorrect. To "liberate" means to set free, which is not opposite in meaning to "vindicate," so answer choice D is incorrect. To "validate" means to confirm or to make legally valid, so answer choice E is incorrect.

12. **The best answer is B.** "Circuitous" means indirect, or taking a roundabout route. Therefore, "direct" is the best choice. Neither "unstable" nor "fundamental" are antonyms of "circuitous," so eliminate answer choices A and C. "Devious" means shifty or departing from the accepted way, so eliminate answer choice D. "Murky" means unclear, which is not an antonym of "circuitous," so eliminate answer choice E.

13. **The best answer is D.** "Waning" means gradually decreasing in size, so "quickly increasing" is the most opposite in meaning. Answer choices A, B, C, and E are not antonyms of "waning."

14. **The best answer is C.** "Derogate" means to take away or detract from. "Extol" means to praise highly or lift up, so it is most opposite in meaning. "Pursue" means to follow, so answer choice A is incorrect. "Broach" means to bring up for discussion, so answer choice B is incorrect. "Eliminate" is not an antonym of "derogate," so answer choice D is incorrect. Answer choice E is incorrect because "detain" means to keep from proceeding.

15. **The best answer is D.** "Embezzle" means to take illegally (as in money), or to appropriate funds for one's own use. "Reimburse" means to pay back or refund money, so it is most opposite in meaning. "Portend" means to warn or predict, so answer choice A is incorrect. "Perform" is not an antonym of "embezzle," so answer choice B is incorrect. When used as a verb, "obscure" means to conceal or hide, so answer choice C is incorrect. "Engender" means to bring into existence, so answer choice E is incorrect.

16. **The best answer is C.** "Obdurate" means hard-hearted or stubborn. Therefore, "willing to comply" is the best choice because "comply" means obedient, or to act in accordance with the wishes of another. Answer choices A, B, D, and E are not antonyms of "obdurate."

17. **The best answer is E.** "Cognizant" means fully informed or aware. "Oblivious" means lacking awareness, so it is the best choice. "Simplified" is not an antonym of "cognizant," so answer choice A is incorrect. "Deferential" means yielding to the opinion of another, so answer choice B is incorrect. "Animated" means lively or spirited, so answer choice C is incorrect. "Forceful" is not an antonym of "cognizant," so answer choice D is incorrect.

18. **The best answer is A.** "Spurious" means lacking relevance or being false. Therefore, "relevant" is the best choice. "Indelible" means permanent, so answer choice B is incorrect. "Effusive" means unrestrained or overflowing, so answer choice C is incorrect. Answer choice D is incorrect because "concise" means clear and precise. "Supportive" is not an antonym of "spurious," so answer choice E is incorrect.

19. **The best answer is B.** "Heinous" means wicked or reprehensible. "Admirable" is the best choice because it is most opposite in meaning to "heinous." "Scandalous" is not an antonym of "heinous," so answer choice A is incorrect. "Ambiguous" means uncertain or lacking clarity, so answer choice C is incorrect. Neither "lazy" nor "critical" are antonyms of "heinous," so answer choices D and E are incorrect.

20. **The best answer is A.** "Enigmatic" means vague or puzzling. Therefore, "completely understood" is the best choice because it is most opposite in meaning to "enigmatic." Answer choices B, C, D, and E are incorrect because they are not antonyms of "enigmatic."

GRE Verbal Section: Analogies

Terms you'll need to know:

✓ Analogy
✓ Antonym
✓ Homonym
✓ Synonym

Concepts you'll need to master:

✓ Establishing a clear relationship between words
✓ Setting up a general relationship sentence
✓ Identifying and using relationship types
✓ Eliminating obviously incorrect answers

An *analogy* is a comparison of two things that seem unrelated, but are actually related or similar to each other in some respect. The GRE Analogies section is designed to test your ability to recognize these relationships between words and successfully identify parallel relationships.

Answering GRE Analogies Questions

Questions in this section will include a pair of words in all capital letters, followed by five lettered pairs of words. You will be required to identify the answer choice that expresses a relationship most similar to that expressed in the original pair. Following is an example of an analogy question similar to those found on the GRE General Test, along with a detailed explanation:

APPRENTICE : PLUMBER ::

- (A) player : coach
- (B) child : parent
- (C) student : teacher
- (D) author : publisher
- (E) intern : doctor

The first step is to establish the relationship between the words in the original pair. An "apprentice" is typically someone who studies or trains to become a "plumber" or some other tradesperson or professional. Likewise, an "intern" trains to become a "doctor," so answer choice E is correct. Although a "player" could train to become a "coach" and a "student" could train to become a "teacher," other, more plausible relationships exist between those words. Therefore, answer choices A and C are not correct. A "child" could eventually become a "parent," but would not likely study or train to become a "parent," so answer choice B is incorrect. Likewise, an "author" could become a "publisher," but there is no direct, logical connection between first being an author, and then becoming a publisher.

The colons in each pair represent placeholders in an analogy phrase. For example: "**AREA : ACRE ::**" can be stated as "Area **is to** Acre **as** _____ **is to** _____."

Several strategies can help you to correctly answer GRE analogy questions. Following is a description of those strategies we have found most helpful:

➤ Establish the relationship

   ➤ Create a general sentence

   ➤ Use the correct part of speech

   ➤ Beware of homonyms

   ➤ Recognize common relationship types

➤ Use the process of elimination

➤ Select the best answer

Establish the Relationship

Before you look at any of the answer choices, attempt to express the relationship between the original pair in your own words. If you can establish a precise connection between the words, you will most likely select the best answer choice.

 The GRE uses only logically strong relationships. If you find yourself saying things like "this could be true" or "sometimes this happens," the relationship, and thus your answer, is probably incorrect. Try for a relationship that must be true or is true all of the time.

Create a General Sentence

One successful technique is to create a sentence that expresses a specific relationship between the stem words, and then replace the original words from your sentence with the words in the answer choices. You should look for the most simple relationship first. If more than one answer choice expresses the same relationship, you might have to revise your original sentence to indicate a more explicit connection between the words. For example:

MUSICIAN : ORCHESTRA ::

   (A) mechanic : car
   (B) songwriter : lyrics
   (C) desk : office
   (D) player : team
   (E) actor : screen

Ask yourself what a musician has to do with an orchestra. A musician plays in an orchestra. Or more specifically, a musician plays an instrument as one part of an orchestra as a whole. Your general sentence becomes "A ____ does something as one part of a ____ as a whole." The correct answer is D: A player participates as one part of a team as a whole. Although answer choice B includes words related to music, the exact relationship is not the same as the relationship in the question stem; a "songwriter" does not participate as one part of "lyrics" as a whole. Likewise, the remaining answer choices do not fit logically into the general sentence that you created. A "mechanic" does not do something as one part of a "car" as a whole. Although a "desk" might be considered one part of an "office," a "desk" is an inanimate object, so it does not do something as one part of an "office" as a whole. An "actor" is portrayed on the "screen," but an "actor" does not do something as one part of a "screen" as a whole.

Use the Correct Part of Speech

Don't forget about other possible, secondary meanings of words. If you are having trouble creating a sentence, you might be thinking of the wrong definition or part of speech. The questions will always ask you to compare the same parts of speech. For example, if one of the words in the original pair can be used as either a noun or a verb, all of the corresponding words in the answer choices will be either nouns or verbs, but not both. You can let the answer choices guide you in this way. Consider the following example:

CORRAL : LIVESTOCK ::

  (A) fence : posts
  (B) capture : thieves
  (C) nest : birds
  (D) devise : plans
  (E) fire : employees

At first glance, you might have created a general sentence such as "A corral is an enclosure for livestock." However, none of the answer choices fits logically into that sentence. Because "corral" is also a verb that means "to take control or possession of," you must now consider this secondary meaning. A closer look at the answer choices shows you that the first word in the pair is either a verb, or a word that can be used as a verb *or* a noun. Create another sentence using "corral" as a verb: "The rancher was unable to corral his livestock after they escaped." Manipulate the sentence slightly, as follows: "The police officer was unable to capture the thieves after they escaped." The remaining answer choices do not fit logically into this general sentence.

Beware of Homonyms

Be aware of *homonyms*, which are words that sound alike but have different meanings. For example, "mettle" is a noun meaning "courage or fortitude," whereas "meddle" is a verb meaning "to interfere." As in the earlier discussion regarding parts of speech, let the answer choices help you to determine the meaning of the words in the original pair. It is likely that you will know the meaning of some of the words in the answer choices and be able to establish a relationship between some of the word pairs listed. Use this knowledge to eliminate answer choices in which the word pairs do not have a clear connection, as well as to identify the correct meaning of the words in the original pair.

It might help to study a list of common homonyms; a search on the Internet will yield many websites devoted to this topic.

 In GRE analogy questions, relationships are paramount. In other words, remember that the relationship between words is more important than the definition of each word. For example, a question stem could contain words about music, and the correct answer could contain words about athletics; in this case, the meaning of each word is irrelevant.

Recognize Common Relationship Types

GRE analogies questions require you to consider many different possible relationships. After you are able to determine a specific relationship for the original pair, select the answer choice that expresses a relationship in the same way. Most GRE questions tend to fall into one of several common categories of relationships. The following list includes many of the common analogy relationships tested on the GRE:

➤ **Definition/Evidence**—One word in a pair helps to define the other word; or, one word in a pair is a defining characteristic of the other word.

> Example: PARAGON : EXCELLENCE ::
>
> A "paragon," by definition, is a "model or example of excellence."
>
> CRATER : CONCAVE ::
>
> A "crater" is "concave"; therefore, being "concave" is a defining characteristic of a "crater."

➤ **Synonym/Antonym**—One word in a pair is a *synonym* or *antonym* of the other word.

Example: FASCINATION: INTEREST ::

The nouns "fascination" and "interest" have a similar meaning. They are synonyms.

STINGY : GENEROUS ::

The adjective "stingy" is the opposite of the adjective "generous." They are antonyms.

Note that synonyms and antonyms do not have to come from the same parts of speech.

Example: CONTRARY : OPPOSE ::

To be "contrary," which is an adjective, is to "oppose," which is a verb. These words have similar meanings, even though the parts of speech are not the same.

SKEPTICAL : BELIEVE ::

"Skeptical," an adjective, means that you "do not believe," which is the opposite of the verb "believe." These words are opposite in meaning, even though the parts of speech are not the same.

➤ **Type/Kind**—One word in a pair is a type or example of the other word.

Example: FRENCH : LANGUAGE ::

"French" is a type of "language."

➤ **Degree/Intensity**—Both words in a pair are similar in concept, but vary in intensity. In other words, one word in the pair is stronger, harsher, or more intense. Words can also vary spatially, by size, weight, and so on.

Example: PHOBIA : FEAR ::

A "phobia" is a "disabling, exaggerated fear," which is far more extreme than a typical "fear."

➤ **Purpose/Function**—One word in a pair describes the purpose or function of the other word.

Example: NEEDLE : STITCH ::

The purpose or function of a "needle" is to "stitch."

Note that "stitch" can be used as either a noun or a verb. You could also say that a "needle" is used to create a "stitch."

➤ **Component/Part**—One word in a pair represents one part of the other word, which represents a whole; or, one word is simply a component of the other.

> Example: ACTOR : CAST ::
>
> An "actor" is one member of an entire "cast" of actors.

> Example: FLOUR : BREAD ::
>
> "Flour" is a component of "bread."

➤ **Cause and Effect**—One word leads to or results in the other word.

> Example: PREPARATION : SUCCESS ::
>
> "Preparation" will most likely lead to "success."

> Example: ANTIBODIES : PROTECTION ::
>
> The presence of "antibodies" results in "protection" against infection.

A correct answer will never contain a relationship that has been reversed. For example, if the analogy given is TOUCH : TACTILE, the answer cannot be AUDIBLE : HEARING. Even though the relationship is the same, the order of the relationship is reversed.

Use the Process of Elimination

This strategy is useful if you are unable to find the correct answer using any of the previously mentioned strategies. Look at each answer choice and determine whether you know something about each word in the pair, and use that information to eliminate answer choices that are clearly incorrect. The process of elimination can be time-consuming, so it should generally be saved for "last-ditch" efforts in selecting the correct answer. You will probably employ this strategy in conjunction with the others mentioned, eliminating answer choices that do not fit logically into the sentence that you created, for instance.

Select the Best Answer

Remember that the test experts create incorrect answers to distract you; if you establish a relationship beforehand, you will be less likely to get caught up in any confusing, incorrect answers the test writers have set up. If your relationship matches a relationship expressed in ONE of the answer choices, it is most likely correct.

It might be difficult to determine an answer choice without eliminating a few incorrect answers first. Beware of obvious answer choices. At first glance, several choices might appear to express a similar relationship to the original pair. The correct relationship will be paralleled in only one of the answer choices; you might have to dig a little deeper to discover the true relationship. For example:

PASSENGERS : AIRPLANE ::

    (A) audience : theater

    (B) birds : nest

    (C) sailors : submarine

    (D) freight : warehouse

    (E) students : classroom

One possible relationship between "passengers" and "airplane" is that passengers are in an airplane. At first glance, several answer choices appear to have the same relationship as the words in the question stem: A "theater" holds an "audience;" "freight" is in a "warehouse," and so on. There cannot be more than one correct answer, so you should look for a more specific relationship. Create a sentence using the words in the question stem: An "airplane" *transports* "passengers" from one place to another. Only the words in answer choice C can be logically inserted into this sentence.

Be sure to consider all of the answer choices before you select a final answer, even if you think you have already found the correct one. If you are struggling to find just one correct answer, make your relationship statement more specific or, if you must, adjust the relationship entirely.

Putting It to Practice

Now that you've got a good feel for how to approach the analogies questions found on the GRE, try the sample questions in the "Exam Prep Questions" section. Be sure to read the explanations in the answers section to help you gain a better understanding of why the correct answer is correct.

Exam Prep Questions

Directions: Each question below contains a pair of words in capital letters and five answer choices. Each answer choice contains a pair of words. Select the pair that best expresses the relationship expressed by the pair in all capital letters.

1. PRIZE : CONTESTANT ::
   - (A) trophy : presenter
   - (B) diploma : principal
   - (C) medal : runner
   - (D) book : author
   - (E) mortgage : lender

2. CLASSROOM : STUDENTS ::
   - (A) podium : lecturers
   - (B) stadium : athletes
   - (C) cafeteria : trays
   - (D) garage : vehicles
   - (E) auditorium : ushers

3. ENDORSE : CANDIDATE ::
   - (A) sign : affidavit
   - (B) endure : trial
   - (C) idolize : celebrity
   - (D) espouse : idea
   - (E) devise : plan

4. STUDY : TEST ::
   - (A) script : composition
   - (B) rehearse : performance
   - (C) interpret : decision
   - (D) operate : cure
   - (E) record : parody

5. CHRONICLE : JOURNEY ::
   - (A) assume : debt
   - (B) enumerate : demands
   - (C) banish : doubts
   - (D) juxtapose : positions
   - (E) clarify : intentions

6. ANNOTATE : ESSAY ::
   - (A) elevate : level
   - (B) research : theory
   - (C) abridge : chapter
   - (D) elaborate : plan
   - (E) mitigate : damage

7. CAPRICIOUS : IMPULSIVE ::

   (A) magnanimous : generous
   (B) articulate : critical
   (C) petty : deceptive
   (D) diligent : precise
   (E) provocative : appealing

8. NOTES : SONG ::

   (A) conductors : orchestra
   (B) pictures : frame
   (C) keys : door
   (D) lawyers : courtroom
   (E) ingredients : recipe

9. MARATHON : RACE ::

   (A) victory : competition
   (B) sprint : finish
   (C) filibuster : speech
   (D) novel : author
   (E) deposition : question

10. CASTLE : MOAT ::

    (A) island : ocean
    (B) king : soldier
    (C) school : playground
    (D) embryo : placenta
    (E) bacteria : germ

11. BLIZZARD : SNOW ::

    (A) harvest : garden
    (B) flood : lake
    (C) water : ice
    (D) exhibits : zoo
    (E) deluge : rain

12. APATHETIC : EMOTION ::

    (A) eloquent : precision
    (B) lenient : permanence
    (C) perceptive : awareness
    (D) zealous : passion
    (E) glib : sincerity

13. EXULTANT : KUDOS ::
    - (A) focused : support
    - (B) joyful : praise
    - (C) honorable : criticism
    - (D) enigmatic : puzzles
    - (E) exceptional : qualities

14. NOXIOUS : POISON ::
    - (A) egregious : crime
    - (B) benign : leader
    - (C) dubious : concoction
    - (D) judicious : statement
    - (E) pragmatic : decision

15. UTILITARIAN : QUIXOTIC ::
    - (A) disconcerting : unsettling
    - (B) ephemeral : fleeting
    - (C) malevolent : kind
    - (D) loquacious : talkative
    - (E) obdurate : stubborn

16. PLAGIARIZE : STEAL ::
    - (A) hoard : dispel
    - (B) placate : provoke
    - (C) concentrate : refine
    - (D) ostracize : exclude
    - (E) perjure : testify

17. CHISEL : CARVE ::
    - (A) athlete : compete
    - (B) courtroom : judge
    - (C) artist : sculpt
    - (D) rake : forage
    - (E) scalpel : operate

18. PHILANTHROPIST : MUNIFICENCE ::
    - (A) skeptic : disbelief
    - (B) symptom : treatment
    - (C) cynic : melancholy
    - (D) aristocrat : gratitude
    - (E) anomaly : plausibility

19. ARTICULATE : MURKY ::
   - (A) credulous : amiable
   - (B) desiccated : moist
   - (C) formidable : dark
   - (D) derelict : neglectful
   - (E) opaque : milky

20. PHLEGMATIC : EXCITEMENT ::
   - (A) insolent : respect
   - (B) penurious : frugality
   - (C) fractious : sarcasm
   - (D) timorous : trepidation
   - (E) sagacious : wisdom

Answers to Exam Prep Questions

1. **The best answer is C.** A "prize" is usually awarded to the winning "contestant." Therefore, a general sentence that can be used to describe the analogy is: A "____" is awarded to the winning "____." Answer choice C is correct because a "medal" is often awarded to the winning "runner" in a race. Answer choices A, B, D, and E include logical relationships, but none are the same as the relationship between "prize" and "contestant." For instance, a "presenter" is not awarded a "trophy," and a "principal" is not awarded a "diploma"; "presenters" and "principals" are generally on the giving end of that transaction.

2. **The best answer is B.** A "classroom" is where "students" gather to learn. A general sentence that can be used to describe the analogy is: A "____" is the place where a group of "____" gather to perform an activity. Therefore, answer choice B is correct because a "stadium" is the place where a group of "athletes" gather to compete. "Lecturers" may perform a speech behind a "podium," but a "podium" is not a place, so answer choice A is incorrect. Answer choices C and D are incorrect because "trays" and "vehicles" are inanimate objects and do not perform activities in a "cafeteria" or a "garage." "Ushers" could perform an activity in an "auditorium," but not in the same way that a group such as "students" or "athletes" perform an activity.

3. **The best answer is D.** People often "endorse," or "give support to," a "candidate" who is being "considered for" something. A general sentence that can be used to describe the analogy is: People "____" a "____" that is being considered for something if they support it. "Espouse" is a synonym of "endorse"; therefore, answer choice D is

correct because people will "espouse" an "idea" that they support. To "endorse" can also mean "to sign," but people "sign" an "affidavit" to "swear" that something is true, so answer choice A is incorrect. To "endure" means "to put up with" or "suffer through," not "support," so answer choice B is incorrect. Although people may "idolize" a "celebrity," a "celebrity" is not a person or cause that is being "considered for" something, so answer choice C is incorrect. People may "devise" a "plan," but to "devise" does not mean to "support," so answer choice E is incorrect.

4. **The best answer is B.** In the same way that you would "study" for a "test," you would "rehearse" for a "performance." A general sentence that can be used to describe the analogy is: A person would "____" in preparation of a "____." To "script" is to "prepare a text," and a "composition" can be the general "structure or makeup" of a certain text, but these words do not have the same relationship as that expressed in the question stem; therefore, answer choice A is incorrect. Likewise, a person would not "interpret" in preparation of a "decision," or "operate" in preparation of a "cure," so answer choices C and D are incorrect. A "parody" is an "imitation of something for comic effect," so it does not make sense that a person would "record" in preparation of a "parody"; answer choice E is incorrect.

5. **The best answer is B.** To "chronicle" is to "record the details of an event," such as a "journey." A general sentence that can be used to describe the analogy is: To "____" is to provide details describing a/an "____." To "enumerate" is to "specifically identify each detail." Therefore, to "enumerate" "demands" is to provide a list of each demand, much like someone would provide a record listing each detail of a journey. Answer choices A, C, D, and E are logical on their own, but none of the answer choices present the same relationship. For example, to "assume" a "debt" means to "take on" the "debt," not provide details of the "debt." "Banish" means to "get rid of," and "juxtapose" means to "place side by side for comparison," so answer choices C and D are incorrect. You might "clarify" your "intentions" by providing details of them, but there is a stronger, more direct relationship between "enumerate" and "demands," so answer choice E is incorrect.

6. **The best answer is D.** The verb "annotate" means to "provide extra information." A general sentence that can be used to describe the analogy is: A person will "____" in order to add something extra and enhance a/an "____." Answer choice D is correct because a person might "elaborate" on a "plan" in order to provide more detail or add

something extra. To "elevate" is to "make higher," but to "elevate" is not a way to enhance a "level," so answer choice A is incorrect. "Research" is typically conducted to support or study a "theory," but is not something that is directly added to a "theory," so answer choice B is incorrect. "Abridge" means to "shorten," so answer choice C is incorrect. To "mitigate" is to "reduce the intensity" of something, so answer choice E is also incorrect.

7. **The best answer is A.** The adjective "capricious" can be used to describe someone who is "impulsive." A general sentence that can be used to describe the analogy is: A "____" person is very "____." To find the answer to this question, look for an answer choice that contains two words that are synonyms. A "magnanimous" person is, by definition, "generous" (for example, with money, gifts, and so on). Although someone who is "articulate" could also be "critical," the words are not synonyms, so answer choice B is incorrect. Likewise, even though someone who is "petty" could also be "deceptive," a "petty" person is not always "deceptive," so answer choice C is incorrect. A "diligent" person is characterized by "carefulness" and "determination," but not necessarily "precision," so answer choice D is incorrect. A "provocative" person could be "appealing," but "provocative" means "tending to provoke or excite," and is not a synonym of "appealing," so answer choice E is incorrect.

8. **The best answer is E.** The "notes" are the primary components of a "song." Likewise, the "ingredients" are the primary components of a "recipe." Answer choices A, B, C, and D include logical relationships, but none are the same as the relationship between "notes" and "song." For example, "conductors" are not the primary components of an "orchestra," "pictures" are not the primary components of "frames," and so on.

9. **The best answer is C.** A "marathon" is a "long-distance race." A general sentence that can be used to describe the analogy is: A "____" is a longer version of a "____." A "filibuster" is a "lengthy speech," or a longer version of a "speech." A "victory" is a possible outcome of a "competition," but not a longer version of a "competition," so answer choice A is incorrect. Someone may "sprint" to "finish," but "sprint" is not a type of "finish," so answer choice B is incorrect. A "novel" is a "lengthy narrative," but not a type of "author," so answer choice D is incorrect. A "deposition" includes several questions (plural), but is not a lengthy "question," so answer choice E is incorrect.

10. **The best answer is D.** A "moat" is a "water-filled ditch" that surrounds and protects a "castle." A general sentence that can be used to

describe the analogy is: The function of a "____" is to surround and form a barrier to protect a "____." The function of the "placenta" is to surround and form a barrier to protect a developing "embryo." The "ocean" surrounds an "island," but does not function to protect the "island," so answer choice A is incorrect. A "soldier" might protect a "king," but does not surround and form a protective barrier, so answer choice B is incorrect. A "playground" might surround a "school," but does not function to protect the "school," so answer choice C is incorrect. A "germ" does not surround and protect "bacteria," so answer choice E is incorrect.

11. **The best answer is E.** A "blizzard" is a noun that is characterized by a lot of "snow." A general sentence that can be used to describe the analogy is: A "____" is characterized by an overabundance of "____." A "deluge" is a noun that is characterized by an overabundance of "rain." A "harvest" does not involve an overabundance of "gardens," so answer choice A is incorrect. Although a "lake" could "flood," these words do not have the same relationship as the words in the question stem, so answer choice B is incorrect. "Water" is not characterized by an overabundance of "ice," so answer choice C is incorrect. A "zoo" could be characterized by its "exhibits," but the relationship is reversed, so answer choice D is incorrect.

12. **The best answer is E.** An "apathetic" person is "unresponsive" and "tends to show little emotion." A general sentence that can be used to describe the analogy is: A "____" person is characterized by a lack of "____." Answer choice E is correct because a person who is "glib" is often characterized by a lack of "sincerity." An "eloquent" person is often described as having "precision," not a lack of it, so answer choice A is incorrect. A "lenient" person might be overly tolerant, but does not necessarily display a lack of "permanence," so answer choice B is incorrect. Being "perceptive" means having "awareness," so answer choice C is incorrect. A "zealous" person often displays "passion," so answer choice D is incorrect.

13. **The best answer is B.** "Exultant" is a "feeling of triumph," and "kudos" is an "expression of praise." A general sentence that can be used to describe the analogy is: Someone who receives "____" often feels very "____." Someone who receives "praise" often feels "joyful," so answer choice B is correct. Although someone who has received "support" may also feel "focused," one does not necessarily cause the other, so answer choice A is incorrect. It is unlikely that someone would feel "honorable" after receiving "criticism," so answer choice C is incorrect. "Puzzles" themselves are "enigmatic," or "perplexing,"

but receiving "puzzles" does not make someone feel "enigmatic." "Exceptional" could be used to describe "qualities," which is not the same relationship as that in the question stem, so answer choice E is incorrect.

14. **The best answer is A.** "Noxious" means "very harmful" and "poison" is a substance that "causes damage or injury." A general sentence that can be used to describe the analogy is: A "____" is something that is always considered very "____." A "crime" is something that is considered very "egregious," or "noticeably wrong," so answer choice A is correct. Not all "leaders" are considered "benign," so answer choice B is incorrect. Likewise, not all "concoctions" are "dubious," not all "statements" are "judicious," and not all "decisions" are "pragmatic," so answer choices C, D, and E are incorrect.

15. **The best answer is C.** "Utilitarian" is an adjective that is used to describe something that is "useful" and "practical." Conversely, the adjective "quixotic" means "idealistic" or "impractical." A general sentence that can be used to describe the analogy is: Something that is appropriately described as "____" cannot be "____." To answer this question, determine which of the answer choices contains two words that are antonyms. Something that is "malevolent" would never be described as "kind" because the two words are opposite in meaning; therefore, answer choice C is correct. Answer choices A, B, D, and E contain words that are synonyms and share the same meaning.

16. **The best answer is D.** To "plagiarize" is to "steal someone else's work and take all of the credit." Therefore, the verb "steal" helps to define the verb "plagiarize," and "plagiarism" is a form of "stealing." A general sentence that can be used to describe the analogy is: To "____" is to "____" something. To "ostracize" is to "exclude" someone from a group, so answer choice D is correct. "Hoard," or "keep," is the opposite of "dispel," or "get rid of," so answer choice A is incorrect. To "placate" is to "calm" something, not "provoke," or "intensify," so answer choice B is incorrect. You can "concentrate" or "refine" something (usually a liquid), but the words do not help to define each other, so answer choice C is incorrect. To "perjure" is "to knowingly lie under oath" and to "testify" is to "tell the truth under oath," so answer choice D is incorrect.

17. **The best answer is E.** A "chisel" is a tool that is used to "carve" or shape materials. A general sentence that can be used to describe the analogy is: A "____" is a tool that makes it possible to "____" something. Answer choice E is correct because a "scalpel" is a tool that is used to "operate" on a patient. An "athlete" "competes," but an athlete

is not a tool. Likewise, a "courtroom" is not a tool that makes it possible to "judge," and an "artist" is not a tool that makes it possible to "sculpt," so answer choices A, B, and C are incorrect. Answer choice E is incorrect because a "rake" is not necessary to "forage."

18. **The best answer is A.** A "philanthropist" is a person who is "concerned with the well-being of people." The noun "munificence" describes someone who is "very generous." A general sentence that can be used to describe the analogy is: A "____" is a type of person who characteristically displays "____." A "skeptic" is a type of person who characteristically displays "disbelief." A "symptom" is not characterized by a "treatment," so answer choice B is incorrect. A "cynic" is characterized by "pessimism" and could very well display "melancholy." "Melancholy," however, is not necessarily a characteristic of a "cynic," so answer choice C is incorrect. Answer choice D is incorrect because an "aristocrat," or someone of the "upper class," does not generally display "gratitude." An "anomaly" is an "abnormal event," which is not characterized by "plausibility," so answer choice E is incorrect.

19. **The best answer is B.** Something that is "articulate" is "clear" and "distinct," whereas something that is "murky" is "unclear" or "vague." To answer this question, look for an answer choice that contains two words that are antonyms. A general sentence that can be used to describe the analogy is: Something that is described as "____" cannot be "____." The adjective "desiccated" is used to describe something that has "dried up from a lack of moisture," which is the opposite of "moist," so answer choice B is correct. Someone who is "credulous," or "naive" and "easy to deceive," may or may not be "amiable," or "friendly," so answer choice A is incorrect. Answer choices C, D, and E are incorrect because they each contain two words that are similar in meaning.

20. **The best answer is A.** By definition, a "phlegmatic" person acts without "excitement." A general sentence that can be used to describe the analogy is: A "____" person is characterized by actions that lack any "____." An "insolent" person is characterized by actions that lack any "respect." A "penurious" person is characterized by "frugality," so answer choice B is incorrect. A "fractious" person is "irritable" and "difficult," but does not necessarily lack "sarcasm," so answer choice C is incorrect. A "timorous" person is characterized by "trepidation," not a lack of it, so answer choice D is incorrect. Likewise, a "sagacious" person is characterized by "wisdom," so answer choice E is incorrect.

GRE Verbal Section: Sentence Completion

Terms you'll need to know:

✓ Connotation
✓ Idiom
✓ Transitional words
✓ Usage
✓ Vocabulary-in-context
✓ Cognates
✓ Antonym
✓ Synonym
✓ Prefix
✓ Suffix

Concepts you'll need to master:

✓ Reading quickly for context
✓ Understanding connotations
✓ Identifying "clue" words and phrases
✓ Predicting answer choices
✓ Recognizing problems in usage and idiom
✓ Using introductory and transitional phrases to select the
  appropriate word or words

Answering GRE Sentence Completion Questions

The sentence completion questions on the GRE Verbal section are designed to measure your ability to understand the intended meaning of a sentence. Each question requires you to analyze the context of a sentence and determine which word or words best complete that sentence. The GRE includes both vocabulary-in-context and logic-based sentence completion questions that are designed to test your grasp of the English language.

A strong vocabulary is the cornerstone of critical reading, and the best way to develop a large and varied vocabulary is to read extensively.

In addition to reading more, you may want to review the Vocabulary List included as Appendix A at the end of this book.

Questions in this section consist of an incomplete sentence that includes one or two blanks, followed by five answer choices. You should be able to determine which answer choice best fills the blank(s) of the given sentence. Keep in mind that a complete sentence is clear and concise, conveys a logical meaning, and is uniform in grammar and style.

Every sentence has hints that will help you select the correct answer. Each of the following strategies will help you decipher those hints, but remember that any given question might require you to use more than one approach.

Remember these general strategies when approaching GRE sentence completion questions:

➤ Understanding the context

   ➤ Using context, prefixes, suffixes, and cognates to define unfamiliar words.

   ➤ Identifying "clue" words and phrases

➤ Using connotation

➤ Watching for idiom

➤ Answering questions with two blanks

➤ Selecting an answer

The following sections cover each of these general strategies in more depth.

Understanding the Context

GRE sentence completion questions usually test the standard meaning of a word. Pay attention to the logic and context of the sentence. Try to predict a word to insert in the blank or blanks as you read the sentence, then look for your word or a *synonym* of your word among the answer choices. A synonym is a word with the same or a similar meaning.

You should also look for *antonyms*, which are words that have the opposite meaning of your predicted word. If you locate any words among the answer choices that have a meaning opposite to the word that you would like to insert in the blank, eliminate those answer choices.

Let the context of the sentences guide you. Make sure that you understand what's going on in the sentence, and pay attention to introductory and transition words and phrases in each sentence that might suggest a continuation, contrast, or comparison. You should immediately begin to pick up on the idea the sentence is trying to convey, as well as any suggestions of tone or mood. Understanding the general meaning and nature of the sentence will help you to choose the most logical and stylistically appropriate answer.

Using Context, Prefixes, Suffixes, and Cognates to Define Unfamiliar Words

Understanding the context of a sentence also helps to determine the meaning of any unfamiliar words you might encounter. Consider the following example:

> Although the fossils were well preserved, paleontologists were unable to _____ the identity of the mammal species.
>
> (A) display
> (B) ascertain
> (C) violate
> (D) embellish
> (E) exploit

You might not have heard the word "paleontologists" before, but you can deduce from the context of the sentence that they are most likely the scientists who study fossils. Another hint provided by the context is the word "although," which suggests a contrast between the condition of the fossils, and the ability of the paleontologists to identify the species. Now, you can insert the words in the answer choices into the sentence to see which one best fits the context. It does not make sense that scientists would "display" or "violate" the identity of a mammal species, so eliminate answer choices A and C. Likewise, scientists might "embellish" or "exploit" certain findings, but these words do not accurately describe what the scientists might do with the identity of a mammal species. If you did not know the meaning of "ascertain," you could arrive at it as the correct choice by using the context of the sentence to help you eliminate incorrect answer choices.

Also, if you have trouble establishing the meaning of an unfamiliar word from the context of the sentence, you can use your knowledge of *prefixes* and *suffixes* to help you. For example, the prefix "multi-" means "many," as in "multinational" and the suffix "-less" means "without," as in "careless."

Lastly, look for any recognizable *cognates* from French, Spanish, or Italian (the modern versions of Latin) in words you are not familiar with. A *cognate* is a word that means the same or nearly the same thing in more than one language. For example, the word *amigo*, which means friend in Spanish, the word *ami*, which means friend in French, and the word *amicable*, which means friendly in English, all come from the Latin root word for friend, *amicus*.

Identifying "Clue" Words and Phrases

When reading, pay attention to words or phrases in the structure of the sentence that indicate a relationship between ideas or tell you where the sentence is going. Consider the following examples:

➤ Due to recent studies touting the health benefits of regular exercise, health club memberships have increased dramatically in the last year.

The phrase "due to" implies a cause of action, or suggests that one thing provides evidence for another: Recent studies promoting the health benefits of regular exercise have led to a dramatic increase in health club memberships.

➤ Just as Lauren's excellent grade in Physics is a result of her diligent study habits, so too is her medal-winning performance at the track meet proof of her adherence to a difficult training regime.

The phrase "just as" indicates a comparison between the first part of the sentence and the last part of the sentence: Lauren received a good grade in Physics because she studied hard, and she won a medal at the track meet because she trained hard. The GRE might have left a blank for "adherence to," and asked you to select that phrase from among the answer choices.

 Transitional words often lead you to the correct answer. Even if you cannot immediately determine the best answer using "clues," you can still use the words to help you establish the nature and meaning of the sentence.

Figure 4.1 contains tables of commonly used introductory and transitional words and phrases.

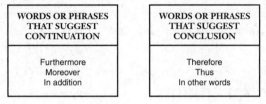

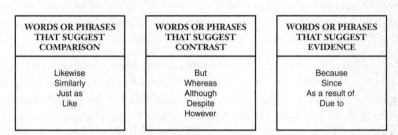

Figure 4.1   Common introductory and transitional words and phrases.

Using Connotation

Each word expresses two things: a *definition* and a *connotation*. A *connotation* is a positive, negative, or neutral feeling that is implied by or associated with a word. Although context is the part of a sentence that surrounds a particular word or passage and determines its meaning, connotation refers to the emotion that is suggested by the word itself.

For example, the adjective "thrifty" implies a positive connotation, whereas the adjective "cheap" implies a negative connotation. Both words have similar definitions, but very different connotations. Using connotations may help you to determine the correct answer or at least eliminate a few wrong answers.

Here is an example of how to use connotation to select the correct answer:

> Because of his ____, Brian's guests felt very welcome and comfortable staying at his house for the weekend.
>
> (A) animosity
> (B) hospitality
> (C) determination
> (D) wittiness
> (E) severity

The sentence has a positive connotation; the transition "because" indicates that something that belongs to Brian has caused his guests to feel welcome and comfortable. "Animosity" and "severity" have a negative connotation and "determination" has a neutral connotation. "Hospitality" and "wittiness" have positive connotations, but "hospitality" best fits the context of the sentence.

Watching for Idiom

Idiom refers to the common or everyday usage of a word or phrase. Learn to recognize idiomatic words and phrases, as they might provide additional clues regarding the intended meaning of the sentence.

Idiom is part of standard written English, and must be considered when answering GRE sentence completion questions. Ask yourself if the completed sentence "sounds" correct, and make sure that the sentence effectively combines words into phrases that express a logical idea. If any portion of the sentence becomes unclear, wordy, or awkward after you insert an answer choice, eliminate that choice. Following is a short list of common idiomatic phrases as they might be used in a sentence:

Correct	Incorrect
Please *look up* that word in the dictionary.	Please *look on* that word in the dictionary.
My sister *listens to* many types of music.	My sister *listens with* many types of music.
That is a very *eye-catching* bracelet.	That is a very *eyeball-catching* bracelet.
The figurine should be placed *on top of* the cake.	The figurine should be placed *at top of* the cake.
He is often *singled out from* a crowd.	He is often *singled out with* a crowd.
I captured a caterpillar that *turned into* a butterfly.	I captured a caterpillar that *turned out of* a butterfly.
I sat *across from* my best friend on the bus today.	I sat *across with* my best friend on the bus today.

Answering Questions with Two Blanks

If a sentence has two blanks, you can quickly eliminate incorrect answer choices if any word alone does not fit into its corresponding blank. When you select an answer choice for a two-blank question, always ensure that both the words make sense in the sentence, both logically and stylistically. It helps to focus on one blank at a time. You can start with either the first or the second blank. Remember that if one word in the answer choice doesn't fit within the context of the sentence, you can eliminate the entire answer choice. Work on both blanks together only if you have not been able to eliminate all of the incorrect answers.

Answer choices for questions with two blanks are commonly structured to trick you into selecting an answer just because one of the words fits perfectly. To avoid making this mistake, choose an answer that effectively uses BOTH words to complete the sentence.

Selecting an Answer

Before you look at the answer choices, try to predict an answer. If your predicted word or words match one of the answer choices, it is most likely the correct choice. Remember that the test writers create incorrect answers in an attempt to distract you—if you predict an answer you are less likely to get caught up on these confusing incorrect answers.

Be careful to consider all of the choices before you confirm your answer, even if your predicted answer is among the choices. The difference between the best answer and the second best answer is sometimes very subtle.

When you think that you have the correct answer, read the entire sentence to yourself, using your choice(s) in the blank(s). If it makes sense, mark your answer on the computer screen and move on to the next question.

Putting It to Practice

Now that you've got a good feel for how to approach the sentence completion questions found on the GRE, try these sample questions. Be sure to read the explanations to help you gain a better understanding of why the correct answer is correct.

Exam Prep Questions

Directions: The following sentences each contain one or two blanks, indicating that one word (or words) has been left out of the sentence. Each answer choice contains one word or a set of words. Select the word or set of words, that, when inserted in the blank(s), best fits the context of the sentence.

1. Investors refused to fund the development of an experimental new aircraft because although it _____ some structural issues, it also produced new mechanical _____.

    (A) resolved..complications

    (B) improved..differences

    (C) alleviated..operations

    (D) initiated..inaccuracies

    (E) interpreted..estimations

2. Although much of the evidence was destroyed or contaminated, enough was _____ to allow investigators to determine the chain of events leading up to the explosion.

    (A) dispersed

    (B) noticeable

    (C) defended

    (D) preserved

    (E) dispelled

3. Environmentalists have expressed a concern over "eutrophication," an ecological process involving the naturally _____ maturation of the world's lakes that is now being _____ by human activity.

    (A) stable..improved

    (B) gradual..accelerated

    (C) beneficial..developed

    (D) decrepit..slowed

    (E) expensive..produced

4. Eager to sell her home and move to another city, Jennifer accepted the proffered purchase agreement with _____.

    (A) reluctance

    (B) humility

    (C) aversion

    (D) probity

    (E) alacrity

5. Muscle aches often yield to a _____ treatment, whereas nerve pain can be quite _____.

    (A) simple..intractable

    (B) complicated..querulous

    (C) mundane..specious

    (D) preventive..calibrated

    (E) cursory..vituperative

6. Instead of relying solely upon circumstantial evidence, the prosecutor sought to gather more _____ proof prior to the trial.

   (A) abstract

   (B) contiguous

   (C) tangible

   (D) variegated

   (E) peripheral

7. Because many novice runners develop knee injuries and many _____ runners do not, experts agree that certain individuals must be more _____ to joint injuries.

   (A) casual..prone

   (B) veteran..susceptible

   (C) amateur..immune

   (D) master..desultory

   (E) fledgling..accustomed

8. The _____ waitress was unusually _____ tonight: Normally, her tiresome chatter kept diners from enjoying their meals.

   (A) apprehensive..boisterous

   (B) garrulous..laconic

   (C) inane..diligent

   (D) scurrilous..ephemeral

   (E) industrious..prompt

9. We were enchanted by the _____ garden: It was full of vibrant roses, with hues ranging from bright yellow to a very deep burgundy.

   (A) homogenous

   (B) iridescent

   (C) achromatic

   (D) pallid

   (E) symmetrical

10. Until Marcia learned to _____ a strict schedule, she seldom managed to complete her tasks in a timely manner.

   (A) infer from

   (B) commingle with

   (C) adhere to

   (D) vacillate from

   (E) inure to

11. After completing the laborious project ahead of schedule, the team felt that it deserved some _____ before beginning the next assignment.
    (A) rigor
    (B) repudiation
    (C) reproach
    (D) respite
    (E) rancor

12. As an ardent _____ of standardized test preparation, Seth had a _____ of supporters at the education conference established to promote the test preparation industry.
    (A) critic..multitude
    (B) proponent..myriad
    (C) advocate..lack
    (D) opponent..plethora
    (E) foe..crowd

13. A wave of _____ swept over the group of students; they could not believe what the principal was saying.
    (A) corruption
    (B) resonance
    (C) indifference
    (D) incredulity
    (E) conviction

14. In light of _____ reports from the investigative teams, Bill decided to discontinue his search for the misappropriated funds.
    (A) ambivalent
    (B) beneficial
    (C) cogent
    (D) diligent
    (E) prolific

15. Many people _____ the ballet for its grace and tranquility; others _____ it for the same reasons.
    (A) despise..abhor
    (B) repudiate..disavow
    (C) cherish..savor
    (D) condemn..revile
    (E) relish..spurn

16. In order to _____ his student's interest in the science experiment, the teacher asked each student to bring a penny to class the next day.

    (A) simulate

    (B) rescind

    (C) pique

    (D) excoriate

    (E) mollify

17. Agriculturists have traditionally considered crop rotation to be _____; it helps to preserve soil nutrients, control disease, and deter weed growth.

    (A) aesthetic

    (B) didactic

    (C) pedantic

    (D) incidental

    (E) crucial

18. Despite the capricious impulses that often impelled him to action in his social life, he was actually quite _____ when it came to making business decisions.

    (A) pretentious

    (B) garrulous

    (C) pragmatic

    (D) guileless

    (E) reclusive

19. Aberrant results in scientific experiments should not be _____; on the contrary, such findings can often be credited as significant break-throughs.

    (A) abraded

    (B) extolled

    (C) predicted

    (D) discounted

    (E) regulated

20. Although often extremely _____ of the legal profession as a whole, people are unwilling to treat their own attorneys with equal criticism.

    (A) reverential

    (B) deferential

    (C) contemptuous

    (D) redemptive

    (E) trusting

Answers to Exam Prep Questions

1. **The best answer is A.** The preposition "although" suggests a contrast. The experimental new aircraft would most likely do something positive regarding structural issues, but have a negative impact on the mechanical issues. A contrast exists between "resolving" structural issues and producing new mechanical "complications." Answer choices B, C, D, and E include words that do not appropriately fit within the context of the sentence. You might have been tempted by answer choice B, but "differences" are not always negative.

2. **The best answer is D.** The context of the sentence indicates that the best word to fill in the blank will have a meaning opposite to that of both "destroyed" and "contaminated." Only "preserved" is appropriate. Answer choices A, B, C, and E do not fit the context of the sentence.

3. **The best answer is B.** Because the environmentalists are concerned, you should look for a word-pair that suggests a contradiction. "Gradual" is the opposite of "accelerated," so answer choice B makes sense. It is not logical that "improving" the natural "stability" of the lakes' maturation would concern environmentalists, so answer choice A is incorrect. Likewise, "developing" something "beneficial" is not generally a cause for concern, so answer choice C is incorrect. "Decrepit" and "slowed" have similar meanings, so answer choice D is incorrect. Answer choice E does not fit the context of the sentence.

4. **The best answer is E.** The best word for the blank will be a synonym of "eager." The word "alacrity" means "eagerness." Answer choice A is incorrect because "reluctance" is the opposite of "eagerness." Neither "humility" nor "aversion" fit the context of the sentence, so answer choices B and C are incorrect. "Probity" refers to "integrity," which is inappropriate based on the context, so answer choice D is incorrect.

5. **The best answer is A.** The word "whereas" indicates that there is a contrast between the ease of treating "muscle aches" and the ease of treating "nerve pain." The first portion of the sentence implies that muscle aches are easy to treat; therefore, the word that best completes the second portion of the sentence will suggest that nerve pain is not easy to treat. "Simple" is an appropriate synonym for "easy" and "intractable" describes something that is "difficult to deal with or fix." Answer choices B, C, D, and E do not fit the context of the sentence. Refer to Appendix A for definitions of some of the words in these answer choices.

6. **The best answer is C.** To answer this question, you should understand that "circumstantial" describes something that is "dependent on other events and conditions," and is "indirect." Hence, the prosecutor is probably looking for "real" or "physical" evidence because "circumstantial evidence" may not be very convincing. "Tangible" is a synonym of "real" and "physical," so answer choice C is correct. Answer choices A, B, D, and E can be eliminated because they are not synonyms of "real" or "physical." Refer to Appendix A for definitions of some of the words in these answer choices.

7. **The best answer is B.** The context of the sentence indicates a comparison between different types of runners. Therefore, the word to insert into the first blank should be an antonym of "novice." Only "veteran" and "master" are antonyms of "novice," so eliminate answer choices A, C, and E. The word "susceptible" best fits the context of the sentence, so eliminate answer choice D. Refer to Appendix A for definitions of some of the words in these answer choices.

8. **The best answer is B.** The context of the sentence indicates that the waitress normally behaves one way, but tonight she was behaving differently. Look for a word to insert into the first blank that describes someone who engages in "tiresome chatter." Only "garrulous," which means "talkative," works in the first blank. Answer choices A, C, D, and E do not fit the context of the sentence. Refer to Appendix A for definitions of some of the words in these answer choices.

9. **The best answer is B.** The context of the sentence indicates that the flowers in the garden were very colorful. Based on the context, the word that best describes the flowers is "iridescent," which means "brilliant, lustrous, or colorful." Answer choice A is incorrect because "homogeneous" means "uniform in composition"; the sentence states that the roses ranged in color from bright yellow to burgundy. Answer choices C and D have meanings opposite to "iridescent." Answer choice E does not fit the context of the sentence.

10. **The best answer is C.** The best word to insert into the blank will clearly indicate that Marcia was unable to complete her tasks in a timely manner until she did something with her schedule. "Adhere to" means "stick to," which makes sense in this sentence. Learning to stick to a strict schedule helped Marcia complete her tasks on time. Answer choices A, B, D, and E do not effectively complete the sentence.

11. **The best answer is D.** The word "respite" means "an interval of rest or relief." It makes sense that the team felt it deserved a rest after completing the "laborious," or "grueling" work. Answer choice A is

incorrect because "rigor" means "strictness," which does not fit the context of the sentence. Likewise, "repudiation," "reproach," and "rancor" all have negative connotations and do not fit the context of the sentence, so B, C, and E are incorrect.

12. **The best answer is B.** According to the sentence, Seth had supporters at the education conference, which was designed to promote the test preparation industry. This suggests that Seth agreed with and supported standardized test preparation. Therefore, you can eliminate answer choices A, D, and E, because the first word in each pair is not appropriate for the first blank in the sentence. It does not make sense that Seth would "lack" supporters, so answer choice C is incorrect. "Myriad" means "a vast number," which best fits the context of the sentence.

13. **The best answer is D.** The information following the semicolon offers a definition for the word that best fits in the blank. "Incredulity" refers to "doubt" or disbelief," so it is the most appropriate word to insert into the blank. Answer choices A, B, C, and E do not mean "doubt" or "disbelief." Refer to Appendix A for definitions of some of the words in these answer choices.

14. **The best answer is A.** The context of the sentence indicates that the reports Bill received led to his decision to discontinue his search. Therefore, the reports could not have included information that was helpful to Bill. "Ambivalence" often refers to "uncertainty" or "lack of clarity." This type of information would not be helpful. Answer choices B and C are incorrect because they suggest that the information was helpful. Answer choice D is incorrect because "diligent" is an adjective that would better describe the investigators; a report is not "diligent." "Prolific" means "in great abundance," which also could be helpful, so eliminate answer choice E.

15. **The best answer is E.** The context of the sentence suggests that the words that best fit the blanks will be antonyms; many people feel one way about ballet, while others feel a different way. "Relish" means "to have a strong appreciation," whereas "spurn" means "to reject with contempt." Answer choices A, B, C, and D contain word pairs that are synonyms. Refer to Appendix A for definitions of some of the words in these answer choices.

16. **The best answer is C.** The best word for the blank will provide a reason for the teacher asking his students to bring a penny to class. It is most likely that the teacher wanted his students to have an increased interest in the science experiment. Therefore, "pique," which means

"to provoke or arouse" is the best choice. "Rescind" means to "take back," and "excoriate" means to "strongly disapprove of," so eliminate answer choices B and D. Likewise, answer choices A and E do not fit the context of the sentence.

17. **The best answer is E.** The information following the semicolon indicates that crop rotation is a good and probably necessary thing. Therefore, the best word for the blank will be a synonym for "good" or "necessary." "Crucial" means "extremely important," so it is the best choice. Both "aesthetic" and "incidental" imply that crop rotation is not necessary or important, so eliminate answer choices A and D. "Didactic" and "pedantic" both relate to "teaching" or "learning" and do not appropriately complete this sentence; eliminate answer choices B and G.

18. **The best answer is C.** The context of the sentence indicates that the best word to insert into the blank will have a meaning opposite to that of "capricious," which means "unpredictable or irrational." The word should also relate to making business decisions. "Pragmatic" means "practical," which best fits the context of the sentence as a whole. Answer choice A is incorrect because "pretentious" does not mean "practical." "Garrulous" means "talkative," which is not supported by the context of the sentence, so answer choice B is incorrect. Eliminate answer choices D and E, because "guileless" means "naïve" and "reclusive" means "preferring isolation," neither of which fit the context of the sentence.

19. **The best answer is D.** The phrase "on the contrary" indicates that a contrast exists between the word in the blank and the information following the semicolon. Because the information following the semicolon states that aberrant results can be credited as significant, the word that best fits in the blank should be an antonym of "credited." "Discount" means to "disregard" or "underestimate the value of" something. Therefore, "discounted" is the best choice. "Abraded" means "worn down"; "extolled" means "praised"; "predicted" means "known about in advance"; "regulated" means "controlled." None of these words is an antonym of "credited."

20. **The best answer is C.** The preposition "although" indicates a contradiction; people believe one thing about the legal profession as a whole, but they believe another thing about their own attorneys. Because they are unwilling to criticize their own attorneys, they must be critical of the legal profession as a whole. You should look for a synonym of "critical." Both "reverential" and "deferential" have a positive connotation

and indicate "respect," so answer choices A and B are incorrect. "Redemptive" also has a positive connotation and refers to being "saved" or "recovered," so answer choice D is incorrect. Answer choice E is incorrect because "trusting" is not a synonym of "critical."

GRE Verbal Section—
Reading Comprehension

Terms you'll need to know:

✓ Vocabulary-in-context
✓ Inference
✓ Imply
✓ Assumption
✓ Extrapolation

Concepts you'll need to master:

✓ Determining the meaning of words using context
✓ Drawing conclusions based on information presented in the reading passage
✓ Locating important details within a reading passage
✓ Comparing and contrasting information presented in one or more reading passages

The GRE Reading Comprehension questions are designed to measure your ability to read, understand, and analyze a written passage. Correctly answering a question requires you to recognize both what is stated and what is implied within the passage, and to establish the relationships and ideas expressed in the passage.

Reading Comprehension questions will appear in the Verbal section of the GRE. The computer adaptive GRE will include a balance of passages across different subject matter areas, such as humanities, social sciences, and natural sciences. Each passage will range from approximately 150 to 500 words in length, and be followed by two to five questions, each with five answer choices. You should select the best possible answer for each question.

 The Verbal section of the GRE contains several other types of questions along with the Reading Comprehension questions. A passage and its questions can appear in any order within the section, and will not necessarily appear near other Reading Comprehension passages.

General Strategies

Probably the biggest mistake that you could make is to read these passages as though you are studying for a college exam. The "open-book" aspect of the passage-based Reading Comprehension sections means that you should read in a way that helps your brain to work through the information efficiently. You should *not* read slowly and carefully as though you will have to remember the information for a long period of time. You should read loosely and only dwell on information that you are sure is important because you need it to answer a question. This type of reading should be very goal-oriented. If the information you are looking at does not help to answer a question that the test writers find important, you should not linger over it. The best scores on this section are usually earned by students who have two key skills: **paraphrasing** and **skimming**. These skills, along with techniques on how to determine the main idea, read and answer the questions, and use the process of elimination, are discussed in more detail in the following sections.

Determining the Main Idea

As you begin to read a passage, your first step should be determining the main idea. This technique will help you to answer the "big picture" questions, as well as assist you in locating information necessary to answer other question types. The main idea has three components:

➤ **Topic** ("What is the passage about?")

➤ **Scope** ("What aspect of the topic does the passage focus on?)

➤ **Purpose**("Why did the author write the passage?")

If you can answer these three questions, then you understand the main idea. Consider the following scenarios:

1. The world's tropical rain forests are being decimated at an alarming rate. Each day, thousands of acres of trees are destroyed in both developing and industrial countries. Nearly half of the world's species of plants and animals will be eliminated or severely threatened over the next 25 years due to this rapid deforestation. Clearly, it is imperative that something be done to curtail this rampant destruction of the tropical rain forests.

2. Tropical rain forests are crucial to the health and welfare of the planet. Experts indicate that over 20% of the world's oxygen is produced by the Amazon rain forest alone. In addition, more than half of the world's estimated 10 million species of plants, animals, and insects live in the tropical rain forests. These plants and animals of the rain forest provide us with food, fuel wood, shelter, jobs, and medicines. Indigenous humans also inhabit the tropical rain forests.

The **Topic** of both passages is tropical rain forests. However, the **Scope** of each passage is very different. The first passage discusses destruction of the tropical rain forests, whereas the second passage introduces the diversity of the rain forests and indicates why the rain forests are important. The **Purpose** of each passage is similar, but the tone of the second passage is more informational than that of the first passage.

 As you read for the main idea, and particularly the author's purpose, avoid arguing with the author. If you disagree with any viewpoints expressed in a passage, do not let your personal opinions interfere with your selection of answer choices. In addition, you should not rely on any prior knowledge you might have about a particular topic. The questions will ask about information that is stated or implied in the passage, not information that you might recall about the topic being discussed.

Too often, students confuse **Topic** with **Main Idea**. The topic of a passage only answers the question "What is the passage about?" If that is all that you notice, you are missing some very important information.

The introductory paragraph often indicates the topic or topics being discussed, the author's point of view, and exactly what the author is trying to prove. So, read a little more slowly at the beginning until you get a grip on the three components of the main idea and then you can shift to the next higher gear and skim the rest of the passage.

The Reading Comprehension section is not meant to test your knowledge about a particular subject. You should answer questions based on the information presented in the passage only, not on any prior knowledge that you might have of the subject. You might be asked to draw a conclusion (inference), but you should only do so based on what the writer's words actually state or imply.

Skimming

Don't use context clues the first time that you skim through a passage. When you come to a word or phrase that is unfamiliar, just read past it. There is always time to come back if you need to. But, there is a strong chance that you won't need to determine exactly what that one word or phrase means to answer the bulk of the questions that accompany the passage. If you waste some of your precious time, you'll never get it back. With perseverance and practice, you will start to get comfortable with a less-than-perfect understanding of the passage.

The goal at this stage is to get a general understanding of the structure of the passage so that you can find what you are looking for when you refer back to the passage. You should pay attention to paragraph breaks: Try to quickly determine the subtopic for each paragraph, the general content of each paragraph, and the purpose of each paragraph. The first sentence is not always the topic sentence. So, don't believe those who say that you can read the first and last sentence of each paragraph and skip the rest of the sentences completely. You are better off skimming over all of the words even if you end up forgetting most of what you read almost immediately.

Remember that the idea at this stage is to not waste time. Keep moving through the material.

Paraphrasing

After you have found the information in the passage that will provide the answer that you are looking for, try to answer the question in your mind. Put the question in your own words so that it makes more sense to you. Try to predict an answer for the question, then skim the choices presented and look for your answer. You might have to be a little flexible to recognize it. Your answer might be there dressed up in different words. If you can recognize a paraphrase of your predicted answer, select it. Developing this skill will help you to become more time-efficient and will lead you to the correct answer more often than not.

Reading and Answering the Questions

Before you read the questions and answers, take a moment to mentally summarize the main idea and the structure of the passage.

Read the question and make sure that you understand it, paraphrasing if necessary. Use the structure of the passage to lead you to the correct answer. Go back to the part of the passage that relates to the question, and that part will probably contain the answer to your question.

Some of the questions on the GRE ask you to draw conclusions based on the information that you read. However, even these questions should be answered based on the information in the passage. There will always be some strong hints, or evidence, that will lead you to an answer.

Some of the questions contain references to specific lines of the passage. The trick in those cases is to read a little before and a little after the specific line that is mentioned. At a minimum, read the entire sentence that contains the line that is referenced.

Some of the questions don't really tell you where to look for the answer, or they are about the passage as a whole. In those cases, think about what you learned about the passage while you were skimming it. Note the subtopics for the paragraphs, and let them guide you to the part of the passage that contains the desired information.

One of the important skills rewarded by the GRE is the ability to sift through text and find the word or concept that you are looking for. This skill improves with practice.

 It is possible for an answer choice to be both true *and* wrong. The answer that you choose must respond correctly to the question being asked. Simply being true is not enough to make an answer correct. The best answer is always supported by details, inference, or tone.

Using the Process of Elimination

Elimination is the process most test-takers use when answering exam questions. It is reliable, but slow. However, it is still useful as a backup strategy for questions where you cannot predict an answer or when you find your prediction is not a choice.

The process of elimination is a good tool. It just shouldn't be the only tool in your box. It can be hard to break the habit of always applying the process of elimination. You have likely developed this habit because on past exams you have been given too much time to answer questions. On the GRE, you will need to be more time-efficient, which is why you should use the process of elimination only when other strategies fail to yield an answer.

Eliminate any answer choices that are clearly incorrect, including answer choices that are outside the scope of the passage. Answer choices that fall outside the scope of the passage are very common in this section. For example, an answer choice might be too specific, too general, or have no relation to the content of the passage itself or to the question being asked.

Finally, be careful to always consider all of the choices before you confirm your answer, even if your predicted answer is among the choices. The difference between the best answer and the second best answer is sometimes very subtle.

It is important that you know the difference between information that is stated directly in the passage, and assumptions and inferences. You might be asked questions based on factual information found in the reading passages. The reading passages might also include information about which you will be asked to make an inference.

An *inference* is a conclusion based on what is stated in the passage. You can infer something about a person, place, or thing by reasoning through the descriptive language contained in the reading passage. In other words, the author's language *implies* that something is probably true.

An *assumption*, on the other hand, is unstated evidence. It is the missing link in an author's argument. Following is a classic example of a conclusion based on stated evidence and unstated evidence (assumption):

Socrates is a man.

Therefore, Socrates is mortal.

Because you are given that Socrates is a man, the conclusion that Socrates is mortal *must* be based on the assumption that men are mortal.

Socrates is a man. (Stated Evidence)

Men are mortal. (Unstated Evidence)

Therefore, Socrates is mortal. (Conclusion)

Some of the evidence is not stated, but the final conclusion leads you to the existence of that missing evidence, or assumption.

Common Question Types

The following list highlights the types of questions you are likely to encounter on the GRE Reading Comprehension section:

➤ Main idea/primary purpose

➤ Specific detail

➤ Purpose of detail

➤ Conclusion/inference

➤ Extrapolation

➤ Vocabulary in context

➤ Structure

➤ Weakening

➤ Except

The following subsections discuss each question type and also include specific approaches to each question type. You will begin to recognize the different question types as you work through the sample questions and practice exams.

Main Idea/Primary Purpose

These questions might ask about the main idea of the passage as a whole, or about a specific paragraph. They also ask about the author's point of view or perspective, and the intended audience. These questions might also ask you to determine the best title for the passage.

Strategy—Answer these questions according to your understanding of the three components of the main idea mentioned previously (Topic, Scope, and Purpose). It is also worth noting that the incorrect choices are usually either too broad or too narrow. You should eliminate the answer choices that focus on a specific part of the passage. Also eliminate the answer choices that are too general and could describe other passages besides the one that you are working on.

Example—"Which of the following titles best describes the passage as a whole?" or "The primary purpose of the passage is to"

Specific Detail

These questions can be as basic as asking you about a fact easily found by referring to a part of the passage. Some questions will even provide specific line references or text from the passage. Questions that begin "According to the author…," or "According to the passage…" might be specific detail questions.

Strategy—When you skim the passage, make sure that you have established the structure of the passage and the purpose of each paragraph. If you have a clear idea of how the passage is organized, you should be able to quickly refer to the portion of the passage that contains the answer. Otherwise, use the line or paragraph references in the questions, if they are given.

Sometimes, the answer choices are paraphrased, so don't just select the answers that contain words that appear in the passage. Make sure that the choice you select is responsive to the question being asked.

Example—"According to the passage, one difference between ... is that"

Purpose of Detail

These questions ask you to determine the author's purpose in mentioning certain details, as well as how details contained within the passage might support the main idea.

Strategy—Making a connection between the supporting details and the main idea of the passage will help you to answer these questions correctly. Think of the details as the "building blocks" of the author's thesis. This should provide you with some insight into why the author included these details in the passage. Refer specifically to any line references given in the questions.

Example—"The author quotes from *The Iron Mountain News* most probably in order to"

Conclusion/Inference

These questions require you to put together information in the passage and use it as evidence for a conclusion. You have to find language in the passage that leads you to the inference that the question demands. Questions that begin "According to the author...," or "According to the passage..." might require you to locate clues or evidence that will lead you to the answer.

Strategy—Understanding the main idea of the passage or paragraph, and particularly the author's tone, is key for these types of questions. Although you have to do a bit of thinking for these questions, you should be able to find very strong evidence for your answers. If you find yourself creating a long chain of reasoning and including information from outside the passage, stop and reconsider your selection.

Example—"It can be inferred from the passage that..." or "The author refers to ... in order to suggest"

Extrapolation

These questions ask you to go beyond the passage itself and find answers that are *probably* true based on what you know from the passage. They can be based on the author's tone, or on detailed information in the passage. You are often required to reason by analogy.

Strategy—You need to be sensitive to any clues about the author's tone or attitude and any clues about how the characters in the passage feel. Eliminate any choices that are outside the scope of the passage. As with the inference questions described previously, the GRE rewards short, strong connections between the passage and the correct answers.

Example—"Which of the following, if true, would be most likely to...?"

Vocabulary in Context

These questions ask what a specific word means from the passage. The context of the passage should lead you to an educated guess, even if you don't know the specific word being asked about.

Strategy—The best way to answer these questions is to read several sentences before and several sentences after the line reference given in the question. Select the answer choice that best fits the context.

Example—"As it is used in the passage, ... most nearly means"

Structure

This type of question might ask you to describe the structure of the passage, or how a particular detail or paragraph functions within the passage as a whole.

Strategy—You need to recognize the author's purpose in writing the passage, and determine how the author develops the main thesis or argument. If the passage is purely informational, for example, the author might simply make a statement, followed by some supporting details. On the other hand, the author might offer comparisons between two different theories to persuade the reader that one theory is better. Pay attention to both the language and the connotation.

Example—"The author's argument is developed primarily by the use of"

Weakening

These questions require you to select the answer choice that weakens the author's argument. Weakening does not necessarily mean to disprove completely; it merely means to make the conclusion of the argument somewhat less likely.

Strategy—The best approach to answering these questions correctly is to first make sure that you understand the author's argument or main point. To weaken the author's argument, you should usually attack the author's assumptions (unstated evidence). In some cases, the correct answer actually contradicts a statement made in the passage.

Example—"Which of the following, if true, would most seriously weaken the author's assertion…"

Except

This type of question is often phrased as follows: "The author probably believes all of the following "EXCEPT," or "All of the following are listed in the passage as examples of biodiversity EXCEPT."

Strategy—The best answer in these instances includes information that is *not* directly stated in the passage, or *cannot* be inferred from information stated in the passage. Eliminate all of the answer choices that are supported by the passage.

Putting It to Practice

Following are simulated GRE Reading Comprehension questions. Read the directions carefully before you begin to answer the questions. Mark the answer sheet with your choices. Make guesses as necessary. Remember that on the actual computer adaptive exam, you will be required to select an answer before you can move on to the next question.

Exam Prep Questions

Now that you've got a good feel for how to approach the reading comprehension questions found on the GRE, try these sample questions. Be sure to read the explanations to help you gain a better understanding of why the correct answer is correct.

Directions: The passage in this section is followed by several questions. The questions correspond to information that is stated or implied in the passage. Read the passage and choose the best answer for each question.

Modern immigration, also known as post-1965 immigration, has forever changed American society. In 1965, amendments to the Immigration and Nationality Act, more commonly known as the Hart-Cellar Act, greatly increased non-European immigration. In the
5   40 years since the Hart-Cellar Act became law, immigration has continued to steadily increase.

Some experts disagree regarding whether the Hart-Cellar Act was the primary reason for the shift in modern immigration. In 1968, the Hart-Cellar Act's goals were to unite fragmented families and to
10   bring in foreign labor. The Hart-Cellar Act eliminated national quotas that were biased against immigrants from Southern and Eastern Europe. In addition, the Hart-Cellar Act removed the longstanding ban on Asian immigrants. The abolishment of the national quotas encouraged immigrants from Eastern Europe, Southern Europe, and
15   Asia to come to America. Other provisions of this law created what became known as the seven preference categories. Unfortunately, the original Hart-Cellar Act and its later amendments also established the first cap on immigrants from the Western Hemisphere. This greatly affected immigration from Central America, South America, and
20   Mexico.

Compared with the immigrants of the nineteenth and early twentieth centuries, post-1965 immigrants are distinctly diverse. These new immigrants settle in different areas, come from a wide variety of countries, and have different socioeconomic backgrounds. In fact,
25   unlike the Ellis Island immigrants, modern immigrants hail principally from non-European nations. Modern immigration will have a significant impact on the size and design of America's population. Since the 1960s, new immigrants have represented over one-third of America's total growth. Although all ethnic groups contribute to
30   America's growth, Asian and Hispanic immigrant populations continue to grow larger and faster than all of the others. Only 30 years ago, Asians and Hispanics made up an infinitesimal percentage of the American population. Since then, the size of these groups has almost quadrupled.

35 In the 1800s, immigrants from Europe tended to settle on the East Coast or in the Midwest. States such as Michigan, Virginia, New York, Pennsylvania, Illinois, Massachusetts, and New Jersey became havens for new Americans. If these immigrants preferred city life, they usually headed for booming cities such as New York, Detroit,
40 Chicago, Philadelphia, St. Louis, and Boston. In the twenty-first century, immigrants continue to flock to those areas. However, today's immigrants also settle on the West Coast, in the Southwest, and in the Southeast. Texas, Arizona, Florida, California, Washington, and Oregon are among the states with the largest immigrant populations.

45 Many of the modern immigrants arrive in America with jobs, college degrees, or technical training. This is in stark contrast to the immigrants of the nineteenth century. After arriving in America, modern immigrants tend to prosper quickly. Networks produced by family ties, friendships, and business contacts enable immigrants to
50 prosper in America far more quickly than they were able to in the past. In the last 30 years, family or friends already in the United States sponsored more than two-thirds of the new immigrants. Other humanitarian institutions, both public and private, also help new immigrants become established in America. In addition to helping
55 immigrants find jobs and homes, these organizations assist in eliminating the abuse and discrimination that many immigrants face.

It is no wonder that family ties are playing such a major role in modern immigration. The Hart-Cellar Act of 1965 and its ensuing amendments made family reunification a priority. This important
60 measure provided immediate family members of American citizens with unlimited visas. Extended relatives were also granted visas based on availability.

Thanks to the Hart-Cellar Act and other legislation, America has become more than a melting pot. With its modern immigration poli-
65 cies, America has become a land filled with united and prosperous families. The Hart-Cellar Act, along with other immigration legislation, has brought increased diversity and new challenges. Like the immigrants before them, modern immigrants require assistance and compassion. However, the strengths and benefits that the new immi-
70 grants bring far outweigh any temporary cost to society.

1. The primary purpose of this passage is to

   (A) criticize modern immigration legislation and discuss its effects on American society

   (B) challenge stereotypes about modern immigrants from Asia and Mexico

   (C) defend immigration from proponents who want to abolish the Hart-Cellar Act

   (D) evaluate the Hart-Cellar Act and discuss modern immigration

   (E) suggest amendments to the Hart-Cellar Act and other immigration legislation

2. The passage states that the Hart-Cellar Act had all of the following effects EXCEPT

   (A) increasing Hispanic immigration after 1965

   (B) uniting families by offering visas to immediate family members

   (C) potentially acting as a catalyst for Southern European immigration

   (D) bringing in much needed foreign labor

   (E) eliminating bans on Asian immigrants

3. It can be inferred from the passage that

   (A) all immigrants benefit from networks established by family ties, friendships, or business contacts

   (B) modern immigrants do not settle in the Midwest or on the East Coast

   (C) the Hart-Cellar Act has eliminated the need for foreign labor

   (D) Asian and Hispanic immigrant populations will continue to grow more quickly than all others

   (E) the Hart-Cellar Act did not benefit all immigrants equally

4. Which of the following measures would the author of the passage probably find to be most helpful?

   (A) Abolishing the Hart-Cellar Act because it has become obsolete

   (B) Continuing to encourage networking among immigrants and more established Americans

   (C) Establishing bans on immigrants from certain regions to promote fairness

   (D) Encouraging the American government to only admit immigrants with college degrees or technical training

   (E) Creating a modern-day version of Ellis or Angel Island for new immigrants

5. The author's attitude toward the Hart-Cellar Act can best be described as

   (A) wholeheartedly appreciative

   (B) hostile and accusatory

   (C) highly disrespectful

   (D) laudatory yet critical

   (E) indifferent yet cautious

Answers to Exam Prep Questions

1. **The best answer is D.** The passage discusses the positive aspects of the Hart-Cellar Act and also criticizes its discrimination against Hispanic immigrants. The author also discusses the characteristics of modern immigrants and their effect on America. Answer choice A might have appeared to be correct because the author does criticize certain elements of the Hart-Cellar Act. However, this is not the primary focus of this passage and the author has more praise than criticism for the Hart-Cellar Act.

2. **The best answer is A.** The passage states, "Unfortunately, the original Hart-Cellar Act and its later amendments also established the first cap on immigrants from the Western Hemisphere. This greatly affected immigration from Central America, South America, and Mexico." All of the other answer choices can be found in the passage.

3. **The best answer is E.** The passage states that immigrants from the Western Hemisphere were negatively affected by the Hart-Cellar Act. Answer choice D might have appeared to be correct because the passage does state that Asian and Hispanic populations are currently growing the fastest. However, the passage does not argue that this growth will necessarily continue.

4. **The best answer is B.** The author argues that networking is helping modern immigrants become successful and established more quickly. It is likely that the author would support any activity that increases these networking opportunities. Answer choice D might have appeared to be correct. However, the author only states that many modern immigrants have college degrees or technical training. The author does not give an opinion about whether this should be a requirement.

5. **The best answer is D.** The author praises the Hart-Cellar Act for uniting families and bringing new ethnic groups to America. However, the author does not seem to approve of the legislation's treatment of immigrants from the Western Hemisphere. Eliminate answer choices A, B, and C because the language is too strong. These attitudes are not supported by the passage. Answer choice E is incorrect because the author is clearly not indifferent to the changes brought about by the Hart-Cellar Act.

GRE Quantitative Section

Terms you'll need to know:

- ✓ Absolute value
- ✓ Acute angle
- ✓ Adjacent angle
- ✓ Area
- ✓ Associative property
- ✓ Average
- ✓ Circumference
- ✓ Commutative property
- ✓ Complementary angle
- ✓ Congruent
- ✓ Coordinate plane
- ✓ Denominator
- ✓ Diameter
- ✓ Distributive property
- ✓ Equilateral triangle
- ✓ Exponent
- ✓ Factor
- ✓ Function
- ✓ Greatest common factor (GCF)

- ✓ Hypotenuse
- ✓ Inequality
- ✓ Integer
- ✓ Intersection
- ✓ Isosceles triangle
- ✓ Least common multiple (LCM)
- ✓ Line
- ✓ Line segment
- ✓ Median
- ✓ Midpoint
- ✓ Mode
- ✓ Numerator
- ✓ Obtuse angle
- ✓ Parallel
- ✓ Perimeter
- ✓ Percent
- ✓ Point
- ✓ Proportion

- ✓ Pythagorean theorem
- ✓ Quadrilateral
- ✓ Radius
- ✓ Range
- ✓ Ratio
- ✓ Reciprocal
- ✓ Right angle
- ✓ Sequence
- ✓ Set
- ✓ Similar triangles
- ✓ Slope
- ✓ Square root
- ✓ Standard deviation
- ✓ System of equations
- ✓ Transversal
- ✓ Vertical angle
- ✓ Volume

Concepts you'll need to master

- ✓ Understanding basic arithmetic operations on real numbers, including integers and fractions
- ✓ Understanding properties of integers
- ✓ Calculating averages and determining median and mode
- ✓ Translating word problems
- ✓ Simplifying algebraic expressions
- ✓ Factoring polynomials
- ✓ Solving algebraic equations and inequalities

- ✓ Working with number sets and sequences
- ✓ Identifying properties of parallel and perpendicular lines
- ✓ Identifying relationships between angles in geometric figures
- ✓ Analyzing properties of triangles, polygons, and circles, including perimeter, area, and circumference
- ✓ Understanding simple coordinate geometry, including using slope and midpoint formulas

The GRE Quantitative section is designed to test your ability to reason mathematically, to understand basic math terminology, and to recall basic mathematic formulas and principles. You should be able to solve problems and apply relevant mathematics concepts in Arithmetic, Algebra, Geometry, and Data Analysis.

The GRE Quantitative sections include multiple choice questions, each with five answer choices (A–E), as well as quantitative comparison questions, each with four possible answers (A–D). All questions cover the content discussed throughout this chapter. As with all sections on the computer adaptive GRE, you must answer each quantitative question before you can move on to the next question.

 Multiple choice questions might include answer choices in the Roman numeral format. Always take each Roman numeral as a true or false statement: Does it answer the question or not? As you evaluate each of the Roman numerals, eliminate answer choices based on whether the answer choices include the Roman numeral. This process might allow you to arrive at the correct answer without looking at every Roman numeral statement.

Quantitative comparison questions ask you to compare the quantities in two columns and determine if one is larger than the other, if the quantities are equal, or if there is not enough information to determine a relationship between the two quantities. Some questions include additional information that is centered above the two columns that concerns one or both of the quantities. If you decide that the quantity in Column A is greater than the quantity in Column B, select answer choice A. If you decide that the quantity in Column B is greater than the quantity in Column A, select answer choice B. If you decide that the quantities are equal, select answer choice C. If there is not enough information to determine a relationship between the two quantities, select answer choice D.

The best way to handle the quantitative comparison questions is to simply determine the value of the quantities in each column. It is often better to apply common sense and estimate values because you are really just trying to decide if one value is greater than the other. After you have calculated the values, you can easily determine the relationship, if one exists.

If one column is sometimes greater than or sometimes less than the other column, the relationship cannot be determined from the information. You should select answer choice D if *no one* can determine the relationship between the two values.

Also, the figures might not be drawn to scale. Rely on the information given, not on the appearance of the figures, to answer the questions.

Remember these general strategies when approaching GRE quantitative, or math questions:

➤ **Draw pictures**—It really helps sometimes to visualize the problem. This strategy should not take a lot of time, and can prevent careless errors. Sometimes, you are given a figure or a table that you can work with; sometimes, you just have to make your own. Consider the following example:

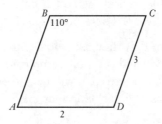

ABCD is a parallelogram.

Column A	Column B
Area of the region	6
ABCD	

To easily solve this problem, re-draw the figure as follows:

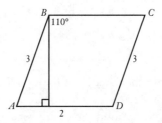

Draw a perpendicular line from point B to the base; this represents the height of the parallelogram. It also creates a right triangle. The hypotenuse of the triangle is 3, which means that the line you just drew must be less than 3. Because the area of a parallelogram is calculated by multiplying the base by the height, and, according to the figure that you just drew, the height is less than 3, the area of ABCD must be less than 6, or (2 × 3). Therefore, answer choice B is correct. Note that the angle measure given is irrelevent to answering the question.

➤ **Apply logic**—You cannot use a calculator, so most of the actual calculations are fairly simple. In fact, the GRE test writers are just as likely to test your logical reasoning ability or your ability to follow directions as they are to test your ability to plug numbers into an equation. Consider the following example:

If $b - c = 2$, and $a + c = 16$, then $a + b =$

To solve this problem, first recognize that $(b - c) + (a + c) = a + b$. This is true because the c values cancel each other out, leaving you with $b + a$, which is equivalent to $a + b$. Therefore, $a + b$ must equal 2 + 16, or 18.

➤ **Answer the question that they ask you**—If the problem requires three steps to reach a solution and you only completed two of the steps, it is likely that the answer you arrived at will be one of the choices. However, it will not be the correct choice! Consider the following example:

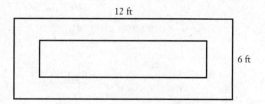

The rectangular garden shown in the figure above has a stone border 2 feet in width on all sides. What is the area, in square feet, of that portion of the garden that excludes the border?

(A) 4
(B) 16
(C) 40
(D) 56
(E) 72

This problem is asking for the area of the middle portion of the garden. To solve this problem, perform the following calculations, and remember that the border goes around the entire garden:

➤ Subtract the border width from the length of the garden: $12 - 2(2) = 8$.

➤ Subtract the border width from the width of the garden: $6 - 2(2) = 2$.

The area of the portion of the garden that excludes the border is 8×2, or 16.

If you only accounted for the border along one length and one width of the garden, you would have gotten answer choice C. Answer choice D is the area of the border around the garden. Answer choice E is the area of the entire garden, including the stone border.

➤ **Don't quit early**—Reason your way through the problem so that it makes sense. Keep in mind, though, that these questions do not usually involve intensive calculations or complicated manipulations.

$$a^2b > 0$$

$$ab^2 < 0$$

Column A	Column B
a	b

At first glance, you might think that you don't have enough information to solve this problem. However, a closer look will reveal some things about both a and b that will allow you to determine the relationship between them. For instance, you know that neither a nor b can be equal to 0, because any number multiplied by 0 equals 0. One given value is greater than 0 and the other is less than 0. In addition, you know that any number squared will always yield a positive result, so both a^2 and b^2 must be positive. Therefore, in order for the quantity a^2b to be greater than 0, b must be positive. Likewise, in order for the quantity ab^2 to be less than 0, a must be negative. This means that b will always be greater than a.

➤ **Check the choices**—Take a quick look at the answer choices as you read the problem for the first time. They can provide valuable clues about how to proceed. For example, many answer choices will be in either ascending or descending order. If the question asks you for the least possible value, try the smallest answer choice first. If it does not correctly answer the question, work through the rest of the answer choices from smallest to largest. Remember that one of them is the correct choice. Consider the following example:

If x is an integer and $y = 7x + 11$, what is the greatest value of x for which y is less than 50?

(A) 7
(B) 6
(C) 5
(D) 4
(E) 3

Because the question asks for the greatest value of x, start with answer choice A. Plug each answer choice into the given equation, as follows:

➤ $y = 7(7) + 11 = 60$. This is not less than 50, so eliminate answer choice A.

➤ $y = 7(6) + 11 = 53$. This is not less than 50, so eliminate answer choice B.

➤ $y = 7(5) + 11 = 46$. This is the greatest of the remaining answer choices, so it must be correct.

➤ **Pick numbers for the variables**—You can sometimes simplify your work on a given problem by using actual numbers as "stand-ins" for variables. This strategy works when you have variables in the question and the same variables in the answer choices. You can simplify the answer choices by substituting actual numbers for the variables. Pick numbers that are easy to work with and that meet the parameters of the information given in the question. If you use this strategy, remember that numbers on the GRE can be either positive or negative and are sometimes whole numbers and sometimes fractions. You should also be careful not to use 1 or 0 as your "stand-ins" because they can create "identities," which can lead to more than one seemingly correct answer choice. In addition, it is sometimes necessary to try more than one number to see if the result always correctly responds to the question. If the numbers that you pick work for more than one answer choice, pick different numbers and try again, focusing on the remaining answer choices.

Consider the following examples:

1. If x and y are both positive even integers, which of the following must be even?

    I. x^y

    II. $(x + 1)^y$

    III. $x^{(y + 1)}$

The question states that both x and y are positive even integers. Therefore, you can pick any positive even integer and substitute that value for x and y in each of the Roman numeral choices, as follows:

➤ Roman numeral I: $2^2 = 4$, which is even; $4^2 = 16$, which is also even. Any positive even integer raised to another positive even integer will result in an even number; therefore, Roman numeral I correctly answers the question. At this point, you could safely eliminate any answer choices that do not contain Roman numeral I.

➤ Roman numeral II: $(2 + 1)^2 = 3^2 = 9$, which is odd; $(4 + 1)^2 = 5^2 = 25$, which is also odd. When you add 1 to a positive even integer and raise the sum to a positive even integer, the result will be odd; therefore, Roman numeral II does not correctly answer the question. At this point, you could safely eliminate any remaining answer choices that contain Roman numeral II.

➤ Roman numeral III: $2^{(2 + 1)} = 2^3 = 8$, which is even; $4^{(2 + 1)} = 4^3 = 64$, which is also even. Any positive even integer raised to an odd power will result in an even number; therefore, Roman numeral III correctly answers the question, and you can eliminate any remaining answer choices that do not contain Roman numeral III.

2. If a and b are positive consecutive odd integers, where $b > a$, which of the following is equal to $b^2 - a^2$?

(A) $2a$

(B) $4a$

(C) $2a + 2$

(D) $2a + 4$

(E) $4a + 4$

You are given that both a and b are positive consecutive odd integers, and that b is greater than a. Pick two numbers that fit the criteria: $a = 3$ and $b = 5$. Now, substitute these numbers into $b^2 - a^2$: $5^2 = 25$ and $3^2 = 9$; therefore, $b^2 - a^2 = 16$. Now, plug the value that you selected for a into the answer choices until one of them yields 16, as follows:

➤ $2(3) = 6$; eliminate answer choice A.

➤ $4(3) = 12$; eliminate answer choice B.

➤ $2(3) + 2 = 8$; eliminate answer choice C.

➤ $2(3) + 4 = 10$; eliminate answer choice D.

➤ $4(3) + 4 = 16$; answer choice E is correct.

As long as the numbers you select meet the criteria given in the question, you will always arrive at answer choice E.

➤ **Read the questions carefully**—When you are looking at ratio problems, for example, note whether the question is giving a part-to-part ratio, or a part-to-whole ratio. The ratio of girls to boys in a class is a part-to-part ratio. The ratio of girls to students in a class is a part-to-whole ratio.

Familiarize yourself with the basic mathematical concepts included in this chapter and be able to apply them to a variety of math problems. Remember that you will not be required to perform any elaborate computations.

Arithmetic

This book assumes a basic understanding of arithmetic. Our focus will be on reviewing some general concepts, and applying those concepts to questions that might appear on the GRE General Test.

Understanding Operations Using Whole Numbers, Decimals, and Fractions

The GRE Quantitative sections require you to add, subtract, multiply, and divide whole numbers, fractions, and decimals. When performing these operations, be sure to keep track of negative signs and line up decimal points in order to avoid careless mistakes.

Following are some simple rules to keep in mind regarding whole numbers, fractions, and decimals:

1. An integer is a positive or negative counting number, including zero.

2. Ordering is the process of arranging numbers from smallest to greatest or from greatest to smallest. The symbol > is used to represent "greater than," and the symbol < is used to represent "less than." To represent "greater than and equal to," use the symbol ≥; to represent "less than and equal to," use the symbol ≤.

3. The Commutative Property of Multiplication can be expressed as $a \times b = b \times a$, or $ab = ba$.

4. The Distributive Property of Multiplication can be expressed as $a(b + c) = ab + ac$.

5. The Associative Property of Multiplication can be expressed as $(a \times b) \times c = a \times (b \times c)$.

6. The Order of Operations for whole numbers can be remembered by using the acronym **PEMDAS**:

➤**P**: First, do the operations within the parentheses, if any.

➤**E**: Next, do the exponents, if any.

➤**M**: Next, do the multiplication, in order from left to right.

➤**D**: Next, do the division, in order from left to right.

➤**A**: Next, do the addition, in order from left to right.

➤**S**: Finally, do the subtraction, in order from left to right.

Consider the following example:

$$\frac{2(5-3)^2 + 16}{4} =$$

➤ First, perform the operation inside the parentheses: $(5 - 3) = 2$

  ➤ Next, work with the exponent: $2(2)^2 = 2 \times 4 = 8$

  ➤ Next, perform the multiplication: $2(8) = 16$

  ➤ Now perform the addition: $16 + 16 = 32$

  ➤ Finally, perform the division: $\frac{32}{4} = 8$

7. When a number is expressed as the product of two or more numbers, it is in factored form. Factors are all of the numbers that will divide evenly into one number. For example, 1, 3, and 9 are factors of 9: $9 \div 1 = 9$; $9 \div 3 = 3$; $9 \div 9 = 1$.

8. A number is called a multiple of another number if it can be expressed as the product of that number and a second number. For example, the multiples of 4 are 4, 8, 12, 16, and so on, because $4 \times 1 = 4$, $4 \times 2 = 8$, $4 \times 3 = 12$, $4 \times 4 = 16$, and so on. Consider the following simulated GRE question:

How many multiples of 3 are there between 15 and 87, inclusive?

(A) 22

(B) 23

(C) 24

(D) 25

(E) 26

➤ One way to solve this problem is to write every multiple of 3 starting with 15 ($3 \times 5 = 15$; $3 \times 6 = 18$, and so on). However, this is time-consuming and leaves opportunity for error. A better way to solve this problem is to recognize that $3 \times 5 = 15$ and $3 \times 29 = 87$; the number of multiples of 3 between 15 and 87, inclusive, is the same as the number of integers between 5 and 29, inclusive, which is 25.

9. The greatest common factor (GCF) is the largest number that will divide evenly into any two or more numbers. The least common multiple (LCM) is the smallest number that any two or more numbers will divide evenly into. For example, the GCF of 24 and 36 is 12

because 12 is the largest number that will divide evenly into both 24 and 36. The LCM of 24 and 36 is 72 because 72 is the smallest number that both 24 and 36 will divide evenly into.

10. Multiplying and dividing both the numerator and the denominator of a fraction by the same nonzero number results in an equivalent fraction. For example, $\frac{1}{4} \times \frac{3}{3} = \frac{3}{12}$, which can be reduced to $\frac{1}{4}$. This works because any nonzero number divided by itself is always equal to 1.

11. When multiplying fractions, multiply the numerators to get the numerator of the product, and multiply the denominators to get the denominator of the product. For example, $\frac{1}{4} \times \frac{5}{6} = \frac{5}{24}$.

12. To divide fractions, multiply the first fraction by the reciprocal of the second fraction. In mathematics, the reciprocal of any number is the number that, when multiplied by the first number, will yield a product of 1. For example: The reciprocal of $\frac{1}{4}$ is $\frac{4}{1}$ because $\frac{1}{4} \times \frac{4}{1} = 1$. So, $\frac{1}{3} \div \frac{1}{4} = \frac{1}{3} \times \frac{4}{1}$, which equals $\frac{4}{3}$. Consider the following example:

$$\frac{50 - 2(12 \div 3)}{\frac{1}{2}}$$

(A) 9
(B) 11
(C) 22
(D) 42
(E) 84

First, perform the calculations in the numerator (remember the order of operations!)

➤ $50 - 2(4) =$

➤ $50 - 8 = 42$

The next step in solving this problem is to get rid of the fraction in the denominator. To do this, multiply the numerator by the reciprocal of the fraction in the denominator:

➤ $\dfrac{42}{\frac{1}{2}}$ is equivalent to $42 \times \dfrac{2}{1}$

➤ $(42)(2) = 84$

13. When adding and subtracting like fractions (fractions with the same denominator), add or subtract the numerators and write the sum or difference over the denominator. So, $\dfrac{1}{8} + \dfrac{2}{8} = \dfrac{3}{8}$, and $\dfrac{4}{7} - \dfrac{2}{7} = \dfrac{2}{7}$.

14. When adding or subtracting unlike fractions, first find the lowest (or least) common denominator (LCD). The LCD is the smallest number that all of the denominators will divide evenly into. For example, to add $\dfrac{3}{4}$ and $\dfrac{5}{6}$, find the smallest number that both 4 and 6 will divide evenly into. That number is 12, so the LCD of 4 and 6 is 12. Multiply $\dfrac{3}{4}$ by $\dfrac{3}{3}$ to get $\dfrac{9}{12}$, and multiply $\dfrac{5}{6}$ by $\dfrac{2}{2}$ to get $\dfrac{10}{12}$. Now add the fractions: $\dfrac{9}{12} + \dfrac{10}{12} = \dfrac{19}{12}$, which can be simplified to $1\dfrac{7}{12}$.

15. To convert a mixed number into an improper fraction, first multiply the whole number by the denominator, add the result to the numerator, and place that quantity over the denominator. For example, $1\dfrac{7}{12} = (1 \times 12) + \dfrac{7}{12}$, or $\dfrac{19}{12}$.

16. When converting a fraction to a decimal, divide the numerator by the denominator. For example, $\dfrac{3}{4} = 3 \div 4$, or .75.

17. Place value refers to the value of a digit in a number relative to its position. Starting from the left of the decimal point, the values of the digits are ones, tens, hundreds, and so on. Starting to the right of the decimal point, the values of the digits are tenths, hundredths, thousandths, and so on.

You are required to add, subtract, multiply, and divide whole numbers, fractions, and decimals. Be careful of decimal points and negative numbers.

Understanding Squares and Square Roots

In mathematics, a square is the product of any number multiplied by itself, and is expressed as $a^2 = n$. A square root is written as $\sqrt{n}$, and is the non-negative value a that fulfills the expression $a^2 = n$. For example, the square root of 25 would be written as $\sqrt{25}$. The square root of 25 is 5, and 5-squared, or 5^2, equals 5×5, or 25. A number is considered a perfect square when the square root of that number is a whole number. So, 25 is a perfect square because the square root of 25 is 5, which is a whole number.

When you square a fraction, simply calculate the square of both the numerator and the denominator, as follows:

$$(\frac{3}{5})^2 =$$

$$\frac{3}{5} \times \frac{3}{5} = \frac{9}{25}$$

Consider the following simulated GRE question:

When $a = -2$, what is the value of $-4a^2$?

(A) -16

(B) -8

(C) 16

(D) 32

(E) 64

To solve this problem, first substitute -2 for a, and then square -2. Remember that a negative number squared results in a positive number. Therefore, $-2^2 = 4$. Now, simply multiply -4×4 to get -16.

Understanding Exponents

When a whole number is multiplied by itself, the number of times it is multiplied is referred to as the exponent. As shown previously with square roots, the exponent of 5^2 is 2 and it signifies 5×5. Any number can be raised to any exponential value. For example:

$$7^6 = 7 \times 7 \times 7 \times 7 \times 7 \times 7 = 117,649$$

Remember that when you multiply a negative number by a negative number, the result is a positive number. When you multiply a negative number by a positive number, the result is a negative number. These rules should be applied when working with exponents, too, as shown next:

➤ $-3^2 = -3 \times -3$

➤ $-3 \times -3 = 9$

➤ $-3^3 = -3 \times -3 \times -3$

➤ $(-3 \times -3) = 9$

➤ $9 \times -3 = -27$

 Remember the Order of Operations mentioned previously, especially when you are working with negative numbers. For example, $-4^2 = 16$, but $-(4^2) = -16$ because you must perform the operation within the parentheses first.

The basic rules of exponents follow:

➤ $a^m \times a^n = a^{(m+n)}$

➤ $(a^m)^n = a^{mn}$

➤ $(ab)^m = a^m \times b^m$

➤ $\left[\dfrac{a}{b}\right]^m = \dfrac{a^m}{b^m}$

➤ $a^0 = 1$, when $a \neq 0$

➤ $a^{-m} = \dfrac{1}{am}$, when $a \neq 0$

➤ $\dfrac{a}{b^{-m}} = ab^m$, when $b \neq 0$

Consider the following simulated GRE questions:

1. What is the value of $-2x^3$ if x equals -2?
    (A) -16
    (B) -12
    (C) 12
    (D) 16
    (E) 64

The PEMDAS order of operations must be followed in order to obtain the correct answer for this problem, with exponents being solved before multiplication. Because $x=-2$, the value of $-2x^3$ is $-2(-2)^3 = -2(-8) = 16$.

2. $(0.1^2)^3 =$
   (A) .001
   (B) .0001
   (C) .00001
   (D) .000001
   (E) .0000001

In multiplying exponents, $(a^m)^n = a^{(mn)}$, which in this case yields $0.1^6 = 0.1 \times 0.1 \times 0.1 \times 0.1 \times 0.1 \times 0.1 = .000001$. Thus, the correct answer is D.

Understanding Ratios and Proportions

A ratio is the relationship between two quantities expressed as one divided by the other.

For example: Jordan works 2 hours for every 3 hours that Al works. This can be expressed as $\frac{2}{3}$ or 2:3, and is known as a part-to-part ratio. If you compared the number of hours that Jordan works in one week to the total number of hours that every employee works in one week, that would be a part-to-whole ratio.

A proportion is an equation in which two ratios are set equal to each other.

For example: Jordan worked 30 hours in one week and earned $480. If he received the same hourly rate the next week, how much would he earn for working 25 hours that week?

➤ $\frac{480}{30} = \frac{x}{25}$; solve for x

➤ $30x = 12,000$

➤ $x = 400$

Jordan would earn $400 that week.

Understanding Percent and Percentages

A percent is a fraction whose denominator is 100. The fraction $\frac{55}{100}$ is equal to 55%.

Or the GRE, percentage problems often deal with calculating an increase or a decrease in number or price.

For example: A jacket that originally sells for $90 is on sale for 30% off. What is the sale price of the jacket (not including tax)?

➤ 30% of $90 =

➤ $\frac{30}{100} \times \$90 =$

➤ .30 × $90 = $27

The discount is equal to $27, but the question asked for the sale price. Therefore, you must subtract $27 from $90.

➤ $90 – $27 = $63

You could also more quickly solve a problem like this by recognizing that, if the jacket is 30% off of the regular price, the sale price must be equal to 100% – 30%, or 70% of the original price.

➤ 70% of $90 =

➤ $\frac{70}{100} \times \$90 =$

➤ .70 × $90 = $63

Remember to answer the question that is asked. You can be certain that $27 would have been an answer choice if the previous problem had appeared on your test, but it is not the correct answer! The GRE will often attempt to distract you from the correct answer by including incorrect answer choices at which you might arrive if you did not complete all of the steps. Be sure you don't forget a step or make calculation errors.

Understanding Number Lines and Sequences

A number line is a geometric representation of the relationships between numbers, including integers, fractions, and decimals. The numbers on a number line always increase as you move to the right, and decrease when you move to the left. Number line questions typically require you to determine the relationships among certain numbers on the line.

Remember that the distance between points on the number line does not always have to be measured in whole units. Sometimes, the distance between points is a fraction of a number.

An arithmetic sequence is one in which the difference between consecutive terms is the same. For example, 2, 4, 6, 8..., is an arithmetic sequence where 2 is the constant difference. In an arithmetic sequence, the nth term can be found using the formula $a_n = a_1 + (n-1)d$, where d is the common difference.

A geometric sequence is one in which the ratio between two terms is constant. For example, $\frac{1}{2}$, 1, 2, 4, 8..., is a geometric sequence where 2 is the constant ratio. With geometric sequences, you can find the nth term using the formula $a_n = a_1(r)^{n-1}$, where r is the constant ratio.

Typically, if you can identify the pattern or the relationship between the numbers, you will be able to answer the question. Following is an example of a sequence question similar to one you might find on the GRE:

$$0,1,2,0,1,2,...$$

The numbers 0, 1, and 2 repeat in a sequence, as shown. If this pattern continues, what will be the sum of the 9th and 12th numbers in the sequence?

To solve this problem, simply recognize that the third number in the sequence is 2, which means that both the 9th number and the 12th number in the sequence will also be 2. Therefore, the sum of the 9th and 12th numbers is 2 + 2, or 4.

Understanding Absolute Value

The absolute value of a number is indicated by placing that number inside two vertical lines. For example, the absolute value of 10 is written as follows: $|10|$. Absolute value can be defined as the numerical value of a real number without regard to its sign. This means that the absolute value of 10, $|10|$, is the same as the absolute value of -10, $|-10|$, in that they both equal 10. Think of it as the distance from -10 to 0 on the number line, and the distance from 0 to 10 on the number line—both distances equal 10 units, as shown in Figure 6.1.

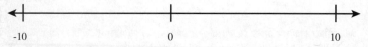

-10   0   10

Figure 6.1 Demonstrating absolute value.

Consider the following example:

$|3-5| =$

$|-2| = 2$

Understanding Mean, Median, and Mode

The arithmetic mean refers to the average of a set of values. For example, if a student received grades of 80%, 90%, and 95% on three tests, the average test grade is 80 + 90 + 95 divided by 3.

The median is the middle value of an ordered list. If the list contains an even number of values, the median is simply the average of the two middle values. It is important to put the values in either ascending or descending order before selecting the median.

The mode is the value or values that appear the greatest number of times in a list of values.

Consider the following simulated GRE question:

1. The average (arithmetic mean) of four numbers is 20. After one of the numbers is removed, the average (arithmetic mean) of the remaining numbers is 17. What number has been removed?
   (A) 3
   (B) 21
   (C) 29
   (D) 37
   (E) It cannot be determined from the information given.

   To answer this question, set the total equal to x, and solve as follows:

   ➤ If the average of four numbers is 20, then $20 = \frac{x}{4}$, and $x = 80$.

   ➤ If one number is removed, and the average of the remaining numbers is 17, then $17 = \frac{x}{3}$, and $x = 51$.

   Therefore, the number that was removed must be $80 - 51$, or 29.

Algebra

This book assumes you have a basic understanding of algebra. Our focus will be on reviewing some general concepts and applying those concepts to questions that might appear on the GRE.

Understanding Linear Equations with One Variable

In a linear equation with one variable, the variable cannot have an exponent or be in the denominator of a fraction. An example of a linear equation is

$2x + 13 = 43$. The GRE will most likely require you to solve for x in that equation. Do this by isolating x on the left side of the equation, as follows:

➤ $2x + 13 = 43$

➤ $2x = 43 - 13$

➤ $2x = 30$

➤ $x = \dfrac{30}{2}$, or 15.

Consider the following simulated GRE question:

> If $3x = -15$, then $4x^2 - 2x - 7 =$
> (A) -117
> (B) 96
> (C) 103
> (D) 117
> (E) 383

The first step is to solve for x in the first equation, as follows:

➤ $3x = -15$

➤ $x = -5$

Now, substitute -5 for x in the second equation, as follows (remember the order of operations, and keep track of the negative signs!):

➤ $4x^2 - 2x - 7 =$

➤ $4(-5)^2 - 2(-5) - 7 =$

➤ $4(25) - (-10) - 7 =$

➤ $100 + 10 - 7 = 103$

Understanding Systems of Equations

A system of equations refers to a number of equations with an equal number of variables. To solve a system of equations you must find the values of the variables that make both equations true at the same time.

The two most common ways to solve systems of equations are the Substitution method and the Addition-Subtraction method. In the Substitution method, simply solve the first equation for one of the variables and substitute the result into the second equation wherever that variable appears. This method is generally suitable when either one or both of the variables does not have a coefficient.

On the GRE, a system of equations will generally take the form of two linear equations with two variables. The following is an example of a system of equations, solved using the Addition-Subtraction method:

$4x + 5y = 21$

$5x + 10y = 30$

With the Addition-Subtraction method, the first step will be to make one set of values, either the x-values or the y-values in this example, cancel the other out. To do this, make the coefficient of one of the variables in one of the equations negative. In the preceding system you can see it will be easier to work with the y-values ($5y$ and $10y$) because 5 is a factor of 10. Therefore, you can simply multiply each element in the first equation by -2 so that the y-values will cancel out, as shown in the following steps:

➤ $-2(4x) + -2(5y) = -2(21)$

➤ $-8x - 10y = -42$

The first equation is now $-8x - 10y = -42$, which is equivalent to the original first equation because you did the same thing to each term. Now, you can add the like terms in each equation:

➤ $(-8x + 5x) = -3x$

➤ $(-10y + 10y) = 0$

➤ $-42 + 30 = -12$

➤ $-3x = -12$

Notice that the two y-terms cancel each other out. Solving for x, you get $x = 4$. Now, choose one of the original two equations, plug 4 in for x, and solve for y:

➤ $4(4) + 5y = 21$

➤ $16 + 5y = 21$

➤ $5y = 5$

➤ $y = 1$

The solutions for the system of equations are $x = 4$ and $y = 1$, which means that when $x = 4$ and $y = 1$, both equations will be true.

Understanding Polynomial Operations and Factoring Simple Quadratic Expressions

A polynomial is the sum or difference of expressions like $2x^2$ and $14x$. The most common polynomial takes the form of a simple quadratic expression, such as $2x^2 + 14x + 8$, with the terms in decreasing order. The standard form of a simple quadratic expression is $ax^2 + bx + c$, where a, b, and c are whole numbers. When the terms include both a number and a variable, such as x, the number is called the coefficient. For example, in the expression $2x$, 2 is the coefficient of x.

The GRE will often require you to evaluate, or solve a polynomial, by substituting a given value for the variable. Consider the following examples:

If $x = -2$, what is the value of $2x^2 + 14x + 8 = ?$

➤ $2(-2)^2 + 14(-2) + 8 =$

➤ $2(-2 \times -2) + 14(-2) + 8$

➤ $2(4) + (-28) + 8 =$

➤ $8 - 28 + 8 = -12$

You will also be required to add, subtract, multiply, and divide polynomials. To add or subtract polynomials, simply combine like terms, as in the following examples:

$(2x^2 + 14x + 8) + (3x^2 + 5x + 32) = 5x^2 + 19x + 40$

Add the like terms

➤ $2x^2 + 3x^2 = 5x^2$

➤ $14x + 5x = 19x$

➤ $8 + 32 = 40$

The same steps apply when subtracting polynomials:

$(8x^2 + 11x + 23) - (7x^2 + 3x + 13) = x^2 + 8x + 10$

Subtract the like terms

➤ $8x^2 - 7x^2 = x^2$

➤ $11x - 3x = 8x$

➤ $23 - 13 = 10$

To multiply polynomials, use the Distributive Property to multiply each term of one polynomial by each term of the other polynomial. Following are some examples:

$(3x)(x^2 + 4x - 2) = (3x^3 + 12x^2 - 6x)$

Let's break this example down:

➤ $3x \times x^2 = 3x^3$

➤ $3x \times 4x = 12x^2$

➤ $3x \times -2 = -6x$

Remember the *FOIL* method for problems like the one that follows. In the *FOIL* method, multiply the first terms of each polynomial, then multiply the outside terms, then multiply the inside terms, and finally, multiply the last terms:

If $(2x + 5)(x - 3) = ax^2 + bx + c$ for all values of x, what is the value of b?

To solve this problem, apply the FOIL method as shown next:

➤ Multiply the *F*irst terms: $(2x)(x) = 2x^2$

➤ Multiply the *O*utside terms: $(2x)(-3) = -6x$

➤ Multiply the *I*nside terms: $(5)(x) = 5x$

➤ Multiply the *L*ast terms: $(5)(-3) = -15$

Now put the terms in decreasing order:

➤ $2x^2 + (-6x) + 5x + (-15) =$

➤ $2x^2 - x - 15$

Therefore, because the middle term has a coefficient of -1, the value of b is -1.

You may also be asked to find the factors or solution sets of certain simple quadratic expressions. A factor or solution set takes the form ($x \pm$ some number). Simple quadratic expressions will usually have two of these factors or solution sets. The GRE might require you to calculate the values of the solution sets. The following example shows you how to work through these problem types.

If $(2x + 5)(x - 3) = 0$, what are all the possible values of x?

To solve, first set both elements of the equation equal to zero.

➤$(2x + 5) = 0$

➤$(x - 3) = 0$

Now solve for x:

➤ $2x + 5 = 0$

➤ $2x + 5 - 5 = 0 - 5$

➤ $2x = -5$

➤ $x = -\dfrac{5}{2}$

and

➤ $x - 3 = 0$

➤ $x - 3 + 3 = 0 + 3$

➤ $x = 3$

The possible values of x are $-\dfrac{5}{2}$ and 3.

Following are some general factoring rules that might prove useful for answering GRE quantitative questions:

➤ Finding the difference between two squares: $a^2 - b^2 = (a + b)(a - b)$

➤ Finding common factors, such as: $x^2 - 2x = x(x + 2)$

➤ Factoring quadratic equations, such as: $x^2 + 2x - 8 = (x + 4)(x - 2)$

 The GRE might ask you to solve one variable in terms of another variable. You may not be able to find a specific numerical value for the variables, but generally you won't need to. Your job will be to manipulate the given expression so that you can isolate one variable on one side of the equation.

Understanding Linear Inequalities with One Variable

Linear inequalities with one variable are solved in almost the same manner as linear equations with one variable: by isolating the variable on one side of the inequality. Remember, though, that when multiplying both sides of an inequality by a negative number, the direction of the sign must be reversed, as follows:

If $3x + 4 > 5x + 1$, then $x =$

First, isolate x on one side of the inequality.

➤ $3x - 5x > 1 - 4$

➤ $-2x > -3$

Now, because you have to divide both sides by -2, remember to reverse the inequality sign.

➤ $x < \dfrac{3}{2}$

Sometimes, the GRE will simply require you to recognize the meaning of an inequality and the relationships among the terms. Consider the following simulated question:

Column A	Column B
	$500 < x < 1,000$	
$1,000 - x$	$x - 500$

This question contains an inequality that says the value of x is somewhere between 500 and 1,000. Because you do not know the exact value of x, you do not know whether the result of subtracting it from 1,000 is greater than, less than, or equal to the result of subtracting 500 from it. For example, if x = 999, then 1,000 – 999 = 1, and 999 – 500 = 499; the quantity in Column B is greater. However, if x = 501, then 1,000 – 501 = 499 and 501 – 500 = 1, and the quantity in Column A is greater.

Remember that when you multiply or divide both sides of an inequality by a negative number, you must reverse the direction of the inequality. This applies to operations involving the greater than or equal to symbol ($\geq$) and the less than or equal to symbol ($\leq$) as well.

Understanding Functions

A function is a set of ordered pairs in which no two of the ordered pairs has the same x-value. In a function, each input (x-value) has exactly one output (y-value). An example of this relationship is $y = x^2$. Here, y is a function of x because for any value of x, there is exactly one value of y. For example, when x = either 4 or -4, y equals 16. However, x is not a function of y because for certain values of y, there is more than one value of x, as we just showed. The *domain* of a function refers to the x-values, while the *range* of a function refers to the y-values, or the $f(x)$ values. If the values in the domain corresponded to more than one value in the range, the relation is not a function.

For example: Let the function f be defined by $f(x) = x^2 - (3x)$. What is the value of $f(5)$?

Solve this problem by substituting 5 for x wherever x appears in the function:

➤ $f(x) = x^2 - 3x$

➤ $f(5) = (5)^2 - (3)(5)$

➤ $f(5) = 25 - 15$

➤ $f(5) = 10$

In this example, whenever $x = 5$, $f(5) = 10$. This is a function because when $x = 5$, $y = 10$; for every x-value, there is only one y-value.

Understanding Simple Probability

Probability is used to measure how likely an event is to occur. It is always between 0 and 1; an event that will definitely not occur has a probability of 0, whereas an event that will certainly occur has a probability of 1.

To determine probability, divide the number of outcomes that fit the conditions of an event by the total number of outcomes. Take the following example:

The chance of getting heads when flipping a coin is 1 out of 2, or $\frac{1}{2}$. There are two possible outcomes (heads or tails) but only one outcome (heads) that fits the conditions of the event. Therefore, the probability of the coin toss resulting in heads is $\frac{1}{2}$ or .5.

When two events are independent, meaning the outcome of one event does not affect the other, you can calculate the probability of both occurring by multiplying the probabilities of each of the events together. For example:

The probability of flipping three heads in a row would be $\frac{1}{2} \times \frac{1}{2} \times \frac{1}{2}$, or $\frac{1}{8}$.

Geometry

This book assumes that you have a basic understanding of both coordinate geometry and plane geometry; however, we will review some general concepts, and then apply those concepts to simulated GRE questions.

Understanding the Coordinate Plane

The xy-coordinate plane has four separate quadrants, as shown in Figure 6.2.

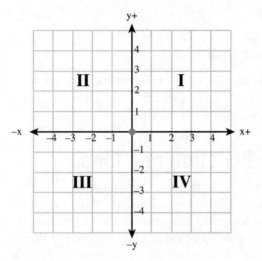

Figure 6.2   The xy-coordinate plane.

The x-coordinates in Quadrants I and IV will be positive, and the x-coordinates in Quadrants II and III will be negative. The y-coordinates in Quadrants I and II will be positive, and the y-coordinates in Quadrants III and IV will be negative.

Consider the following simulated GRE question:

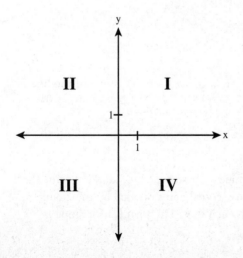

Points $(a,-2)$ and $(-3,b)$, not shown in the figure above, are in quadrants IV and II, respectively. If $ab \neq 0$, in which quadrant is point (a,b)?

(A) I

(B) II

(C) III

(D) IV

(E) It cannot be determined from the information given.

You are given that point $(a,-2)$ is in quadrant IV, which means that a is positive. You are also given that point $(-3,b)$ is in quadrant II, which means that b is positive. The quadrant in which both a and b are positive is quadrant I.

Understanding the Equation of a Line

The GRE will include questions concerning the slope-intercept form of a line, which is expressed as $y = mx + b$, where m is the slope of the line and b is the y-intercept (that is, the point at which the graph of the line crosses the y-axis). You might be required to put the equation of a line into the slope-intercept form to determine either the slope or the y-intercept of a line, as follows:

In the xy-plane, a line has the equation $3x + 7y - 16 = 0$. What is the slope of the line?

The first step is to isolate y on the left side of the equation:

➤ $3x + 7y - 16 = 0$

➤ $3x - 3x + 7y - 16 + 16 = 0 - 3x + 16$

➤ $7y = -3x + 16$

➤ $y = -\dfrac{3}{7} x + \dfrac{16}{7}$

According to the slope-intercept formula, $y = mx + b$, the slope of the line is $-\dfrac{3}{7}$.

Understanding Slope

The slope of a line is commonly defined as "rise over run," and is a value that is calculated by taking the change in y-coordinates divided by the change in x-coordinates from two given points on a line. The formula for slope is

$$m = \frac{(y_2 - y_1)}{(x_2 - x_1)}$$

where (x_1, y_1) and (x_2, y_2) are the two given points. For example, if you are given (3,2) and (5,6) as two points on a line, the slope would be $m = \dfrac{(6\text{-}2)}{(5\text{-}3)} = \dfrac{4}{2} = 2$.

A positive slope will mean the graph of the line will go up and to the right. A negative slope will mean the graph of the line will go down and to the right. A horizontal line has a slope of 0, whereas a vertical line has an undefined slope. Figure 6.3 shows you these various slope possibilities.

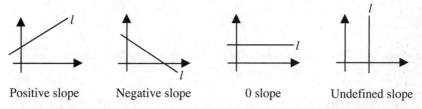

Positive slope   Negative slope   0 slope   Undefined slope

Figure 6.3   Directions of slopes.

Understanding Parallel and Perpendicular Lines

Two lines are parallel if they lie in the same plane and never intersect. Two lines are perpendicular if they intersect at right angles. Figure 6.4 demonstrates this concept. Note that in the figure, the two parallel lines intersect a third, perpendicular line to form two right angles.

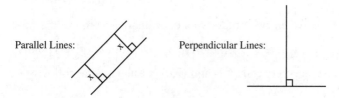

Figure 6.4   Perpendicular and parallel lines.

This concept is important for GRE quantitative questions such as the following:

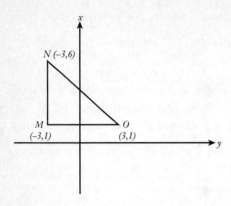

In the figure above, if *MO* and *MN* are parallel to the *x* and *y* axes, respectively, what is the area of triangle *MNO*?

The area of a triangle is $\frac{1}{2}(bh)$. Because you know that *MO* (the base, *b*) is parallel to the *x*-axis, you know that it is a straight line segment with a length of 6 (the distance from -3 to 3 along the *x*-axis). Likewise, because you know that *MN* (the height, *h*) is parallel to the *y*-axis, you know that it is a straight line segment with a length of 5 (the distance from 1 to 6 along the *y*-axis). Therefore, the area of triangle *MNO* is $\frac{1}{2}$ (6 × 5), or 15.

Understanding Distance and Midpoint Formulas

To find the distance between two points on a coordinate graph, use the formula $\sqrt{([x_2-x_1]^2+[y_2-y_1]^2)}$, where (x_1, y_1) and (x_2, y_2) are the two given points. For instance, the distance between (3,2) and (7,6) is calculated as follows:

➤ $\sqrt{([7-3]^2+[6-2]^2)}$ =

➤ $\sqrt{(16+16)} = \sqrt{32}$

➤ $\sqrt{(4)(8)} = 2\sqrt{8}$.

To find the midpoint of a line given two points on the line, use the formula $\left(\frac{[x_1+x_2]}{2}, \frac{[y_1+y_2]}{2}\right)$.

For example, the midpoint between (5,4) and (9,2) is

$$\left(\frac{[5+9]}{2}, \frac{[4+2]}{2}\right), \text{ or } (7,3).$$

The GRE might also simply require you to understand that the midpoint of any line segment is the point halfway between the endpoints of the line segment. Consider the following simulated GRE question:

If Q is the midpoint of line segment PS and R is the midpoint of line segment QS, what is the value of $\dfrac{PQ}{PR}$?

(A) $\dfrac{1}{4}$

(B) $\dfrac{1}{3}$

(C) $\dfrac{1}{2}$

(D) $\dfrac{2}{3}$

(E) $\dfrac{3}{4}$

To answer this question, draw a picture of the line segments indicated:

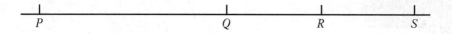

Because Q is halfway between P and S, set the value of PQ to $\dfrac{1}{2}$. Likewise, because R is three-fourths of the distance between P and S, set the value of PR to $\dfrac{3}{4}$. Now reduce the fraction, as follows:

➤ $\dfrac{\frac{1}{2}}{\frac{3}{4}}$ (multiply the numerator by the reciprocal of the denominator.

➤ $\dfrac{1}{2} \times \dfrac{4}{3} = \dfrac{4}{6}$

➤ $\dfrac{4}{6} = \dfrac{2}{3}$

Understanding Properties and Relations of Plane Figures

Plane figures include circles, triangles, rectangles, squares, and other parallelograms. While this book assumes a basic understanding of the properties of these figures, we will review some basic concepts and apply them to simulated GRE exam questions.

Triangles

A *triangle* is a polygon with three sides and three angles. If the measure of all three angles and all three sides of the triangle are the same length, the triangle is an *equilateral triangle*. If the measure of two angles and two sides of the triangle are the same, the triangle is an *isosceles triangle*. A triangle in which none of the sides are the same is called a *scalene triangle*.

The sum of the interior angles in a triangle is always 180 degrees. If the measure of one of the angles in the triangle is 90 degrees (a right angle), the triangle is a right triangle, as shown in Figure 6.5.

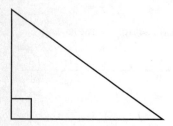

Figure 6.5 A right triangle.

Some right triangles have unique relationships between the angles and the lengths of the sides. These are called "Special Right Triangles." It might be helpful to remember the information in Figure 6.6.

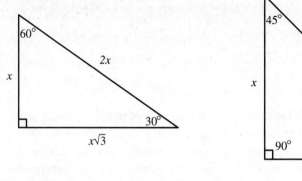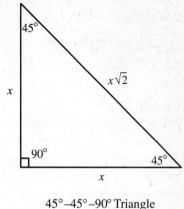

30°–60°–90° Triangle   45°–45°–90° Triangle

Figure 6.6 Special right triangles.

The perimeter of a triangle is the sum of the lengths of the sides. The area of a triangle is calculated by using the formula $A = \frac{1}{2}$ (base)(height). For any right triangle, the Pythagorean theorem states that $a^2 + b^2 = c^2$, where a and b are legs (sides) and c is the hypotenuse. For example:

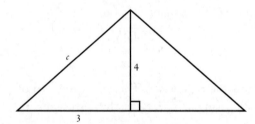

What is the value of c in the figure above?

Solve this problem using the Pythagorean theorem, as follows:

➤ $a^2 + b^2 = c^2$

➤ $3^2 + 4^2 = c^2$

➤ $9 + 16 = c^2$

➤ $25 = c^2$

➤ $5 = c$

Similar triangles always have the same shape, and each corresponding pair of angles has the same measure. The lengths of the pairs of corresponding sides that form the angles are proportional.

Circles

The radius of a circle is the distance from the center of the circle to any point on the circle. The diameter of a circle is twice the radius. The formula for the circumference of a circle is $C = 2\pi r$, or πd, whereas the formula for the area of a circle is $A = \pi r^2$. A circle contains 360 degrees. These concepts are important for GRE questions such as the following:

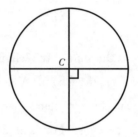

The circle has a center C and a diameter of 6.

Column A	Column B
The area of the circle	6π

Because the diameter is 6, you know the radius is 3. Therefore, the area of circle C is $\pi 3^2$, or 9π, which is greater than 6π. Therefore, the correct answer is A.

Rectangles

A rectangle is a quadrilateral with four sides (two sets of congruent, or equal sides) and four right angles.

Figure 6.7 shows a rectangle.

Figure 6.7   A rectangle.

The sum of the angles in a rectangle is always 360 degrees. The perimeter of a rectangle is P = 2*l* + 2*w*, where *l* is the length and *w* is the width.

The area of a rectangle is A = *lw*, where *l* is the length and *w* is the width.

The lengths of the diagonals of a rectangle are congruent, or equal. Consider the following rectangle:

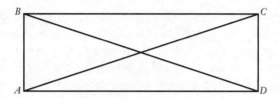

Line segment AC is equal in length to line segment BD.

A square is a special rectangle where all four sides are of equal length, and where the diagonals are congruent, perpendicular bisectors.

Consider the following simulated GRE questions:

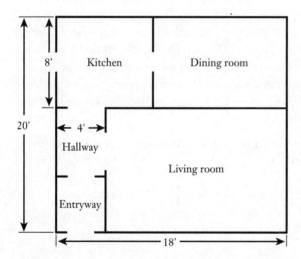

Questions 1–3 refer to the following floor plan.

Note: Figure drawn to scale.

The figure above shows the plan for the ground floor of a townhouse. The thickness of the walls should be ignored when answering the questions. The dimensions shown are in feet, and each region is rectangular.

1. What is the area, in square feet, of the living room?

(A) 38

(B) 168

(C) 216

(D) 280

(E) 360

According to the floor plan, the dimensions of the living room are 14 feet (18 – 4) by 12 feet (20 – 8). Therefore, the area is 14 × 12, or 168 square feet. If you failed to subtract the width of the hallway (4), you would likely have selected answer choice C. If you failed to subtract the length of the kitchen (8), you would likely have selected answer choice D. If you calculated the area of the entire ground floor, you would have selected answer choice E.

2. What is the perimeter, in feet, of the ground floor of the townhouse?

(A) 38

(B) 46

(C) 76

(D) 92

(E) 360

The perimeter is the distance around an object. Therefore, the perimeter of the rectangular townhouse is 2(20) + 2(18), or 76. Answer choice A accounts for only two of the four sides of the townhouse. If you add 8 feet to the length of the townhouse and made some calculation errors, you would likely have selected answer choices B or D. Answer choice E is the area of the ground floor of the townhouse.

3. If the kitchen is square, what is the ratio of the area of the kitchen to the area of the dining room?

(A) 1 : 3

(B) 9 : 20

(C) 1 : 2

(D) 8 : 11

(E) 2 : 1

If the kitchen is square, that means the area is 8^2, or 36 square feet. The area of the dining room must be 8 × (18 – 8), or 80 square feet. Therefore, the ratio of the area of the kitchen to the area of the dining room is 36:80, which can be reduced to 9:20.

Parallelograms

A parallelogram is a quadrilateral with four sides and four angles. A parallelogram has two sets of congruent sides and two sets of congruent angles; see Figure 6.8.

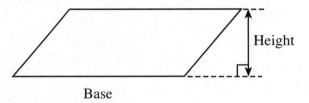

Base

Figure 6.8   A parallelogram.

In addition, the following are special properties of parallelograms:

➤ The sum of the angles of a parallelogram is 360 degrees.

➤ The perimeter of a parallelogram is P = 2*l* + 2*w*.

➤ The area of a parallelogram is A = (base)(height). The height is the distance from top to bottom.

Consider the following simulated GRE question:

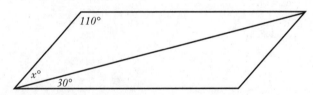

In the parallelogram above, *x* =

(A) 20°

(B) 30°

(C) 40°

(D) 50°

(E) 60°

Because the sum of the angles in a parallelogram is 360°, and the opposite angles are congruent, you can set up the following equation and solve for x:

➤ $2(110) + 2(x + 30) = 360$

➤ $220 + 2x + 60 = 360$

➤ $280 + 2x = 360$

➤ $2x = 80$

➤ $x = 40$

Trapezoids

A trapezoid is a quadrilateral with four sides and four angles. Figure 6.9 shows a trapezoid.

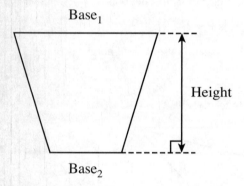

Figure 6.9 A trapezoid.

In addition, the following are special properties of trapezoids:

➤ The bases of the trapezoids (top and bottom) are never the same length.

➤ The sides of the trapezoid can be, but are not always, the same length.

➤ The perimeter of the trapezoid is the sum of the lengths of the sides.

➤ The area of a trapezoid is A = $\frac{1}{2}$ (base$_1$ + base$_2$)(height).

➤ Height is the distance between the bases.

Following is an example of a GRE question testing some additional concepts regarding quadrilaterals:

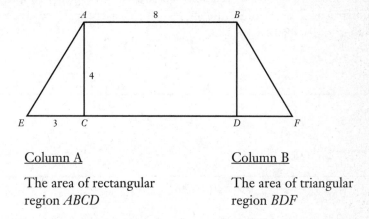

Column A	Column B
The area of rectangular region *ABCD*	The area of triangular region *BDF*

You can calculate the area of rectangular region *ABCD* by multiplying the length (8) by the width (4) to get 32. You can calculate the area of the triangular region as follows: $\frac{1}{2}(3)(4)$, which equals 6. Therefore, the quantity in Column A is greater than the quantity in Column B.

Understanding Angles

Angles can be classified as *acute*, *obtuse*, or *right*. An *acute angle* is any angle less than 90 degrees. An *obtuse angle* is any angle that is greater than 90 degrees and less than 180 degrees. A *right angle* is a 90 degree angle.

When two parallel lines are cut by a perpendicular line, right angles are created, as shown in Figure 6.10.

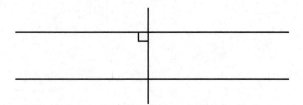

Figure 6.10   Creating right angles.

When two parallel lines are cut by a *transversal*, or an intersecting line, the angles created have special properties. Each of the parallel lines cut by the transversal has four angles surrounding the intersection, which are matched in measure and position with a counterpart at the other parallel line. The vertical (opposite) angles are congruent, and the adjacent angles are supplementary; that is, the sum of the two supplementary angles is 180°. Figure 6.11 shows these special relationships, where the angles with measure a are congruent to each other, the angles with measure b are congruent to each other, and angles $a + b = 180$.

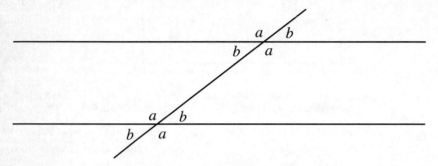

Figure 6.11 Congruent and supplementary relationships formed by a transversal.

Following are simulated GRE questions that test this concept:

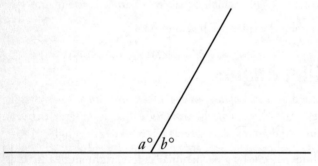

1. In the figure above, if $\dfrac{a}{(a+b)} = \dfrac{3}{4}$, then $a =$

(A) 65°

(B) 75°

(C) 135°

(D) 150°

(E) 175°

You are given that $\dfrac{a}{(a+b)} = \dfrac{3}{4}$. Cross multiply to eliminate the denominators, as follows:

➤ $\dfrac{a}{(a+b)} = \dfrac{3}{4}$

➤ $4a = 3(a + b)$

Angles *a* and *b* are supplementary, which means that $a + b = 180°$. Therefore, $4a = 3(180)$. Solve for *a*:

➤ $4a = 540°$

➤ $a = 135°$

Column A	Column B

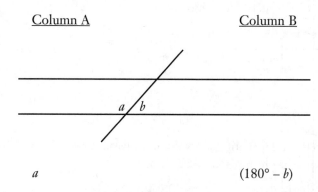

2.　　　　*a*　　　　　　　　　　　　　　　　$(180° - b)$

Because angles *a* and *b* are supplementary, that is, their sum is 180°, the quantity in Column B must equal the quantity in Column A: $180° = a + b$, so $180° - b = a$.

Recapping Perimeter, Area, and Volume

The area, perimeter, and volume of geometric figures involve the size and amount of space taken up by a particular figure. The following sections give you formulas for perimeter, area, and volume that you may encounter on the GRE. We have provided this section as a quick reference so you can see all the pertinent formulas in one location.

Perimeter

The formulas for calculating the perimeter of shapes that might appear on the GRE math sections are as follows:

➤ Triangle: sum of the sides

➤ Rectangle and parallelogram: $2l + 2w$

➤ Square: $4s$ (*s* is the length of each side)

➤ Trapezoid: sum of the sides

➤ Circle (Circumference): $2\pi r$, or πd

Area

The formulas for calculating the area of shapes that might appear on the GRE are as follows:

➤ Triangle: $\frac{1}{2}$ (base)(height)

➤ Rectangle and square: (length)(width)

➤ Parallelogram: (base)(height)

➤ Trapezoid: $\frac{1}{2}$ (base 1 + base 2)(height)

➤ Circle: πr^2

Volume

The formulas for calculating the volume of basic three-dimensional shapes that might appear on the GRE are as follows:

➤ Rectangular box and cube: (length)(width)(height)

➤ Sphere: $(\frac{4}{3})\pi r^3$

➤ Right circular cylinder: $\pi r^2 h$ (h is the height)

Word Problems

Many GRE quantitative questions are presented as word problems that require you to apply math skills to everyday situations. It is important that you carefully read the questions and understand what is being asked. Some of the information given might not be relevant to answering the question, so it is your job to focus on the information necessary to answer the question. Table 6.1 represents the relationship between some words and their mathematical counterparts.

Table 6.1   Relationships Between Words and Mathematical Counterparts

Description	Mathematical Translation
5 more than *n*	*n* + 5
5 less than *n*	*n* - 5
2 times the quantity (*x* + 3)	2(*x* + 3)
the sum of *a* and *b*	*a* + *b*
the difference between *a* and *b*	*a* – *b*
the product of *a* and *b*	*a* × *b*
the quotient of *a* and *b*	*a* ÷ *b*
50 miles per hour	50 miles/60 minutes, or 50 miles/1 hour
3 more than twice *n*	2*n* + 3
3 less than twice *n*	2*n* – 3
the average of *a* and *b*	$\frac{a + b}{2}$
20 percent of *n*	*n*(.2)

It is a good idea to actually set up tables or equations based on the relevant information in word problems. Do not try to solve these problems in your head. Visualizing the situation presented in the problem will help you to keep track of the important information and prevent you from making silly mistakes.

Consider the following simulated GRE question:

Melissa gave Nancy *x* books. She gave Sofia one book more than she gave Nancy and she gave Paul two books fewer than she gave Nancy. In terms of *x*, how many books did Melissa give Nancy, Sofia, and Paul altogether?

(A) $\frac{x}{3}$

(B) *x* –1

(C) 3*x* –1

(D) 3*x*

(E) 3*x* + 1

To solve this problem, set up a table such as the one that follows:

	Nancy	Sofia	Paul
	x	$x + 1$	$x - 2$

Now, add the number of books together:

➤ $x + (x + 1) + (x - 2)$

➤ $x + x + x + 1 - 2$

➤ $3x - 1$

Data Interpretation

Data interpretation questions require you to interpret information that is presented in charts, graphs, or tables. Also, you will need to be able to compare quantities, recognize trends and changes in the data, and perform basic calculations based on the information contained in the figures.

Get a general understanding of the charts, graphs, or tables before you look at the questions. If you can determine the relationships between the data elements, the questions will be much easier to answer.

The GRE data interpretation questions also include analysis of measurement, such as average, median, and percent, which was discussed previously in this chapter.

The best approach to data interpretation questions is to first gain an understanding of how the data is represented, and then look for patterns or trends in the data. When there are charts or graphs given, take a moment to figure out which variables are being charted and note any apparent relationships between them. For example, a *direct relationship* is when one variable increases as the other increases. An *inverse relationship* is when one variable decreases as another increases. Remember that these questions test your ability to interpret and understand relationships and trends in data, and that most of the math calculations will be fairly simple. Read the questions carefully and let the answer choices guide you.

Following are examples of data interpretation questions such as you might encounter on the GRE:

Questions 1–2 refer to the following graph.

County M's total annual expenditures compared to County O's total annual expenditures, 1995-2000

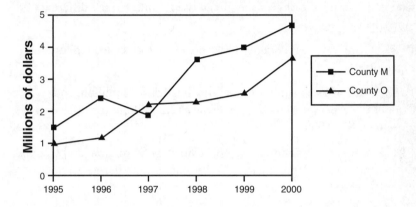

1. For which year shown on the graph did County O's annual expenditures exceed County M's annual expenditures?

   (A) 1995
   (B) 1997
   (C) 1998
   (D) 1999
   (E) 2000

According to the graph, in 1997, County O's expenditures were slightly more than $2 million, and County M's expenditures were slightly less than $2 million. For every other year, County M's expenditures were higher than County O's expenditures. Therefore, answer choice B is correct.

2. For how many years shown on the graph did County M's expenditures exceed County O's expenditures by more than $750,000?

   (A) 2
   (B) 3
   (C) 4
   (D) 5
   (E) 6

You can eliminate answer choice E immediately, because you already know that during at least one year, County O's expenditures exceeded County M's expenditures (refer to the previous question). Because only 6 years are shown on the graph, County M's expenditures could not have exceeded County O's expenditures in any amount for 6 years. The next step is to look carefully at the amounts of the expenditures for each year:

➤ 1995: County M's expenditures = approximately $1.5 million, and County O's expenditures = approximately $1 million; the difference is less than $750,000.

➤ 1996: County M's expenditures = approximately $2.3 million, and County O's expenditures = approximately $1.2 million; the difference is more than $750,000.

➤ 1997: During this year, County O's expenditures exceeded County M's expenditures.

➤ 1998: County M's expenditures = approximately $3.6 million, and County O's expenditures = approximately $2.2 million; the difference is more than $750,000.

➤ 1999: County M's expenditures = approximately $4 million, and County O's expenditures = approximately $2.5 million; the difference is more than $750,000.

➤ 2000: County M's expenditures = approximately $4.7 million, and County O's expenditures = approximately $3.5 million; the difference is more than $750,000.

You can see that during 4 years as shown on the graph, County M's expenditures exceeded County O's expenditures by more than $500,000, answer choice C.

Refer to the sample questions in the "Rectangles" section on pages 111-112 for additional examples of data interpretation questions.

Understanding Measures of Dispersion and Distribution

Discrete sets of numerical values can be measured in many ways. The GRE data interpretation questions commonly test the simplest measure of dispersion, known as *range*. Range is defined as the greatest measured value minus the least measured value. Consider the following example:

Week 1 Temperatures	72°	74°	76°	80°	80°	74°	78°
Week 2 Temperatures	68°	70°	70°	72°	76°	74°	72°

In the table shown, the difference between the highest and lowest temperatures is what percent of the highest temperature?

(A) 10%

(B) 12%

(C) 15%

(D) 68%

(E) 80%

The first step in answering this question is to find the highest and lowest temperatures recorded in the table. The highest recorded temperature is 80°, and the lowest recorded temperature is 68°. Now, find the difference: $80 - 68 = 12$. Next, divide the difference (12) by the highest temperature (80) to calculate the percent:

➤ $12 \div 80 = .15$

➤ $.15 = \dfrac{15}{100}$, or 15%

Now that you've got a good feel for how to approach the quantitative questions found on the GRE, try these sample questions. Be sure to read the explanations to help you gain a better understanding of why the correct answer is correct.

Putting It to Practice

Following are simulated GRE Quantitative questions. Read the directions carefully before you begin to answer the questions. Make guesses as necessary. Remember that on the actual computer adaptive exam, you will be required to select an answer before you can move on to the next question.

Exam Prep Questions

Numbers: All of the numbers used in this section are real numbers.

Figures: Assume that the position of all points, angles, and so on are in the order shown and the measures of angles are positive.

Straight lines can be assumed to be straight.

All figures lie in a plane unless otherwise stated.

The figures shown for each question provide information to solve the problem. The figures are not drawn to scale unless otherwise stated. To solve the problems, use your knowledge of mathematics; do not estimate lengths and sizes of the figures to answer questions.

Directions: Some of the following questions give you two quantities, one in Column A and one in Column B. Compare the two quantities and choose one of the following answer choices:

➤ **A** if the quantity in Column A is greater

➤ **B** if the quantity in Column B is greater

➤ **C** if the two quantities are equal

➤ **D** if you cannot determine the relationship based on the given information

Do not mark answer choice E because there are only four choices from which to choose.

Information and/or figures pertaining to one or both of the quantities may appear above the two columns. Any information that appears in both columns has the same meaning in Column A and in Column B.

Directions: Select the best answer for the remaining multiple choice questions.

	Column A	Column B
1.	$-(3)^4$	$(-3)^4$
2.	$1 - \dfrac{1}{6}$	$1 - \dfrac{1}{9}$
3.	$(x + 2)(x + 4)$	$x^2 + 8$

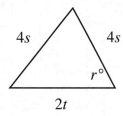

$t = 2s$

4.	r	60

A decrease in the number of factory workers at Company L to 75 percent of the original number of factory workers resulted in a decrease of 2,000 in the number of parts produced.

5. The percent decrease in the number of factory workers at Company L The percent decrease in the number of parts produced

6. When jogging, a certain person takes 24 complete steps in 10 seconds. At this rate, approximately how many complete steps does the person take in 144 seconds?
   (A) 34
   (B) 104
   (C) 154
   (D) 240
   (E) 346

Questions 7-8 refer to the following graph.

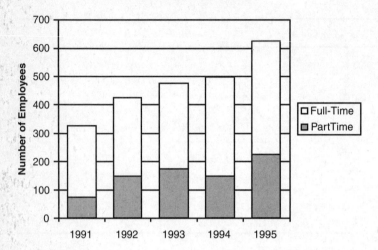

**TOTAL NUMBER OF
EMPLOYEES AT STARBANK**

7. What was the total number of employees at StarBank in 1995?

(A) 225

(B) 325

(C) 400

(D) 500

(E) 625

8. By approximately what percent did the number of full-time employees at StarBank increase from 1993 to 1995?

(A) 25%

(B) 33%

(C) 50%

(D) 66%

(E) 75%

9. If $y = 5x$ and $z = 3y$, then in terms of x, $x + y + z =$

(A) $21x$

(B) $16x$

(C) $15x$

(D) $9x$

(E) $8x$

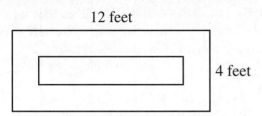

12 feet

4 feet

10. The rectangular garden shown above has a stone center that is 2 feet wide and 7 feet long. What is the area, in square feet, of the portion of the garden surrounding the stone center?

(A) 14

(B) 30

(C) 34

(D) 48

(E) 78

Answers to Exam Prep Questions

1. **The correct answer is B.** To answer this question, it is necessary to apply the rules regarding order of operations, as follows:

   ➤ $-(3)^4 = -81$; this is the negative of 3 raised to the fourth power.

   ➤ $(-3)^4 = 81$; this is -3 raised to the fourth power.

   Therefore, the quantity in Column B (81) is greater than the quantity in Column A (-81).

2. **The correct answer is B.** To solve this problem, first convert 1 in Column A to $\frac{6}{6}$ and subtract $\frac{1}{6}$; the quantity in Column A = $\frac{5}{6}$. Next convert 1 in Column B to $\frac{9}{9}$ and subtract $\frac{1}{9}$; the quantity in Column B = $\frac{8}{9}$, which is greater than $\frac{5}{6}$. Test this by finding the lowest common denominator of 9 and 6. Because both 9 and 6 divide evenly into 18, this is the lowest common denominator. Now, determine whether $\frac{8}{9}$ is greater than $\frac{5}{6}$ as follows:

   ➤ $\frac{8}{9} = \frac{16}{18}$

   ➤ $\frac{5}{6} = \frac{15}{18}$

3. **The correct answer is D.** Because the value of x is not given, x could be any number. For example, when $x > 1$, the quantity in Column A is larger, and when $0 < x < 1$, the quantity in Column B is larger. Therefore, it is not possible to determine a relationship between the two quantities.

4. **The correct answer is C.** You are given that $t = 2s$, which means that $2t = 4s$, and all three sides of the triangle are equal; thus, all three interior angles of the triangle must be equal. Because the sum of the interior angles of a triangle is 180°, each angle, r, must be equal to $\frac{180°}{3}$, or 60°. The quantity in Column A is equal to the quantity in Column B.

5. **The correct answer is D.** The question asks you to compare the percent decrease in the number of workers with the percent decrease in the number of parts. Because the percent decrease in the number of parts produced is not given, and you do not have enough information to calculate the percent decrease, you cannot determine a relationship between the two quantities.

6. **The correct answer is E.** To solve this problem, you should recognize that 144 seconds represents fourteen 10-second intervals, plus .4 of another 10-second interval. Therefore, a person who takes 24 complete steps in 10 seconds, will take 24(14.4) steps in 144 seconds. This value will certainly be greater than 34, 104, 154, and 240 because 24 × 10 is 240, and you will be multiplying 24 by a value greater than 10; eliminate answer choices A, B, C, and D. When you multiply 24(14.4), you get 345.6, which, when rounded up, gives you 346.

7. **The correct answer is E.** The graph shows that, in 1995, there were a total of approximately 625 employees at StarBank. Answer choice A is incorrect because it is the number of part-time employees only. Answer choice C is incorrect because it is the number of full-time employees only. Answer choices B and D represent other numbers found on the graph, but not the total number of employees in 1995.

8. **The correct answer is B.** Based on the graph, there were approximately 300 full-time employees in 1993 and approximately 400 full-time employees in 1995. Therefore, there were 100 more full-time employees in 1995 than there were in 1993. Calculate the percent increase as follows:

➤ The increase in full-time employees (100) over the number of full-time employees in 1993 (300)

➤ $\frac{100}{300}$ = .333, which is equivalent to approximately 33%

9. **The correct answer is A.** You are given that $y = 5x$, which means that $3y$ must equal $3(5x)$, or $15x$. Therefore, $z = 15x$. Substitute $5x$ for y and $15x$ for z and solve for x, as follows:

➤ $x + 5x + 15x = 21x$, answer choice A

10. **The correct answer is C.** The first step in solving this problem is to calculate the area of the rectangular garden. The area of a rectangle is calculated using the formula A = l(length) × w(width), so the area of the garden is 12 × 4, or 48 square feet. Next calculate the area of the stone center: 7 × 2 = 14 square feet. The area of the portion of the garden surrounding the stone center will be the difference between the area of the garden and the area of the stone center: 48 – 14 = 34.

Practice Exam 1

This practice GRE consists of 58 multiple-choice questions and two essay tasks, divided into four main sections. Please allow approximately 2 hours and 30 minutes to complete the following test. Each of the test sections should be taken in the time indicated at the beginning of the sections, and in the order in which the sections appear on this test. There are several different types of questions within each section. Make sure that you read and understand all directions before you begin. To achieve the best results, time yourself strictly on each section. Use the answer sheet at the end of the chapter to mark your answers.

You may write on the test itself, but you should indicate your answers the your answer sheet after you have made your selections. The number of questions that you answer correctly on the separate answer sheet determines your score. If you leave a question blank or fill in more than one circle, that question will not be counted in scoring. Your score is not reduced if you answer incorrectly, so it is in your best interest to guess on a question rather than to not answer the question at all. The computer adaptive GRE does not allow you to skip questions, so you should get in the habit of answering all of the questions on your practice exams.

Section 1—Issue Task

45 Minutes

1 Question

You have 45 minutes to select one topic, organize your thoughts, and compose a response that represents your point of view on the topic that you chose. Do not respond to any topic other than the one you select; a response to any other topic receives a score of 0.

You will be given a choice between two general issues on a broad range of topics. You will be required to discuss your perspective on one of the issues, using examples and reasons drawn from your own experiences and observations.

The space given for writing your response is limited, so use scratch paper to organize your response before you begin writing. For this practice test, allow approximately two 8.5- by 11-inch lined sheets of paper.

Present your viewpoint on <u>one</u> of the following claims. Use relevant reasons and examples to support your point of view.

Topic 1.

"Government should not fund any artistic endeavor that might be viewed as controversial."

Topic 2.

"To be a good substance abuse rehabilitation counselor, a person should have no history of any illegal drug use."

Section 2—Argument Task

30 Minutes

1 Question

You have 30 minutes to organize your thoughts and compose a response that critiques the given argument. Do not respond to any topic other than the one given; a response to any other topic receives a score of 0.

You are not being asked to discuss your point of view on the statement. You should identify and analyze the central elements of the argument, the underlying assumptions that are being made, and any supporting information that is given. Your critique can also discuss other information that would strengthen or weaken the argument or make it more logical.

The space given for writing your response is limited, so use scratch paper to evaluate the given argument and organize your response before you begin writing. For this practice test, allow approximately two 8.5- by 11-inch lined sheets of paper.

Critique the reasoning used in the following argument.

> The following appeared in *The Iron Mountain Daily News*.
>
> "Recently, there has been an increase in crimes involving duct tape and plastic trash bags. Some of the criminals have used these materials to commit their crimes directly, as in the tragic kidnapping that held us all riveted to our televisions last week. In other cases, the duct tape and plastic bags were used to dispose of evidence after a crime had been committed, as in the case of a criminal who disposed of the clothes he was wearing while committing the crime. In still other instances, the tape and plastic bag were used to conceal loot, as in the case of the rare painting that was recovered earlier this year from a stolen car retrieved from a local lake. If the painting had not been wrapped in plastic bags and sealed with duct tape, it might not have been recognizable after so many weeks underwater. Thus, it is clear that there must be a new law requiring that members of the public submit to an identification check and sign a registry whenever they purchase plastic bags or duct tape."

Section 3—Verbal

30 Minutes

30 Questions

This section consists of four different types of questions. To answer the questions, select the best answer from the answer choices provided.

<u>Directions:</u> Sentence Completion Questions—The following sentences each contain one or two blanks, indicating that something has been left out of the sentence. Each answer choice contains one word or a set of words. Select the word or set of words, that, when inserted in the blank(s), best fits the context of the sentence.

<u>Directions:</u> Analogies Questions—The following questions contain a set of related words in capital letters and five answer choices. Each answer choice also contains a set of words. Select the set of words that represents a relationship similar to the original set of words.

<u>Directions:</u> Antonyms Questions—The following questions contain a word in capital letters and five answer choices. Each answer choice contains a word or phrase. Select the word or phrase that best expresses a meaning opposite to the word in capital letters.

<u>Directions:</u> Reading Comprehension Questions—The passages in this section are followed by several questions. The questions correspond to information that is stated or implied in the passage. Read the passage and choose the best answer for each question.

1. SKILL : PRACTICE ::
   - (A) game : observe
   - (B) physique : exercise
   - (C) tragedy : endure
   - (D) book : write
   - (E) style : dress

2. DROUGHT : RAIN ::
   - (A) famine : hunger
   - (B) wealth : money
   - (C) despair : hope
   - (D) certitude : confidence
   - (E) flood : water

3. Even though they tended to be _____ toward each other in private, Dr. Smith and Dr. Evans maintained an _____ demeanor whenever they appeared together in public.

- (A) malicious .. affable
- (B) absurd .. enigmatic
- (C) lenient .. aristocratic
- (D) cordial .. honest
- (E) spiteful .. inimical

4. Consider the ongoing pessimism of the mayor, whose ideas are increasingly _____.

- (A) versatile
- (B) astute
- (C) euphoric
- (D) political
- (E) bleak

5. PUGILIST : FISTS ::

- (A) forest : trees
- (B) glove : hands
- (C) teacher : books
- (D) runner : legs
- (E) artist : pencils

6. AGITATE:

- (A) quiet
- (B) determine
- (C) overpower
- (D) prevent
- (E) preclude

7. TARNISH:

- (A) vibrate
- (B) admit
- (C) polish
- (D) reluctantly change
- (E) suddenly appear

8. DIVEST : PROPERTY ::

- (A) till : soil
- (B) molt : feather
- (C) seize : asset
- (D) divulge : secret
- (E) reject : proposal

9. LIMITED:
- (A) persuasive
- (B) infinite
- (C) consistent
- (D) vague
- (E) mediocre

10. FOSTER:
- (A) remove
- (B) minimize
- (C) suppress
- (D) enlighten
- (E) digress

11. TENUOUS:
- (A) capacious
- (B) drenched
- (C) isolated
- (D) abandoned
- (E) substantial

12. EMULATE:
- (A) dissect
- (B) pretend
- (C) exculpate
- (D) ruminate
- (E) originate

13. INCIPIENT : NASCENT ::
- (A) manifest : conspicuous
- (B) insidious : naive
- (C) frenetic : onerous
- (D) incorrigible : malleable
- (E) insular : plausible

14. Because it is _____ to _____ all of the costs associated with starting a new business, a certain level of flexibility should be built in to any initial business plan.
- (A) necessary .. incur
- (B) challenging .. anticipate
- (C) pragmatic .. assess
- (D) beneficial .. determine
- (E) negligent .. decipher

15. INTERMITTENT:

(A) continuous
(B) transient
(C) asymmetrical
(D) vacillating
(E) permanent

16. The issue of establishing a dress code at the office has caused so much _____ among the employees that several high-level managers have threatened to resign.

(A) buoyancy
(B) effrontery
(C) rancor
(D) civility
(E) regard

Questions 17 and 18 are based on the following passage.

Deconstructive reading of texts is a source of controversy at universities across the country. Scholars accuse deconstruction of being ridiculous and nihilistic. In the media, deconstruction is seen as evidence that academia has become too involved in useless endeavors. Although

5 deconstruction appears to be attacked from almost every angle, it continues to be a prominent force in modern philosophy and literary studies.

There are three main criticisms of deconstruction. First, critics argue that deconstruction lacks significance. In addition, deconstruction is

10 seen as a political ploy against traditional modernism. Hence, deconstruction is often equated with nihilism and relativism. Critics also challenge the utility of deconstruction. Some argue that deconstruction is nothing more than a pseudo intellectual theory used to question a text while ignoring the text's arguments.

15 Although deconstruction succeeds by questioning Western rationality, deconstruction tends to be relatively obscure, unconventional, and unoriginal. Deconstruction is only taken seriously on the fringes of modernist discourse. Despite the hype over deconstruction, scholars and critics are continually questioning whether deconstruction is no more

20 than complicated language and vague ideas disguised as an academic theory.

17. According to the passage, the author indicates that all of the following are criticisms of deconstruction EXCEPT:

(A) deconstruction is uninspired

(B) deconstruction imitates Western rationality

(C) deconstruction is compared with nihilism and relativism

(D) deconstruction lacks importance

(E) deconstruction is a political ploy against traditional modernism

18. The author's attitude toward deconstruction can be best described as

(A) shocked and appalled

(B) suspicious and apprehensive

(C) laudatory and admiring

(D) unsympathetic and critical

(E) impartial and disinterested

19. BRUSQUE : COURTEOUS ::

(A) nimble : wily

(B) tenuous : ambiguous

(C) stoic : gracious

(D) ethical : corrupt

(E) bereft : impoverished

20. The designer's use of gaudy paint colors and mismatched fabrics was intended to be innovative, but instead it highlighted her _____ talent.

(A) dubious

(B) primordial

(C) resolute

(D) venal

(E) idyllic

Questions 21–24 are based on the following passage.

The Great Pyramid at Giza is arguably the most fascinating and contentious piece of architecture in the world. In the 1980s, researchers began focusing on studying the mortar from the pyramid hoping it would reveal important clues about the pyramid's age and construction.

5 Instead of clarifying or expunging older theories about the Great Pyramid's age, the results of the study left the researchers mystified.

Robert J. Wenke from the University of Washington received authorization to collect mortar samples from some famous ancient construction sites. Among these sites was the Great Pyramid. The mortar that

10 Wenke discovered was formed by particles of pollen, charcoal, and other

organic matter. By using radiocarbon dating, scientists were able to reveal some disconcerting discoveries. After adjusting the data, the mortar revealed that the pyramid must have been built between 3100 B.C. and 2850 B.C. with an average date of 2977 B.C. This discovery was
15 controversial because these dates claimed that the structure was built over 400 years earlier than most archaeologists originally believed. Furthermore, archaeologists discovered something even more anomalous. Most of the mortar samples collected appeared to be little more than processed gypsum with traces of sand and limestone. The sand and
20 limestone found in the gypsum were not added but were actually contaminants of the processed gypsum. The mortar used to build the Great Pyramid is of an unknown origin. It has been analyzed repeatedly and its chemical composition has been established. However, even using modern techniques, scientists have been unable to reproduce it. The gypsum
25 mortar is stronger than the stone on the pyramid and the mortar is still intact thousands of years later. This mortar was not used to bond the heavy stone blocks together like cement mortar does with modern bricks. The gypsum mortar's role was to buffer the joints and to reduce friction as the enormous blocks were placed.

30   Examining the mortar from the Great Pyramid assists scientists in making inferences about Egypt's past. Researchers questioned why the Egyptian builders would choose to use gypsum mortar over lime mortar. Egypt had numerous limestone mines that could have been used to create a more durable lime mortar. Despite the abundance of lime, there is
35 no evidence of lime mortar being used in Egypt until 2500 years after the pyramids were built. Researchers then began to determine why the more water-soluble gypsum would have been preferred. They discovered that gypsum would have been easier to mine than limestone. In addition, the Egyptian builders discovered that when gypsum is heated to approxi-
40 mately 265 degrees Fahrenheit, some of the moisture is excluded. When the processed gypsum is mixed with water again, the resulting substance is used for the mortar. Despite having significant mineral resources, Egypt has few natural fuels available. The 265 degree Fahrenheit temperatures needed to process the gypsum and turn it into mortar can be
45 achieved with only the heat of an open fire. On the other hand, to make lime mortar, extremely high temperatures around 1800 degrees Fahrenheit are needed. Most historians conjecture that the high heat needed to process limestone is the reason why lime mortar was not used. The shortage of natural fuel sources would most likely have made the
50 creation of lime mortar highly uneconomical.

21. The primary purpose of the passage is to
    (A) discuss the chemical properties of limestone and gypsum
    (B) propose a way to create a better mortar
    (C) resolve a dispute about whether gypsum or limestone should be used to make mortar
    (D) describe the deficiencies of radiocarbon dating
    (E) offer an explanation about why the mortar from the Great Pyramid is important to scientists

22. The author mentions that "Egypt has few natural fuels available" to
    (A) give a reason why gypsum might have been used instead of limestone for the mortar
    (B) illustrate the deprivation that was characteristic of ancient Egyptian society
    (C) show the need for mortar to contain large amounts of limestone in order to be effective
    (D) illustrate the impossibility of knowing when the Great Pyramid was built
    (E) explain how gypsum is used to create mortar

23. The author suggests which of the following about structures built during the same time period as the Great Pyramid?
    (A) The structures would have all used gypsum as the base for their mortar.
    (B) The structures would not have contained lime mortar.
    (C) The structures would have mortar that was not chemically verifiable.
    (D) The structures would all have mortars that could be replicated with modern science.
    (E) The structures would not have mortar that could be replicated with modern science.

24. According to the passage, the mortar in the Great Pyramid contains which of the following?
    I. charcoal
    II. sand
    III. limestone
    (A) I only
    (B) II only
    (C) III only
    (D) II and III only
    (E) I, II, and III

Questions 25 and 26 are based on the following passage.

Contrary to popular belief, radioactivity is not merely a derivative of nuclear activity or science fiction. In fact, all rocks and minerals on Earth contain radioactive elements. These radioactive elements were integrated into the Earth's mantle and crust when the solar system was formed.

5 Radioactive elements are initially incredibly unstable. Over time, these elements break down and become more stable. This scientific process is commonly referred to as *radioactive decay*. Although the initial radioactive elements are unstable, once radioactive decay occurs, it continues at a constant rate. The rate of radioactive decay varies depending on the

10 radioactive isotope.

For centuries, scientists have tried to determine the age of rocks. Fifty years ago, geologists discovered that radioactive elements could help determine the age of many rocks. Geologists have used radiometric dating to determine the approximate ages of meteorites, moons, fossils, and

15 the Earth. Scientists have even been able to determine when ice ages, earthquakes, and volcanic eruptions occurred on Earth. One popular radiometric dating method concentrates on the breakdown of potassium to argon. When dating younger rocks that contain organic matter, carbon-14 dating is used. Carbon-14 dating is employed primarily with

20 sedimentary rocks that are less than 50,000 years old. Scientists using carbon-14 dating test the remains of organic material embedded in the rock. The amount of carbon in the remains of the deceased organisms helps accurately predict the age of the rock.

25. The author of the passage is primarily concerned with

(A) comparing and contrasting carbon-14 dating with other radiometric dating methods

(B) arguing for the use of carbon-14 dating over radiometric dating methods using potassium and argon

(C) exploring the history and tradition of radiometric dating

(D) discussing radioactive elements and their contribution to science

(E) pointing out scientific strides that have been made using carbon-14 dating

26. The passage suggests that carbon-14 dating might not be appropriate when

(A) the rock is suspected to be younger than 50,000 years old

(B) material from once-living organisms is not present in the rock

(C) trying to predict the occurrence of volcanic eruptions or earthquakes

(D) methods using the breakdown of potassium to argon are available

(E) rocks have been subjected to nuclear activity or unstable isotopes

27. He approached the witness stand with a(n) _____ sense of doom; his confession would certainly be his undoing.

    (A) judicious
    (B) frivolous
    (C) inadvertent
    (D) inexorable
    (E) assiduous

28. RAREFY:

    (A) transcend
    (B) regulate
    (C) adulterate
    (D) modernize
    (E) assuage

29. OBTUSE:

    (A) sly
    (B) organic
    (C) leisurely
    (D) precise
    (E) intricate

30. VICTORY : CELEBRATION ::

    (A) apology : exoneration
    (B) marriage : license
    (C) injustice : elucidation
    (D) anomaly : extenuation
    (E) triumph : impunity

Section 4—Quantitative

30 Minutes

28 Questions

Numbers: All of the numbers used in this section are real numbers.

Figures: Assume that the position of all points, angles, and so on are in the order shown and the measures of angles are positive.

Straight lines can be assumed to be straight.

All figures lie in a plane unless otherwise stated.

The figures given for each question provide information to solve the problem. The figures are not drawn to scale unless otherwise stated. To solve the problems, use your knowledge of mathematics; do not estimate lengths and sizes of the figures to answer questions.

Directions: Some of the following questions give you two quantities, one in Column A and one in Column B. Compare the two quantities and choose one of the following answer choices:

A if the quantity in Column A is greater

B if the quantity in Column B is greater

C if the two quantities are equal

D if you cannot determine the relationship based on the given information

Do not mark answer choice E because there are only four choices from which to choose.

Information and/or figures pertaining to one or both of the quantities might appear above the two columns. Any information that appears in both columns has the same meaning in Column A and in Column B.

Directions: Select the best answer for the remaining multiple-choice questions.

	Column A	Column B
1.	160,000	$(397.65)^2$

	Column A	Column B
2.	60 percent of 30	30 percent of 60

$$4x - 5y = 10$$
$$2x + 6y = 22$$

	Column A	Column B
3.	$x + y$	10

$$x = 7$$

	Column A	Column B
4.	$5x^2$	250

5. If $5(n + 3) = 35$, what is the value of n?

(A) 4

(B) $\dfrac{32}{5}$

(C) 7

(D) $\dfrac{38}{5}$

(E) 10

6. If $r = f(f + 6)$, then $r + 5 = $?

(A) $f^2 + 11$

(B) $f^2 + 6f + 5$

(C) $f^2 - 6f + 5$

(D) $f^2 + f$

(E) $f^2 + 11f$

	<u>Column A</u>	<u>Column B</u>

x is an integer greater than 1.

7.	2^{x+3}	3^x

8.	$(\sqrt{8}\,)^2$	$8\sqrt{8}$

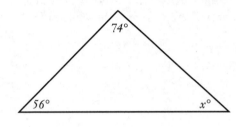

9.	x	$45°$

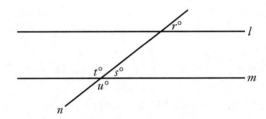

10. In the figure above, $l // m$ and angle $t = 135°$. What is the value of $3r - 4s + u$?

(A) $45°$

(B) $90°$

(C) $135°$

(D) $180°$

(E) $315°$

Column A	Column B
11. The average (arithmetic mean) of 12, 19, and 45	The average (arithmetic mean) of 12, 20, and 45

12. The total daily profit p, in dollars, from producing and selling x units of a certain product is given by the function $p(x) = 19x - (13x - b)$, where b is a constant. If 200 units were produced and sold yesterday for a total profit of $3,575, what is the value of b?

(A) -2,375
(B) -1,200
(C) 0
(D) 975
(E) 2,825

Column A	Column B
13. The number of minutes in a day	The number of days in 4 years

Refer to the following graph for Questions 14 and 15.

NEW CONSTRUCITON IN DAISY HILL SUBDIVISION

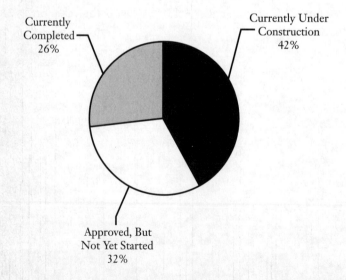

Currently Completed
26%

Currently Under Construction
42%

Approved, But Not Yet Started
32%

14. When construction is completed in Daisy Hill Subdivision, there will be a total of 40 homes. Approximately how many homes have not yet been completed?

(A) 15
(B) 20
(C) 25
(D) 30
(E) 40

15. When construction is completed in Daisy Hill Subdivision, there will be a total of 40 homes. What is the approximate ratio of new homes currently completed to new homes currently under construction?

(A) 1:2
(B) 5:8
(C) 3:4
(D) 4:3
(E) 8:5

Column A	Column B
A rectangular box is 4 feet wide by 2 feet high and has a volume of 38 cubic feet.	

16.   5 feet   The length of the box

In the rectangular coordinate plane, points F, G, and H have coordinates (4,5), (7,8), and (4,8), respectively.

17. FH FG

18. When the average of a list of test scores is multiplied by the number of test scores, the result is k. What does k represent?

(A) The sum of the test scores
(B) The average of the test scores
(C) The number of test scores
(D) Half the number of test scores
(E) Half the sum of the test scores

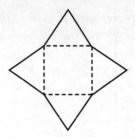

19. If the area of the square in the figure above is 64 and the perimeter of each of the four triangles is 40, what is the perimeter of the figure outlined by the solid line?

    (A) 32
    (B) 64
    (C) 96
    (D) 128
    (E) 160

Refer to the following graph for Questions 20 and 21.

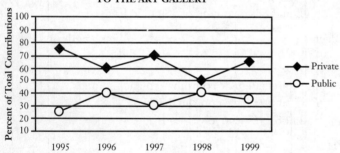

20. In which of the years from 1995 through 1999 were private and public contributions most nearly the same?

    (A) 1995
    (B) 1996
    (C) 1997
    (D) 1998
    (E) 1999

21. For how many of the years shown was the amount of private contributions more than double the amount of public contributions?

(A) None
(B) One
(C) Two
(D) Three
(E) Four

22. After the first term, each term in a sequence is 4 less than $\frac{2}{3}$ of the preceding term. If t is the first term of the sequence, and $t \neq 0$, what is the ratio of the second term to the first term?

(A) $(\frac{2t-12}{3t})$

(B) $(\frac{2}{3})t - 4$

(C) $(\frac{2t-12}{3})$

(D) $(\frac{2t-4}{3t})$

(E) $(\frac{2t-4}{3})$

	Column A	Column B
23.	$2(6.3)$	$7(6.3) + 0.2(6.3)$
24.	The area of a rectangle with a perimeter of 20	The area of a square with a perimeter of 16
25.	The cost of p apples at a cost of $r + 3$ cents each	The cost of r peaches at a cost of $p + 3$ cents each

26. The number that results when an integer is multiplied by itself and then tripled CANNOT end in which of the following digits?

(A) 3
(B) 5
(C) 6
(D) 7
(E) 8

27. If the total surface area of a cube is 54, what is the volume of the cube?

    (A) 3
    (B) 9
    (C) 27
    (D) 54
    (E) 162

28. $2,600 = 50(3n - 8)$, then $n = ?$

    (A) 0
    (B) 2
    (C) 16
    (D) 20
    (E) 58

GRE PRACTICE EXAM 1
ANSWER SHEET

These answer sheets are provided for your convenience only. You will not receive answer sheets for the actual computer-based test.

SECTION 3

1 Ⓐ Ⓑ Ⓒ Ⓓ Ⓔ	11 Ⓐ Ⓑ Ⓒ Ⓓ Ⓔ	21 Ⓐ Ⓑ Ⓒ Ⓓ Ⓔ	31 Ⓐ Ⓑ Ⓒ Ⓓ Ⓔ
2 Ⓐ Ⓑ Ⓒ Ⓓ Ⓔ	12 Ⓐ Ⓑ Ⓒ Ⓓ Ⓔ	22 Ⓐ Ⓑ Ⓒ Ⓓ Ⓔ	32 Ⓐ Ⓑ Ⓒ Ⓓ Ⓔ
3 Ⓐ Ⓑ Ⓒ Ⓓ Ⓔ	13 Ⓐ Ⓑ Ⓒ Ⓓ Ⓔ	23 Ⓐ Ⓑ Ⓒ Ⓓ Ⓔ	33 Ⓐ Ⓑ Ⓒ Ⓓ Ⓔ
4 Ⓐ Ⓑ Ⓒ Ⓓ Ⓔ	14 Ⓐ Ⓑ Ⓒ Ⓓ Ⓔ	24 Ⓐ Ⓑ Ⓒ Ⓓ Ⓔ	34 Ⓐ Ⓑ Ⓒ Ⓓ Ⓔ
5 Ⓐ Ⓑ Ⓒ Ⓓ Ⓔ	15 Ⓐ Ⓑ Ⓒ Ⓓ Ⓔ	25 Ⓐ Ⓑ Ⓒ Ⓓ Ⓔ	35 Ⓐ Ⓑ Ⓒ Ⓓ Ⓔ
6 Ⓐ Ⓑ Ⓒ Ⓓ Ⓔ	16 Ⓐ Ⓑ Ⓒ Ⓓ Ⓔ	26 Ⓐ Ⓑ Ⓒ Ⓓ Ⓔ	36 Ⓐ Ⓑ Ⓒ Ⓓ Ⓔ
7 Ⓐ Ⓑ Ⓒ Ⓓ Ⓔ	17 Ⓐ Ⓑ Ⓒ Ⓓ Ⓔ	27 Ⓐ Ⓑ Ⓒ Ⓓ Ⓔ	37 Ⓐ Ⓑ Ⓒ Ⓓ Ⓔ
8 Ⓐ Ⓑ Ⓒ Ⓓ Ⓔ	18 Ⓐ Ⓑ Ⓒ Ⓓ Ⓔ	28 Ⓐ Ⓑ Ⓒ Ⓓ Ⓔ	38 Ⓐ Ⓑ Ⓒ Ⓓ Ⓔ
9 Ⓐ Ⓑ Ⓒ Ⓓ Ⓔ	19 Ⓐ Ⓑ Ⓒ Ⓓ Ⓔ	29 Ⓐ Ⓑ Ⓒ Ⓓ Ⓔ	39 Ⓐ Ⓑ Ⓒ Ⓓ Ⓔ
10 Ⓐ Ⓑ Ⓒ Ⓓ Ⓔ	20 Ⓐ Ⓑ Ⓒ Ⓓ Ⓔ	30 Ⓐ Ⓑ Ⓒ Ⓓ Ⓔ	40 Ⓐ Ⓑ Ⓒ Ⓓ Ⓔ

SECTION 4

1 Ⓐ Ⓑ Ⓒ Ⓓ Ⓔ	11 Ⓐ Ⓑ Ⓒ Ⓓ Ⓔ	21 Ⓐ Ⓑ Ⓒ Ⓓ Ⓔ	31 Ⓐ Ⓑ Ⓒ Ⓓ Ⓔ
2 Ⓐ Ⓑ Ⓒ Ⓓ Ⓔ	12 Ⓐ Ⓑ Ⓒ Ⓓ Ⓔ	22 Ⓐ Ⓑ Ⓒ Ⓓ Ⓔ	32 Ⓐ Ⓑ Ⓒ Ⓓ Ⓔ
3 Ⓐ Ⓑ Ⓒ Ⓓ Ⓔ	13 Ⓐ Ⓑ Ⓒ Ⓓ Ⓔ	23 Ⓐ Ⓑ Ⓒ Ⓓ Ⓔ	33 Ⓐ Ⓑ Ⓒ Ⓓ Ⓔ
4 Ⓐ Ⓑ Ⓒ Ⓓ Ⓔ	14 Ⓐ Ⓑ Ⓒ Ⓓ Ⓔ	24 Ⓐ Ⓑ Ⓒ Ⓓ Ⓔ	34 Ⓐ Ⓑ Ⓒ Ⓓ Ⓔ
5 Ⓐ Ⓑ Ⓒ Ⓓ Ⓔ	15 Ⓐ Ⓑ Ⓒ Ⓓ Ⓔ	25 Ⓐ Ⓑ Ⓒ Ⓓ Ⓔ	35 Ⓐ Ⓑ Ⓒ Ⓓ Ⓔ
6 Ⓐ Ⓑ Ⓒ Ⓓ Ⓔ	16 Ⓐ Ⓑ Ⓒ Ⓓ Ⓔ	26 Ⓐ Ⓑ Ⓒ Ⓓ Ⓔ	36 Ⓐ Ⓑ Ⓒ Ⓓ Ⓔ
7 Ⓐ Ⓑ Ⓒ Ⓓ Ⓔ	17 Ⓐ Ⓑ Ⓒ Ⓓ Ⓔ	27 Ⓐ Ⓑ Ⓒ Ⓓ Ⓔ	37 Ⓐ Ⓑ Ⓒ Ⓓ Ⓔ
8 Ⓐ Ⓑ Ⓒ Ⓓ Ⓔ	18 Ⓐ Ⓑ Ⓒ Ⓓ Ⓔ	28 Ⓐ Ⓑ Ⓒ Ⓓ Ⓔ	38 Ⓐ Ⓑ Ⓒ Ⓓ Ⓔ
9 Ⓐ Ⓑ Ⓒ Ⓓ Ⓔ	19 Ⓐ Ⓑ Ⓒ Ⓓ Ⓔ	29 Ⓐ Ⓑ Ⓒ Ⓓ Ⓔ	39 Ⓐ Ⓑ Ⓒ Ⓓ Ⓔ
10 Ⓐ Ⓑ Ⓒ Ⓓ Ⓔ	20 Ⓐ Ⓑ Ⓒ Ⓓ Ⓔ	30 Ⓐ Ⓑ Ⓒ Ⓓ Ⓔ	40 Ⓐ Ⓑ Ⓒ Ⓓ Ⓔ

Practice Exam 1 Answer Key

Analysis of an Argument and Analysis of an Issue

Because grading the essay is subjective, we've chosen not to include any "graded" essays here. Your best bet is to have someone you trust, such as your personal tutor, read your essays and give you an honest critique. Make the grading criteria mentioned in Chapter 1 available to whomever grades your essays. If you plan on grading your own essays, review the grading criteria and be as honest as possible regarding the structure, development, organization, technique, and appropriateness of your writing. Focus on your weak areas and continue to practice in order to improve your writing skills.

Verbal

1. **The answer is B.** To perfect a "skill," a person must "practice." A general sentence that can be used to describe the analogy is: To perfect his or her "____," a person must "____." "Physique" refers to the muscular development of the body. It makes sense that a person would "exercise" to perfect his or her "physique." Answer choices A, C, D, and E contain word pairs that are related, but not in the same way as "skill" and "practice." If you insert the other word pairs into your test sentence, it does not make sense.

2. **The answer is C.** A "drought" is caused by a severe shortage of "rain." A general sentence that can be used to describe the analogy is: _____ is caused by a severe shortage of _____. Because "despair" is brought on by a severe lack or shortage of "hope," answer choice C is the best selection. "Famine" leads to "hunger," not the other way around, so answer choice A is incorrect. A severe shortage of "money" does not lead to "wealth," so answer choice B is incorrect. "Certitude" means "confidence," so answer choice D is incorrect. A severe shortage of "water" does not lead to a "flood," so answer choice E is incorrect.

3. **The answer is A.** The phrase "even though" indicates that the words in the blanks will contradict each other. The context suggests that the doctors behave differently toward each other in private than they do in public. "Malicious" means "deliberately harmful, or spiteful," whereas "affable" means "pleasant and gracious." Answer choice B is incorrect because "absurd" does not contradict "enigmatic," which means "puzzling." Answer choices C and D are incorrect because the word pairs do not indicate contradiction. Likewise, although "spiteful" might have been a good choice for the first blank, "inimical," which means "adverse or unfriendly" does not contradict "spiteful" and does not work in the second blank, therefore, answer choice E is incorrect.

4. **The answer is E.** The context indicates that the mayor was pessimistic, so it makes sense that his ideas would be increasingly "bleak" or "gloomy." Although it is possible that the mayor's ideas are "political," answer choice D is incorrect because it does not fit the context of the sentence. Likewise, answer choices A, B, and C are not appropriate. Refer to Appendix A for definitions of some of the words in these answer choices.

5. **The answer is D.** A "pugilist" is a boxer, or fighter. "Fists" are the tools of the trade for a "pugilist." A general sentence that can be used to describe the analogy is: A "_____" uses his "_____" to do his job. Eliminate answer choices A and B because they do not contain words with a similar relationship. It is true that "teachers" use "books" and "artists" use "pencils" to do their jobs, so you must refine your sentence. A "pugilist" *must* use his "fists" to fight; likewise a "runner" *must* use his legs to run.

6. **The answer is A.** "Agitate" means to "disturb or stir up." The word that is most nearly opposite is "quiet," which, when used as a verb, means to "cause to become calm." Answer choices B, C, D, and E are incorrect because none have a meaning that is opposite to "agitate."

7. **The answer is C.** "Tarnish" means to "dull or diminish," whereas "polish" means to "make shiny." Answer choices A, B, D, and E are incorrect because none have a meaning that is opposite to "tarnish."

8. **The answer is C.** To "divest" means to "deprive or rid of." It is possible for someone to "divest" you of your "property" by taking it away from you. It is also possible for someone to "seize" your "assets" by taking them away from you. Answer choices A, B, D, and E contain word pairs that are related, but not in the same way as "divest" and "property."

9. **The answer is B.** "Limited" means "confined or restricted," whereas "infinite" means "having no boundaries or limits." "Persuasive" means "capable of convincing"; "consistent" means "in agreement with"; "vague" means "not clearly expressed"; "mediocre" means "average or ordinary." None of these words has a meaning that is opposite to "limited," so answer choices A, C, D, and E are incorrect.

10. **The answer is C.** The word "foster" can mean to "cultivate, or advance the progress of" something. "Suppress" means to "subdue or prohibit the activities" of something. Answer choices A, B, D, and E are incorrect because none have a meaning that is opposite to "foster." Refer to Appendix A for definitions of some of the words in the answer choices.

11. **The answer is E.** "Tenuous" means "slender or flimsy," whereas "substantial" means "having substance or strength." "Capacious" means "spacious or roomy," which is not opposite in meaning to "tenuous," so answer choice A is incorrect. Likewise, answer choices B, C, and D are incorrect because none have a meaning that is opposite to "tenuous."

12. **The answer is E.** To "emulate" means to "imitate or copy." To "originate" means to "create, or bring into being." These two words are most opposite in meaning. "Dissect" means to "cut apart"; "prevaricate" means to "evade the truth"; "exculpate" means to "clear of guilt"; "ruminate" means to "reflect on." None of these words has a meaning that is opposite to "emulate," so answer choices A, B, C, and D are incorrect.

13. **The answer is A.** Something that is "incipient" is just beginning to appear or develop. Likewise, something that is "nascent" has just begun to develop. Therefore, the best answer choice will contain a word pair that is nearly synonymous. Something that is "manifest" is clearly demonstrated or obvious. Something that is "conspicuous" is easy to notice or obvious. "Insidious" means "stealthy" and "naïve"

means "simple or unsophisticated"; "frenetic" means "wildly excited" and "onerous" means "burdensome"; "incorrigible" means "unable to be corrected, or difficult to manage"; "malleable" means "easily formed or changed";"insular" means "isolated" and "plausible" means "believable." None of these word pairs are synonymous, so eliminate answer choices B, C, D, and E.

14. **The answer is B.** The word "flexibility" used in the second part of the sentence suggests that one should be willing to adjust to unpredictable changes when starting a new business. A certain level of flexibility is necessary because it is "challenging" to "anticipate" or predict all of the costs associated with starting a new business. Answer choices A, C, D, and E contain words that might be associated with starting a new business, but none of them fit the context of the sentence.

15. **The answer is A.** "Intermittent" means "stopping and starting at intervals." Therefore, "continuous" is the best choice. "Transient" means "passing in time, or temporary"; "asymmetrical" means "having no balance"; "vacillating" means "wavering, or swaying from side to side"; therefore, answer choices B, C, and D are incorrect. "Permanent" might have seemed to be correct, but it means "lasting or enduring," which is not quite the opposite of "intermittent."

16. **The answer is C.** The context of the sentence indicates that something about the dress-code issue has caused high-level managers to threaten to resign. The connotation, therefore, is negative. Eliminate answer choices A, D, and E, which all have a positive connotation. "Rancor" means "bitter resentment," and "effrontery" means "boldness," so answer choice C best fits the context of the sentence.

17. **The answer is B.** The passage states that "Although deconstruction succeeds by questioning Western rationality, deconstruction tends to be relatively obscure, unconventional, and unoriginal." This implies that deconstruction challenges Western rationality instead of imitating it. Answer choices A, C, D, and E can be found in the passage as criticisms of deconstruction.

18. **The answer is D.** The author writes that "Although deconstruction succeeds by questioning Western rationality, deconstruction tends to be relatively obscure, unconventional, and unoriginal." This is an unflattering assessment of deconstruction. Answer choice E might have appeared to be correct. However, the author takes a decisive stance against deconstruction and does not remain impartial. Likewise, the other answer choices are not supported by the passage.

19. **The answer is D.** "Brusque" means "abrupt or discourteous"; there-fore, the words in the question stem are antonyms. Someone who is "ethical" is, by definition, not "corrupt"; these two words are also antonyms. Answer choices A, B, C, and E are incorrect because the word pairs are not antonyms. Refer to Appendix A for definitions of sosme of the words in these answer choices.

20. **The answer is A.** The word "instead" indicates a contradiction. The context of the sentence suggests that the designer's intent was to appear innovative, but the gaudy paint and mismatched fabrics instead caused her to appear as if she had no talent for decorating. "Dubious" means "doubtful," which best fits the context of the sentence. "Primordial" means "original," "resolute" means "determined," "venal" means "corruptible," and "idyllic" means "simple and care-free," none of which fit the context of the sentence.

21. **The answer is E.** The passage mentions that the mortar from the Great Pyramid was used to help determine the age of the pyramid and to make inferences about why certain materials were used to create the pyramid. Answer choice C might have appeared to be correct. However, the passage only states that gypsum was a better choice for mortar for the Great Pyramid. The passage is not primarily about whether gypsum or limestone should be used to make mortar. Answer choices A, B, and D are not supported by the passage.

22. **The answer is A.** The passage mentions that limestone needs to reach a temperature of 1800 degrees Fahrenheit to be made into lime mortar. It is likely that the author mentioned that there was a lack of natural fuels to produce these high temperatures to show that lime mortar would be uneconomical. Answer choice E might have appeared to be correct. Although heat is needed to turn gypsum into mortar, this sentence refers to scarcity of natural fuels, not the process of cre-ating gypsum mortar. Answer choices B, C, and D are not supported by the passage.

23. **The answer is B.** The passage states that "Despite the abundance of lime, there is no evidence of lime mortar being used in Egypt until 2500 years after the pyramids were built." Answer choices A, C, D, and E could be true, but the passage does not suggest or specifically state that these are true.

24. **The answer is E.** The passage states that "The mortar that Wenke discovered was formed by particles of pollen, charcoal, and other organic matter." The passage also states, "Most of the mortar samples collected appeared to be little more than processed gypsum

with traces of sand and limestone." This information best supports answer choice E.

25. **The answer is D.** The passage begins by discussing the origin and location of radioactive elements. The rest of the passage is concerned with discussing how radioactive elements have helped scientists. Answer choice C might have appeared to be correct because the passage does mention when radiometric dating began. However, this is only a small portion of the passage. Answer choices A, B, and E are not supported by the passage.

26. **The answer is B.** By definition, "organic" material is material derived from living organisms. The passage states that the presence of organic matter is necessary to date rocks using the carbon-14 dating method. Answer choices A, C, D, and E are not supported by the passage.

27. **The answer is D.** The context of the sentence indicates that the witness was certain that his confession would most likely yield negative consequences. Therefore, it makes sense that his sense of doom in approaching the witness stand would not be changed. "Inexorable" means "relentless, or not likely to be diverted." "Judicious" is a word often associated with a courtroom or a witness stand, but it does not fit the context, so answer choice A is incorrect. "Frivolous" means "trivial, or silly"; "inadvertent" means "careless, or accidental"; "assiduous" means "diligent," but has a positive connotation. None of these words fit the context of the sentence, so answer choices B, C, and E are incorrect.

28. **The answer is C.** "Rarefy" means "to purify," whereas "adulterate" means to "make impure." "Transcend" means to "surpass"; "regulate" means to "control, or adjust"; "modernize" means to "make modern"; "assuage" means to "make less intense." None of these words has a meaning that is opposite to "rarefy," so answer choices A, B, D, and E are incorrect.

29. **The answer is D.** "Obtuse" refers to something that "lacks sharpness or definition." "Precise" refers to something that is "definite, or clear." Answer choices A, B, C, and E are incorrect because none have a meaning that is opposite to "obtuse." Refer to Appendix A for definitions of sosme of the words in these answer choices.

30. **The answer is A.** "Victory" is the "state of having won or triumphed." A "celebration" is "a joyful occasion to mark a happy event." A general sentence that can be used to describe the analogy is: A _____ is cause for _____. An "exoneration" refers to "the act of freeing someone from

blame," and would likely stem from an "apology." Therefore, an "apology" is cause for "exoneration." Answer choices B, C, D, and E contain word pairs that are related, but not in the same way as "victory" and "celebration." Refer to Appendix A for definitions of sosme of the words in these answer choices.

Quantitative

1. **The answer is A.** To solve this problem, you should first recognize that 160,000 is equal to $(400)^2$. Because 400 is greater than 397.65, $(400)^2$ will be greater than $(397.65)^2$, so the quantity in Column A is greater than the quantity in Column B.

2. **The answer is C.** The easiest way to solve this problem is to first convert 60% into its decimal equivalent, .6, and multiply by 30 to get 18. Next, convert 30% into its decimal equivalent, .3, and multiply by 60 to get 18. The quantities are equal, so answer choice C is correct.

3. **The answer is B.** To solve this system of equations, first multiply the bottom equation by -2 to get $-4x - 12y = -44$. Next, add the two equations together:

   ➤ $(4x - 5y = 10) + (-4x - 12y = -44)$

   ➤ The x values cancel out, so you get $-17y = -34$.

   ➤ Divide both sides by -17 to get $y = 2$.

   Using the first equation, solve for x given that $y = 2$:

   ➤ $4x - 5(2) = 10$

   ➤ $4x - 10 = 10$

   ➤ $4x = 20$. Divide both sides by 4 to get $x = 5$.

   Therefore, the quantity in Column A, $x + y$, equals 5 + 2, or 7. The quantity in Column B = 10, which is greater than 7.

4. **The answer is B.** The problem states that $x = 7$, which means that, in the quantity in Column A, x^2, equals 49. You should recognize that $250 \div 5 = 50$, which is greater than 49. Therefore, the quantity in Column B, 250 (5 × 50) is greater than the quantity in Column A, $5x^2$ (5 × 49).

5. **The answer is A.** To solve this problem, use the distributive property, which states that $a(b + c) = ab + bc$:

> ➤ $5(n + 3) = 35$

> ➤ $5n + 15 = 35$

> ➤ Subtract 15 from both sides to get $5n = 20$

> ➤ Divide both sides by 5 to get $n = 4$, answer choice A.

6. **The answer is B.** To solve this problem, first use the distributive property to expand the binomial, as follows:

> ➤ $r = f(f + 6)$

> ➤ $r = f^2 + 6f$

If $r = f^2 + 6f$, then $r + 5 = f^2 + 6f + 5$. You cannot simplify this because there are no like terms.

7. **The answer is D.** The problem states that x is an integer greater than 1. To solve the problem, pick some numbers for x and insert them into the exponents in each quantity. For example, when $x = 2$, the quantity in Column A is 2^5, or 32, which is greater than the quantity in Column B when $x = 2$ ($3^2 = 9$). When $x = 7$, the quantity in Column B ($3^7 = 2,187$) is greater than the quantity in Column A ($2^{10} = 1,024$). Because you cannot determine a relationship, the correct answer is D.

8. **The answer is B.** To answer this question, you must recognize that $(\sqrt{8})^2 = 8$; the quantity in Column A is 8. The quantity in Column B is $8\sqrt{8}$, which is greater than 8.

9. **The answer is A.** The sum of the interior angles of a triangle is 180°. Therefore, x must equal $180° - 74° - 56°$, or 50°. The quantity in Column A, 50°, is greater than the quantity in Column B, 45°.

10. **The answer is B.** When two parallel lines are cut by a transversal, the resulting angles have special relationships. For example, the measure of angle t equals the measure of angle u. Therefore, angle u is 135°. Angle t plus angle s must equal 180°; therefore, angle s must equal $180° - 135°$, or 45°. In addition, because line n is a transversal, angle r = angle s = 45°. Plug in the values of the angles and solve the equation, as follows:

> ➤ $3r - 4s + u =$

> ➤ $3(45°) - 4(45°) + (135°) =$

> ➤ $135° - 180° + 135° = 90$

11. **The answer is B.** The average is calculated by dividing the sum of the values by the number of values. Both quantities include the same number of values (3). Therefore, because the sum of the values in Column B (12 + 20 + 45 = 77) is greater than the sum of the values in Column A (12 + 19 + 45 = 76), the average of the values in Column B is greater than the average of the values in Column A.

12. **The answer is D.** The problem gives you the equation $p(x) = 19x - (13x - b)$. The problem also gives you the profit ($3,575) and sets the value of x at 200. To calculate the value of b, substitute 3,575 for p (profit) and 200 for x (units sold) as follows:

➤ $3,575 = 19(200) - [13(200) - b]$

Solve for b (remember to watch your negatives!)

➤ $3,575 = 3,800 - 2,600 + b$

➤ $3,575 = 1,200 + b$

➤ $2,375 = b$, answer choice D.

13. **The answer is B.** To solve this problem, calculate the quantity in each column. The number of minutes in a day is 24×60, or 1,440. The number of days in 4 years is 365×4, or 1,460. Therefore, the quantity in Column B is greater than the quantity in Column A.

14. **The answer is D.** According to the graph, 42% of the homes are currently under construction and 32% of the homes have not yet been started. To calculate the number of homes that have not yet been completed, you must determine what 42% + 32%, or 74% of 40 is. Because the question asks for an approximation, you can simply calculate 75% of 40 by first recognizing that 50% of 40 is 20, and 25% of 40 is 10 therefore, approximately 30 homes have not yet been completed. If you only counted the number of homes currently under construction, you might have guessed answer choice A. You could have eliminated answer choice E right away because it is the total number of homes in the subdivision.

15. **The answer is B.** To solve this problem, first calculate the number of homes currently completed and the number of homes currently under construction. The question states that there will be a total of 40 homes in the subdivision when construction is completed. Because you are asked for an approximate ratio, you can simplify the percentages.

   ➤ Currently completed: 40 × approximately 25% = 10

   ➤ Currently under construction: 40 × approximately 40% = 16

   Now, set up a ratio and simplify.

   ➤ 10:16 = 5:8

16. **The answer is A.** To solve this problem, you must determine what the length of the box is. The formula for the volume of a cube is $l \times w \times h$. The problem states that the width is 4, the height is 2, and the volume is 38. Calculate the length as follows:

   ➤ $l \times 4 \times 2 = 38$

   ➤ $l \times 8 = 38$

   ➤ $l = \dfrac{38}{8}$

   You can determine that 38 divided by 8 will be less than 5 because 40 divided by 8 is equal to 5. Therefore, the quantity in Column A (5) is greater than the quantity in Column B ($\dfrac{38}{8}$).

17. **The answer is B.** The easiest way to solve this problem is to draw a picture as follows:

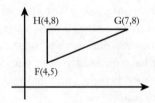

   You can see that *FG* is the hypotenuse and *FH* is a side; the hypotenuse is always longer than the sides, so the quantity in Column B (*FG*) is greater than the quantity in Column A (*FH*).

18. **The answer is A.** The average (a) of the test scores equals the sum of the test scores (s) divided by the number of test scores (n): $a = s/n$. The question states that k is equal to the average of the test scores (a) multiplied by the number of test scores (n): $an = k$. This is equivalent to $a = k/n$ (divide both sides by n), which means that $k = s$, the sum of the test scores, answer choice A.

19. **The answer is D.** The problem states that the perimeter of each of the four triangles is 40. Perimeter is the distance around any object. If the area of the square is 64, each side of the inner square must be equal to 8 ($8^2 = 64$). Each side of the square is also one side of each of the four triangles. It follows that the sum of the two remaining sides of each triangle is 32 ($40 - 8$). There are four triangles, so the perimeter of the figure is 4×32, or 128, answer choice D.

20. **The answer is D.** The contributions will be most nearly the same in the year during which the lines are closest together. Based on the graph, the lines are closest together during 1998. In that year, approximately 50% of the contributions came from private donations, and approximately 40% of contributions came from public donations.

21. **The answer is C.** To answer this question, simply calculate the percent of contributions made during each year as follows:

➤ **1995**: Private = approximately 75%; Public = approximately 25%. The amount of private contributions was more than double the amount of public contributions.

➤ **1996**: Private = approximately 60%; Public = approximately 40%. The amount of private contributions was NOT more than double the amount of public contributions.

➤ **1997**: Private = approximately 70%; Public = approximately 30%. The amount of private contributions was more than double the amount of public contributions.

➤ **1998**: Private = approximately 50%; Public = approximately 40%. The amount of private contributions was NOT more than double the amount of public contributions.

➤ **1999**: Private = approximately 65%; Public = approximately 35%. The amount of private contributions was NOT more than double the amount of public contributions.

Therefore, the amount of private contributions was more than double the amount of public contributions during two years: 1995 and 1997.

22. **The answer is A.** Based on information given in the problem, if the

    first term is t, then the second term is $\frac{2}{3}t-4$. So, the ratio of the sec-

    ond term to the first term is $\dfrac{(\frac{2t}{3} - 4)}{t}$

    To get rid of the fraction in the numerator, multiply both the numera-
    tor and denominator by 3 as follows:

    ➤ $\dfrac{3}{3}\left[\dfrac{(\frac{2t}{3} - 4)}{t}\right]$

    ➤ $\dfrac{2t-12}{3t}$

23. **The answer is C.** To solve this problem, you should first recognize
    that you can factor 6.3 out of Column B to get 6.3(7 + 0.2), which is
    equivalent to 6.3(7.2). This quantity is equal to the quantity in
    Column A.

24. **The answer is D.** A square with a perimeter of 16 has sides of length
    4 and an area of 4^2, or 16. A rectangle with a perimeter of 20 can have
    two sides of length 8 and two sides of length 2 (area = 16) or two sides
    of length 7 and two sides of length 3 (area = 21), and so on. Because
    you are not given the length and width of the rectangle in Column A,
    you cannot calculate the area of the rectangle. Therefore, you do not
    have enough information to determine the relationship between the
    quantities in Column A and Column B.

25. **The answer is D.** To determine the relationship between the quanti-
    ties in Column A and Column B, you need to know the value of both
    p and r. Because this information is not given, D is the correct answer.

26. **The answer is C.** The easiest way to solve this type of problem is to
    make a table (such as the following table). Based on the calculations in
    the table, the number 6 will never be the last digit.

Original number	Last digit of number squared	Last digit of column two tripled
1	$1^2 = 1$	$1 \times 3 = 3$
2	$2^2 = 4$	$4 \times 3 = 12$
3	$3^2 = 9$	$9 \times 3 = 27$
4	$4^2 = 16$	$16 \times 3 = 48$
5	$5^2 = 25$	$25 \times 3 = 75$
6	$6^2 = 36$	$36 \times 3 = 108$
7	$7^2 = 49$	$49 \times 3 = 147$
8	$8^2 = 64$	$64 \times 3 = 192$
9	$9^2 = 81$	$81 \times 3 = 243$

27. **The answer is C.** To solve this problem, you must recognize that a cube has six sides, and that the total surface area is the total "amount" of the surface of the cube. You are given that the total surface area of the cube is 54, which means that the area of one side of the cube is $54 \div 6$, or 9. This, in turn, means that the length of each side of the cube is 3 because the area of a square is equivalent to a side squared ($9 = 3^2$). The formula for the volume of a cube is length × width × height, so the volume is equal to $3 \times 3 \times 3$, or 27. Draw a diagram to help visualize the solution:

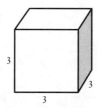

28. **The answer is D.** To solve this problem, apply the distributive property, which says that $a(b + c) = ab + bc$, and solve for n.

➤ $2,600 = 50(3n - 8)$

➤ $2,600 = 150n - 400$

➤ $3,000 = 150n$

➤ $20 = n$

Practice Exam 2

This practice GRE consists of 58 multiple-choice questions and two essay tasks, divided into four main sections. Please allow approximately 2 hours and 30 minutes to complete the following test. Each of the test sections should be taken in the time indicated at the beginning of the sections, and in the order in which the sections appear on this test. There are several different types of questions within each section. Make sure that you read and understand all directions before you begin. To achieve the best results, time yourself strictly on each section. Use the answer sheet at the end of the chapter to mark your answers.

You may write on the test itself, but you should indicate your answers on the answer sheet after you have made your selections. The number of questions that you answer correctly on the separate answer sheet determines your score. If you leave a question blank or fill in more than one circle, that question will not be counted in scoring. Your score is not reduced if you answer incorrectly, so it is in your best interest to guess on a question rather than to not answer the question at all. The computer adaptive GRE does not allow you to skip questions, so you should get in the habit of answering all of the questions on your practice exams.

Section 1—Issue Task

45 Minutes

1 Question

You have 45 minutes to select one topic, organize your thoughts, and compose a response that represents your point of view on the topic that you choose. Do not respond to any topic other than the one you select; a response to any other topic receives a score of 0.

You will be given a choice between two general issues on a broad range of topics. You will be required to discuss your perspective on one of the issues, using examples and reasons drawn from your own experiences and observations.

The space given for writing your response is limited, so use scratch paper to organize your response before you begin writing. For this practice test, allow approximately two 8.5- by 11-inch lined sheets of paper.

Present your viewpoint on one of the following claims. Use relevant reasons and examples to support your point of view.

Topic 1.

> "Technological development must continue in order to solve the problems that have been created by technological development in the past."

Topic 2.

> "Publicly funded schools should not offer any courses that cannot be shown to be a direct benefit to a majority of students."

Section 2—Argument Task

30 Minutes

1 Question

You have 30 minutes to organize your thoughts and compose a response that critiques the given argument. Do not respond to any topic other than the one given; a response to any other topic receives a score of 0.

You are not being asked to discuss your point of view on the statement. You should identify and analyze the central elements of the argument, the underlying assumptions that are being made, and any supporting information that is given. Your critique can also discuss other information that would strengthen or weaken the argument or make it more logical.

The space given for writing your response is limited, so use scratch paper to evaluate the given argument and organize your response before you begin writing. For this practice test, allow approximately two 8.5- by 11-inch lined sheets of paper.

Critique the reasoning used in the following argument.

The following appeared in an educational trade journal.

"Various studies examining the connection between a student's home environment and the student's success in school, as measured by grade point average, reveal that there is a strong correlation between the presence of books in the student's home and better grades. A similar correlation exists between the number of televisions and a student's grade success as well as the number of channels of cable television available in the student's home and his or her grade point average. This leads to the inescapable conclusion that in order to best prepare a student for school success, we must be certain that he or she has access to both books and cable or satellite television in the home. While government can and should shoulder some of the burden by subsidizing pay television services for lower income homes that cannot now afford it, we can do our part by encouraging students and their families to own books. Perhaps, we could donate obsolete textbooks to underprivileged families rather than simply disposing of the old books when we receive replacement texts in our schools."

Section 3—Verbal

30 Minutes

30 Questions

This section consists of four different types of questions. To answer the questions, select the best answer from the answer choices provided.

Directions: Sentence Completion Questions—The following sentences each contain one or two blanks, indicating that something has been left out of the sentence. Each answer choice contains one word or a set of words. Select the word or set of words, that, when inserted in the blank(s), best fits the context of the sentence.

Directions: Analogies Questions—The following questions contain a set of related words and five answer choices. Each answer choice also contains a set of words. Select the set of words that represents a relationship similar to the original set of words.

Directions: Antonyms Questions—The following questions contain a word in capital letters and five answer choices. Each answer choice contains a word or phrase. Select the word or phrase that best expresses a meaning opposite to the word in capital letters.

Directions: Reading Comprehension Questions—The passages in this section are followed by several questions. The questions correspond to information that is stated or implied in the passage. Read the passage and choose the best answer for each question.

1. ACROBAT : AGILITY ::
    (A) pianist : dexterity
    (B) author : grammar
    (C) artist : creativity
    (D) inventor : capital
    (E) physician : responsibility

2. ALIENATE : UNITE ::
    (A) alleviate : cure
    (B) rebel : garnish
    (C) endure : conjoin
    (D) estrange : conciliate
    (E) feign : deceive

3. To determine the _____ of statements made by witnesses, a prosecutor must be adept at _____ the truth.

(A) veracity..discerning

(B) meaning..condemning

(C) accuracy..ignoring

(D) importance..discounting

(E) fortuity..epitomizing

4. Michael had a _____ for storytelling; the words seemed to flow out of him quite naturally.

(A) zenith

(B) lavishness

(C) propensity

(D) benevolence

(E) prejudice

5. PEEK : LOOK ::

(A) glance : glimpse

(B) speak : talk

(C) suppose : propose

(D) acquire : divest

(E) skim : peruse

6. FLEXIBLE:

(A) mild

(B) frozen

(C) impetuous

(D) taut

(E) resilient

7. UNDETERRED:

(A) pending

(B) indefinite

(C) easily discouraged

(D) extremely temperamental

(E) emotionally indifferent

8. PERCOLATE : WATER ::

(A) sift : flour

(B) flow : blood

(C) foreclose : mortgage

(D) burn : fire

(E) conceal : truth

9. IMPLY:

    (A) define

    (B) mention

    (C) suddenly implicate

    (D) arrive at a conclusion

    (E) directly express

10. DISTRACT:

    (A) draw attention to

    (B) cause turmoil

    (C) cut short

    (D) extricate

    (E) prolong

11. Impressed by the exceptional potential of the findings, scientists predict that a cure for the _____ disease will be forthcoming.

    (A) innocuous

    (B) pernicious

    (C) didactic

    (D) miniscule

    (E) sedulous

12. Despite all of the advertisements _____ the new product, its first quarter sales were _____.

    (A) criticizing..protracted

    (B) praising..extraordinary

    (C) lauding..abysmal

    (D) abrogating..profound

    (E) censuring..marred

13. FEIGN : COUNTERFEIT ::

    (A) abrogate : nullify

    (B) amortize : adjudicate

    (C) foil : encourage

    (D) sanction : interdict

    (E) whet : dull

14. For some time now, the dissenters have been held in _____; they have suspended their activities.

    (A) contempt

    (B) obscurity

    (C) contrast

    (D) awe

    (E) abeyance

15. ADULTERATED:

(A) distilled

(B) maligned

(C) assimilated

(D) amalgamated

(E) diversified

16. It is surprising to observe that Murray's performances have recently been criticized as _____, because his advocates have been touting his great _____.

(A) ambiguous..uncertainty

(B) exceptional..fidelity

(C) feckless..incompetence

(D) banal..imagination

(E) placid..serenity

Questions 17 and 18 are based on the following passage.

It is a popular misconception among consumers that wind power is unreliable because wind plants are controlled by nature and not by utility operators. This fear has kept wind power development to a minimum while increasing dependency on nonrenewable energy resources. In addition, the unsubstantiated belief that wind power is undependable has led many to believe that wind plants would need 100% backup from an alternate power generation system at all times. If this were true, wind power might indeed be a precarious option. However, although it is true that wind plants are not administered in the usual fashion, it is important to remember that electricity demand is not created or controlled by utility operators. The average utility system is designed to accommodate varying supply and demand. The wind plants are no exception to this rule. It is also imperative to remember that no power plant of any nature is completely reliable. Electrical plants experience outages and use backup provided by the entire interconnected power system. If wind plants were added to this intricate system, deficiencies in their abilities could be compensated for as well.

17. It can be inferred from the passage that the author believes which of the following about the current state of public awareness concerning wind power and wind plants?

    (A) Consumers have been intentionally misinformed about the advantages and disadvantages of wind power.

    (B) Consumers are unaware of the primary advantage of using wind power as an energy source.

    (C) The public perception of wind power is at least partially distorted.

    (D) Consumers are not interested in learning more about the advantages and disadvantages of wind power.

    (E) Consumers prefer nonrenewable resources to wind power for economic reasons.

18. Which of the following statements concerning energy is most directly suggested in the passage?

    (A) All energy sources require 100% backup from an alternate generation source.

    (B) Electrical power plants are more likely than wind plants to require an alternate generation source.

    (C) Wind plants are completely reliable because they rely on nature instead of utility operators.

    (D) Some problems with wind plants could be solved using techniques already in place.

    (E) Consumers completely control the supply and demand of energy sources.

19. ICONOCLAST : DOCTRINE ::

    (A) xenophobe : fear

    (B) magistrate : judgment

    (C) rebel : convention

    (D) incumbent : politics

    (E) attorney : law

20. Certain methods of instruction are quite _____, making it difficult to _____ novel techniques.

    (A) benign..assume

    (B) cogent..understand

    (C) derivative..agree with

    (D) prevalent..introduce

    (E) deliberate..arrive at

Questions 21–24 are based on the following passage.

Maya Angelou's masterpiece *I Know Why the Caged Bird Sings* tells the story of a heroine named Marguerite Johnson. Throughout the text, Marguerite faces the challenges of being African American in the American South. During the Depression era, Marguerite and her family

5   continuously struggle against prejudice and racism. The novel chroni-
cles Marguerite's childhood, and relates the shame Marguerite suffers
when she is raped as a young girl and the pride she feels when she earns
a place as the first African American female streetcar conductor in San
Francisco. The book explores amazing characters that influence and
10   shape young Marguerite and provides a glimpse of the American South
in the 1930s.

The story quickly became a favorite among literary critics because the
text did not shy away from difficult subjects like rape, racism, and the
struggles of young women fighting to find their identity in a hostile soci-
15   ety. *I Know Why the Caged Bird Sings* was popular among white audiences
because it did not have an openly hostile attitude or hold grudges about
the effects of slavery. Despite this, *I Know Why the Caged Bird Sings* does
reveal the ruthless realities of segregation while refraining from being
hostile or accusatory.

20   Angelou's story is so unique because it is autobiographical. Marguerite
Johnson is a reflection of Maya Angelou in every way that matters.
Knowing this, readers can view the story in many different ways. The
book can be seen as an historical narrative that explores African
American life across America, or as a touching autobiography. Since the
25   book's publication, it has been revered for its emotional depiction of the
economic hardships and social injustices that faced African Americans
during the 1930s. Other critics view the book as a moving description of
a young African American woman's coming of age. In the years since it
was first published, scholars have studied *I Know Why the Caged Bird*
30   *Sings* using different viewpoints. The book has been interpreted using
feminist readings and as an example of African American literary scholarship. African American scholars argue that *I Know Why the Caged Bird*
Sings is mostly an African American text because of its examination of
racism and African American heritage. However, this theory fails to rec-
35   ognize Marguerite's fight for femininity and her role in society as a
woman.

Through the story and speaking in the voice of Marguerite Johnson,
Angelou finds inspiration from her childhood memories and includes
these experiences to develop the book. Angelou's goal in writing this
40   story was to promote hope. Angelou tells the story of a young African
American girl growing up amidst great hardships and shows how this
same girl was able to overcome horrifying obstacles and challenges.

I Know Why the Caged Bird Sings is as relevant and important today as
it was when it was initially published. Every subsequent generation can
45   find lessons and truths in this book. The book remains a classic because

it is more than just a story about Marguerite Johnson. *I Know Why the Cages Bird Sings* captures the essence of humanity and restores one's ability to believe in a better tomorrow.

21. Which of the following would be the most appropriate title for the passage?

   (A) An Examination of the Effects of Racism and Prejudice on African American Women

   (B) Trends in Autobiographical Literature and Novels

   (C) *I Know Why the Caged Bird Sings:* Critical Reflections on Maya Angelou's Masterpiece

   (D) An Exploration of Violence Against Women in the American South During the 1930s

   (E) The Great Depression: Its Effects, Consequences, and Lessons, as told by Maya Angelou

22. In the last paragraph of the passage, the author's attitude toward *I Know Why the Caged Bird Sings* can best be described as

   (A) disparaging

   (B) facetious

   (C) disillusioned yet hopeful

   (D) incredulous but acquiescent

   (E) appreciative and approving

23. It can be inferred from the passage that Angelou used the character, Marguerite Johnson, as

   (A) a fictional representation of herself to create a subtle autobiographical effect

   (B) a scapegoat for the hardships and challenges of the American South during the 1930s

   (C) a mechanism to promote outrage over slavery and its atrocities against African Americans

   (D) a supporting character to reveal the main character's prejudice and malice

   (E) an example of society's ability to create individuals who are unable to experience real emotion during troubled times

24. The passage supplies information for answering which of the following questions?

   (A) Why was *I Know Why the Caged Bird Sings* accepted by some white readers?

   (B) What were the effects of the Great Depression on African American families?

   (C) What are some criticisms and complaints about Maya Angelou's writing style?

   (D) What was Maya Angelou/Marguerite Johnson's educational background?

   (E) What is the impact of this novel on the autobiographical genre?

Questions 25 and 26 are based on the following passage.

Seed dispersal is crucial for the survival of many species of plants. Long distance dispersal of seeds affects many ecological and evolutionary processes. Wind dispersal is especially important and has been attributed to spreading the seeds of certain plants more than 100 meters away.
5 The common dandelion is one of the best examples of plant species that relies on wind dispersal for its ability to populate and flourish across countries and even continents.

For years, scientists have sought to discover what weather conditions are ideal for long distance wind dispersal of seeds. The effect of differ-
10 ent weather conditions on long distance dispersal of seeds was virtually unknown. Many assumed that the speed of the wind would be of utmost importance. High horizontal wind speeds were believed to have been the cause of long distance dispersal. However, studies show that it is in fact vertical turbulence and notably, convective updrafts, that are most cru-
15 cial for the wind dispersal of seeds. Data even suggests that dandelion seeds are more likely to be released during periods of calm conditions. This anomaly greatly confused scientists until it was discovered that it only takes very small gusts of wind to separate the seeds from the mother plant.

25. The author of the passage is primarily concerned with

(A) discussing the usefulness of dandelions to scientists

(B) discussing the drawbacks of wind dispersal

(C) discussing the impact of certain weather conditions to seed dispersal

(D) resolving a dispute about the merits of studying seed dispersal

(E) resolving a dispute about the ability of plants to disperse seeds long distances

26. It can be inferred from information in the passage that the existence of dandelions

(A) is entirely dependent on the dandelion's ability to release seeds during calm conditions

(B) is perpetuated partly because of the dandelion's ability to disperse its seeds across long distances

(C) is in danger of extinction due to the lack of high wind speeds across countries and continents

(D) is important because the dandelion is one of the only plants in existence that relies on wind dispersal of it seeds

(E) is unique because its seed dispersal is unaffected by vertical turbulence

27. One theory _____ that the organisms have a common ancestor.

    (A) instigates

    (B) deplores

    (C) postulates

    (D) subsumes

    (E) transposes

28. IRASCIBLE:

    (A) serious

    (B) choleric

    (C) tolerant

    (D) finicky

    (E) adroit

29. VILIFY:

    (A) censure

    (B) eulogize

    (C) incinerate

    (D) parse

    (E) squelch

30. SCALE : NOTES ::

    (A) song : singers

    (B) family : children

    (C) recipe : ingredients

    (D) test : grades

    (E) spectrum : colors

Section 4—Quantitative

30 Minutes

28 Questions

Numbers: All of the numbers used in this section are real numbers.

Figures: Assume that the position of all points, angles, and so on are in the order shown and the measures of angles are positive.

Straight lines can be assumed to be straight.

All figures lie in a plane unless otherwise stated.

The figures given for each question provide information to solve the problem. The figures are not drawn to scale unless otherwise stated. To solve the problems, use your knowledge of mathematics; do not estimate lengths and sizes of the figures to answer questions.

Directions: Some of the following questions give you two quantities, one in Column A and one in Column B. Compare the two quantities and choose one of the following answer choices:

A if the quantity in Column A is greater

B if the quantity in Column B is greater

C if the two quantities are equal

D if you cannot determine the relationship based on the given information

Do not mark answer choice E because there are only four choices from which to choose.

Information and/or figures pertaining to one or both of the quantities might appear above the two columns. Any information that appears in both columns has the same meaning in Column A and in Column B.

Directions: Select the best answer for the remaining multiple-choice questions.

	Column A	Column B
1.	The greatest odd factor of of 360	The greatest even factor 360 less than 90
2.	$3x^2 + 3y^2$	$(x^2 + y^2)^3$

	Column A	Column B

$$a > b > c > 0$$

| 3. | $\dfrac{ca}{b}$ | $\dfrac{c^2}{a}$ |

| 4. | $3 + 7\sqrt{3}$ | $7 + 3\sqrt{3}$ |

5. If $\dfrac{4x}{3y} = \dfrac{8}{6}$, what is the value of $\dfrac{9x}{12y}$?

(A) $\dfrac{3}{2}$

(B) $\dfrac{3}{4}$

(C) $\dfrac{2}{3}$

(D) $\dfrac{5}{12}$

(E) $\dfrac{3}{8}$

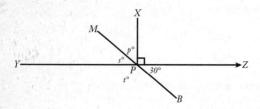

6. In the figure above, YZ and MB intersect at P and XP is perpendicular to YZ. What is the value of $2p + 3s - t$?
   (A) 30°
   (B) 60°
   (C) 90°
   (D) 120°
   (E) 150°

	Column A	Column B
7.	$3,200 \div 79$	45

| 8. | $\dfrac{6}{13}$ | $\dfrac{15}{28}$ |

Column A	Column B
9. 80 percent of 40	60 percent of 50

10. If $|4 - 3x| = 5$, which of the following is a possible value of x?

(A) $-\dfrac{1}{3}$

(B) $\dfrac{1}{3}$

(C) $\dfrac{2}{3}$

(D) 3

(E) 6

Column A	Column B

$$\frac{3}{4}x + 7 = 28$$

11. x 28

12. Which of the following is the sum of two positive integers whose product is 18?

(A) 5

(B) 11

(C) 12

(D) 18

(E) 36

Column A	Column B

In a geography class that consisted of 25 students, the number of Seniors was 5 more than twice the number of Sophomores, and $\dfrac{1}{5}$ were neither Seniors nor Sophomores.

13.   The number of Seniors in   15
the class

Refer to the following table for Questions 14 and 15.

PRIMARY ENERGY SOURCES

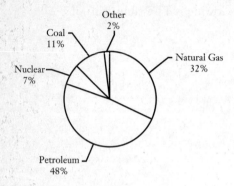

"Other" includes: wood and waste
hydroelectricity
wind, geothermal, solar

14. Hydroelectricity makes up approximately what percentage of the primary energy sources?

    (A) 0.6%

    (B) 1.3%

    (C) 2%

    (D) 3%

    (E) It cannot be determined from the information given.

15. What is the ratio of nuclear power to coal as a primary energy source?

    (A) $\dfrac{7}{100}$

    (B) $\dfrac{2}{7}$

    (C) $\dfrac{7}{11}$

    (D) $\dfrac{9}{7}$

    (E) $\dfrac{11}{7}$

Column A	Column B

The morning shift of a certain manufacturing plant produced 250 parts before their first break. The second shift produced 200 parts before their first break.

16.   The number of parts produced before the first shift's first break   The number of parts produced after the second shift's first break

The height of right circular cylinder K is 5 times the radius of its base.

17. The height of K The circumference of the base of K

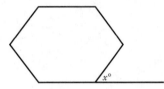

18. If all interior angles of the polygon above are congruent, then $x = $?

(A) 45°

(B) 60°

(C) 75°

(D) 90°

(E) 120°

19. What is the remainder when 7^3 is divided by 9?

(A) 5

(B) 4

(C) 3

(D) 2

(E) 1

Refer to the following graph for Questions 20 and 21.

RECOMMENDED DAILY DIETARY INTAKES OF SPECIFIC NUTRIENTS		
Nutrients	**2,000 calories per day**	**2,500 calories per day**
Fat	< 65 grams	< 80 grams
Sodium	< 2,400 milligrams	< 2,400 milligrams
Carbohydrates	300 grams	375 grams
Fiber	25 grams	30 grams
Potassium	3,500 milligrams	3,500 milligrams

Note: Daily intake will vary depending on whether you eat a total of 2,000 calories or 2,500 calories per day.

20. The daily intake values are the same for which of the following nutrients, regardless of total calories consumed per day?

    I. Fat

    II. Sodium

    III. Carbohydrates

    IV. Potassium

(A) I only

(B) I and II only

(C) II and III only

(D) II and IV only

(E) II, III, and IV

21. If you eat a total of 2,000 calories per day, which of the following would be an appropriate amount of fat to consume each day?

(A) 80 grams

(B) 74 grams

(C) 70 grams

(D) 68 grams

(E) 60 grams

22. If $a + c = 17$ and $b - c = 2$, then $a + b =$

(A) 15

(B) 17

(C) 19

(D) 21

(E) 34

<u>Column A</u>   <u>Column B</u>

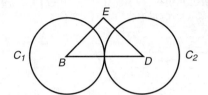

In circles C_1 and C_2, the length
of segment BE equals
the length of segment ED.

23. The circumference of circle C_2 The circumference of
                                                   circle C_1

The wheel of a bicycle has a 9-inch
radius and is rotating at a rate of
32 revolutions per minute

24.   The number of inches traveled   The number of inches
             per minute by a point 6 inches   traveled per minute by
             from the center of the wheel   a point on the
                                                     circumference of the
                                                     wheel

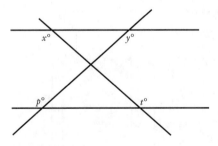

25. $p + t$ $x + y$

26. If a certain car has been traveling at the constant rate of x miles per hour, how many miles has the car traveled in the last y minutes?

(A) $\dfrac{x}{60y}$

(B) $\dfrac{y}{60x}$

(C) $\dfrac{x(60)}{y}$

(D) $\dfrac{xy}{60}$

(E) $\dfrac{60}{xy}$

27. $\sqrt{(37-9)(13+15)}$

(A) 5
(B) 14
(C) 28
(D) 37
(E) 56

28. $81.24 \times \dfrac{1}{100} =$

(A) 0.008124
(B) 0.08124
(C) 0.8124
(D) 8.124
(E) 81.24

GRE PRACTICE EXAM 2
ANSWER SHEET

These answer sheets are provided for your convenience only. You will not receive
answer sheets for the actual computer-based test.

SECTION 3

1 Ⓐ Ⓑ Ⓒ Ⓓ Ⓔ	11 Ⓐ Ⓑ Ⓒ Ⓓ Ⓔ	21 Ⓐ Ⓑ Ⓒ Ⓓ Ⓔ	31 Ⓐ Ⓑ Ⓒ Ⓓ Ⓔ
2 Ⓐ Ⓑ Ⓒ Ⓓ Ⓔ	12 Ⓐ Ⓑ Ⓒ Ⓓ Ⓔ	22 Ⓐ Ⓑ Ⓒ Ⓓ Ⓔ	32 Ⓐ Ⓑ Ⓒ Ⓓ Ⓔ
3 Ⓐ Ⓑ Ⓒ Ⓓ Ⓔ	13 Ⓐ Ⓑ Ⓒ Ⓓ Ⓔ	23 Ⓐ Ⓑ Ⓒ Ⓓ Ⓔ	33 Ⓐ Ⓑ Ⓒ Ⓓ Ⓔ
4 Ⓐ Ⓑ Ⓒ Ⓓ Ⓔ	14 Ⓐ Ⓑ Ⓒ Ⓓ Ⓔ	24 Ⓐ Ⓑ Ⓒ Ⓓ Ⓔ	34 Ⓐ Ⓑ Ⓒ Ⓓ Ⓔ
5 Ⓐ Ⓑ Ⓒ Ⓓ Ⓔ	15 Ⓐ Ⓑ Ⓒ Ⓓ Ⓔ	25 Ⓐ Ⓑ Ⓒ Ⓓ Ⓔ	35 Ⓐ Ⓑ Ⓒ Ⓓ Ⓔ
6 Ⓐ Ⓑ Ⓒ Ⓓ Ⓔ	16 Ⓐ Ⓑ Ⓒ Ⓓ Ⓔ	26 Ⓐ Ⓑ Ⓒ Ⓓ Ⓔ	36 Ⓐ Ⓑ Ⓒ Ⓓ Ⓔ
7 Ⓐ Ⓑ Ⓒ Ⓓ Ⓔ	17 Ⓐ Ⓑ Ⓒ Ⓓ Ⓔ	27 Ⓐ Ⓑ Ⓒ Ⓓ Ⓔ	37 Ⓐ Ⓑ Ⓒ Ⓓ Ⓔ
8 Ⓐ Ⓑ Ⓒ Ⓓ Ⓔ	18 Ⓐ Ⓑ Ⓒ Ⓓ Ⓔ	28 Ⓐ Ⓑ Ⓒ Ⓓ Ⓔ	38 Ⓐ Ⓑ Ⓒ Ⓓ Ⓔ
9 Ⓐ Ⓑ Ⓒ Ⓓ Ⓔ	19 Ⓐ Ⓑ Ⓒ Ⓓ Ⓔ	29 Ⓐ Ⓑ Ⓒ Ⓓ Ⓔ	39 Ⓐ Ⓑ Ⓒ Ⓓ Ⓔ
10 Ⓐ Ⓑ Ⓒ Ⓓ Ⓔ	20 Ⓐ Ⓑ Ⓒ Ⓓ Ⓔ	30 Ⓐ Ⓑ Ⓒ Ⓓ Ⓔ	40 Ⓐ Ⓑ Ⓒ Ⓓ Ⓔ

SECTION 4

1 Ⓐ Ⓑ Ⓒ Ⓓ Ⓔ	11 Ⓐ Ⓑ Ⓒ Ⓓ Ⓔ	21 Ⓐ Ⓑ Ⓒ Ⓓ Ⓔ	31 Ⓐ Ⓑ Ⓒ Ⓓ Ⓔ
2 Ⓐ Ⓑ Ⓒ Ⓓ Ⓔ	12 Ⓐ Ⓑ Ⓒ Ⓓ Ⓔ	22 Ⓐ Ⓑ Ⓒ Ⓓ Ⓔ	32 Ⓐ Ⓑ Ⓒ Ⓓ Ⓔ
3 Ⓐ Ⓑ Ⓒ Ⓓ Ⓔ	13 Ⓐ Ⓑ Ⓒ Ⓓ Ⓔ	23 Ⓐ Ⓑ Ⓒ Ⓓ Ⓔ	33 Ⓐ Ⓑ Ⓒ Ⓓ Ⓔ
4 Ⓐ Ⓑ Ⓒ Ⓓ Ⓔ	14 Ⓐ Ⓑ Ⓒ Ⓓ Ⓔ	24 Ⓐ Ⓑ Ⓒ Ⓓ Ⓔ	34 Ⓐ Ⓑ Ⓒ Ⓓ Ⓔ
5 Ⓐ Ⓑ Ⓒ Ⓓ Ⓔ	15 Ⓐ Ⓑ Ⓒ Ⓓ Ⓔ	25 Ⓐ Ⓑ Ⓒ Ⓓ Ⓔ	35 Ⓐ Ⓑ Ⓒ Ⓓ Ⓔ
6 Ⓐ Ⓑ Ⓒ Ⓓ Ⓔ	16 Ⓐ Ⓑ Ⓒ Ⓓ Ⓔ	26 Ⓐ Ⓑ Ⓒ Ⓓ Ⓔ	36 Ⓐ Ⓑ Ⓒ Ⓓ Ⓔ
7 Ⓐ Ⓑ Ⓒ Ⓓ Ⓔ	17 Ⓐ Ⓑ Ⓒ Ⓓ Ⓔ	27 Ⓐ Ⓑ Ⓒ Ⓓ Ⓔ	37 Ⓐ Ⓑ Ⓒ Ⓓ Ⓔ
8 Ⓐ Ⓑ Ⓒ Ⓓ Ⓔ	18 Ⓐ Ⓑ Ⓒ Ⓓ Ⓔ	28 Ⓐ Ⓑ Ⓒ Ⓓ Ⓔ	38 Ⓐ Ⓑ Ⓒ Ⓓ Ⓔ
9 Ⓐ Ⓑ Ⓒ Ⓓ Ⓔ	19 Ⓐ Ⓑ Ⓒ Ⓓ Ⓔ	29 Ⓐ Ⓑ Ⓒ Ⓓ Ⓔ	39 Ⓐ Ⓑ Ⓒ Ⓓ Ⓔ
10 Ⓐ Ⓑ Ⓒ Ⓓ Ⓔ	20 Ⓐ Ⓑ Ⓒ Ⓓ Ⓔ	30 Ⓐ Ⓑ Ⓒ Ⓓ Ⓔ	40 Ⓐ Ⓑ Ⓒ Ⓓ Ⓔ

Practice Exam 2
Answer Key

Analysis of an Argument and Analysis of an Issue

Because grading the essay is subjective, we're chosen not to include any "graded" essays here. Your best bet is to have someone you trust, such as your personal tutor, read your essays and give you an honest critique. Make the grading criteria mentioned in Chapter 1 available to whomever grades your essays. If you plan on grading your own essays, review the grading criteria and be as honest as possible regarding the structure, development, organization, technique, and appropriateness of your writing. Focus on your weak areas and continue to practice in order to improve your writing skills.

Verbal

1. **The answer is A.** An "acrobat" requires great physical "agility." A general sentence that can be used to describe the analogy is: For a person to be a(n) "____," he or she must possess a high level of physical "____." A "pianist" must be skilled in the use of his or her hands, and someone who possesses this skill has a high level of "dexterity." The remaining answer choices are incorrect because "grammar," "creativity," "capital," and "responsibility" are not physical characteristics.

2. **The answer is D.** The verbs "alienate" and "unite" are opposite in meaning; therefore, the correct answer will contain two words that

have opposite meanings. Answer choice D is correct because the verb "estrange" is a synonym for "alienate" and the verb "conciliate" is a synonym for "unite." In other words, "estrange" and "conciliate" are opposite in meaning. Answer choices A and E are incorrect because they contain verbs that are synonyms of each other. Answer choice B is incorrect because "rebel" and "garnish" are not opposite in meaning. Although "conjoin" is a synonym for "unite," "endure" is neither a synonym for "alienate" nor an opposite of "endure," so answer choice C is incorrect.

3. **The answer is A.** In this sentence, the word that best fits in the first blank will be related to the word that best fits in the second blank. The first word describes what a prosecutor needs to determine about the statements, and the second word describes the action that must take place to make that determination. "Veracity" means "truth," so it makes sense based on the context of the sentence that a prosecutor must be adept at "discerning," or "mentally recognizing," the truth. It would not make sense if the prosecutor was "condemning," "ignoring," or "discounting" the truth, so answer choices B, C, and D are incorrect. Likewise, "fortuity" refers to a "chance event," so answer choice E is incorrect.

4. **The answer is C.** The phrase "words seemed to flow...quite naturally" helps to describe how Michael told stories. Because the phrase indicates that storytelling came "naturally," you can assume that Michael was a natural storyteller, or had a "propensity" for storytelling. The remaining answer choices do not describe a "natural ability," so answer choices A, B, D, and E are incorrect. Refer to Appendix A for definitions of some of the words in these answer choices.

5. **The answer is E.** The verbs "peek" and "look" are similar actions, but to "peek" is to "look" quickly. A general sentence that can be used to describe the analogy is: To "____" is to "____" quickly. To "skim" is to "peruse" or "examine" something quickly, so answer choice E is correct. To "glance" is not to quickly "glimpse," so answer choice A is incorrect. Likewise, to "speak" is not to quickly "talk," so answer choice B is incorrect. Although "suppose" and "propose" could be related, neither action is necessarily quicker than the other, so answer choice C is incorrect. Answer choice D is incorrect because "acquire" and "divest" are opposite in meaning.

6. **The answer is D.** "Flexible" means "capable of being bent or adapted." "Taut" means "pulled or stretched tight," which suggests "inflexibility." Answer choices A and B are incorrect because neither

"mild" nor "frozen" have meanings that are opposite to "flexible." "Impetuous" means "impulsive" and "resilient" means "capable of returning to an original condition," neither of which are antonyms of "flexible."

7. **The answer is C.** The root word "deter" means to "discourage or stop, usually through intimidation or fear." Therefore, someone who is "undeterred" is not "easily discouraged." "Pending" means "not yet decided" and "indefinite" means "unclear or not stated," so answer choices A and B are incorrect. Likewise, answer choices D and E are not antonyms of "undeterred."

8. **The answer is A.** "Water" can "percolate," or "pass through," the soil. A general sentence that can be used to describe the analogy is: "____" is a substance that will "____," or pass through, something. "Flour" is a substance that will "sift," or pass through, a sieve, or straining device. Answer choice B is incorrect because, while "blood" "flows," to "flow" is not the same as "to pass through." Likewise, the remaining answer choices are incorrect because, although they contain related word pairs, they do not include a verb that means "to pass through."

9. **The answer is E.** To "imply" means to "suggest, or indirectly express" an idea. Therefore, "directly express" is most opposite in meaning to "imply." To "mention" means to "casually refer to," and is not an antonym of "imply," so answer choice B is incorrect. Likewise, answer choices A, C, and D are not antonyms of "imply," so they are incorrect as well.

10. **The answer is A.** To "distract" means to "divert or draw attention away from." "Turmoil" means "a state of extreme agitation," so to "cause turmoil" is not an antonym of "distract"; answer choice B is incorrect. "Extricate" means to "release from entanglement," which is not an antonym of "distract," so answer choice D is incorrect. Likewise, answer choices C and E are incorrect because they are not opposite in meaning to "distract."

11. **The answer is B.** The context of the sentence indicates that the scientists believe, or predict, that a cure will be found for some type of disease. You can assume that the scientists would like to cure a "harmful" or "deadly" disease, so answer choice B is most likely correct because both of these adjectives define "pernicious." To be certain that this is the correct answer, eliminate the remaining answer choices. "Innocuous" means "harmless," so eliminate answer choice A. It does not make sense for a disease to be "instructional," so eliminate answer

choice C. Because "miniscule" means "tiny," answer choice D can also be eliminated. "Sedulous" is an adjective that describes something "careful" and "persistent." A disease could be "persistent," but "sedulous" is not the best word to describe a disease, so eliminate answer choice E.

12. **The answer is C.** The preposition "despite" indicates that the information in the first portion of the sentence contradicts the information in the second portion of the sentence. In other words, the advertisements said one thing about the new product, but the first quarter sales proved another. Look for answer choices that contain two words that have opposing connotations. If you insert the words from answer choice C into the sentence, the advertisements would be "lauding," or "praising," the new product, while the sales would be "abysmal," or "very bad." "Criticizing" and "protracted" have contradictory connotations. "Protracted," however, means "extended," which does not appropriately describe sales. Therefore, answer choice A is incorrect. "Praising" and "extraordinary" both have positive connotations, so answer choice B is incorrect. It does not make sense that advertisements would "repeal," or "revoke" a product, so answer choice D is incorrect. Answer choice E contains two words that both have negative connotations, so it is incorrect.

13. **The answer is A.** The verb "feign" describes an activity that implies "imitation" and "deception." The verb "counterfeit" is a synonym of "feign," so the correct answer will contain two words that have similar meanings. "Abrogate" and "nullify" both mean to "end" or "annul," so answer choice A is correct. "Amortize" means to "gradually reduce an amount, usually money" and "adjudicate" means to "hear and settle a dispute," so answer choice B is incorrect. Likewise, "foil" is similar to the stem words, but "encourage" is not a synonym of "foil," so answer choice C is incorrect. "Sanction," which means "to give permission," is opposite in meaning to "interdict," which means "to prohibit," so answer choice D is incorrect. Similarly, "whet" means "to sharpen," which is the opposite of to "dull," so answer choice E is incorrect.

14. **The answer is E.** In this sentence, the phrase "activities have been suspended" defines the missing word. An "abeyance" is a "suspension," so answer choice E is correct. "Contempt" has several meanings that fit the context of the first portion of the sentence, but none of the meanings relate to "suspension," so answer choice A is incorrect. Likewise, "obscurity," "contrast," and "awe," do not have meanings that relate to "suspension," so answer choices B, C, and D are incorrect.

15. **The answer is A.** Something that is "adulterated" has been "polluted, or made impure by adding improper or inferior ingredients." Something that is "distilled" has been "purified, or has had the essential elements separated out." Someone or something that has been "maligned" has had "harmful, often untrue statements made about him or it"; something that has been "assimilated" has been "absorbed or incorporated" into something; "amalgamated" means "combined or mixed"; "diversified" means "varied or spread out." None of these words are antonyms of "adulterated," so answer choices B, C, D, and E are incorrect.

16. **The answer is D.** The context of the sentence indicates a contrast between the words that best fit the two blanks. On one hand, Murray's performances have been criticized for being a certain way; on the other hand, his advocates have been "touting," or "publicly promoting" Murray for a certain quality. "Banal" means "boring or ordinary," so a "banal" performance would not be expected from a person with great "imagination." "Ambiguous" means "uncertain," "feckless" means "incompetent," and "placid" means "serene," so answer choices A, C, and E are incorrect. Answer choice B is incorrect because the words do not contradict each other, and "fidelity" does not fit within the context of the sentence.

17. **The answer is C.** The author addresses some misconceptions about wind power because he or she believes that consumers and the public are not as well informed about wind power as they could be. Answer choice A might have appeared to be correct. However, there is no evidence that the author believes that anyone or anything has intentionally tried to mislead the consumer. Answer choices B, D, and E are not supported by the passage.

18. **The answer is D.** The passage states, "Electrical plants experience outages and use backup provided by the entire interconnected power system. If wind plants were added to this intricate system, deficiencies in their abilities could be compensated for as well." Therefore, the author argues that outages in wind plants could be handled in the same way that outages at electrical plants are. Answer choice E might have appeared to be correct. However, the author only states, "It is important to remember that electricity demand is not created or controlled by utility operators." The author does not state who or what controls the supply and demand of energy resources. Likewise, answer choices A, B, and C are not supported by the passage.

19. **The answer is C.** An "iconoclast" is a "person who challenges beliefs or ideas." The noun "doctrine" refers to a group of "beliefs." A general sentence that can be used to describe the analogy is: A(n) "____" is a person who challenges "____." A "rebel" is a person who challenges "convention." A "xenophobe" does not challenge "fear"; a "xenophobe" is a person "afraid of things that are unfamiliar or different," so answer choice A is incorrect. A "magistrate" is a person who "has the power to enforce laws," but does not challenge "judgment," so answer choice B is incorrect. An "incumbent" is the politician "currently in office"; an "incumbent" does not necessarily challenge "politics," so answer choice D is incorrect. Answer choice E is incorrect for the same reason.

20. **The answer is D.** The context of the sentence indicates that something about certain methods of instruction has a negative impact on novel, or new, techniques. A method of instruction that is "prevalent" is "widely or commonly practiced," which could make the "introduction" of new techniques difficult. Answer choices A, B, C, and E are incorrect because they do not fit within the context of the sentence. Refer to Appendix A for definitions of some of the words in these answer choices.

21. **The answer is C.** The passage reflects on the book's influence and different interpretations or ways to view the story. Answer choice A might have appeared to be correct. However, although the actual book does explore racism and African American women, the passage is not focused on examining these issues. Likewise, answer choices B, D, and E are not supported by the passage.

22. **The answer is E.** In the last paragraph, the author of the passage refers to the book as "relevant," "classic," and "important," which best supports answer choice E. Answer choices A, B, C, and D are incorrect because the author of the passage reveals a thoughtful appreciation for the book, and these choices all have a negative connotation.

23. **The answer is A.** The passage states, "Angelou's story is so unique because it is autobiographical. Marguerite Johnson is a reflection of Maya Angelou in every way that matters." The passage also states, "Through the story and speaking in the voice of Marguerite Johnson, Angelou finds inspiration from her childhood memories and includes these experiences to develop the book." Answer choices B, C, D, and E are beyond the scope of the passage.

24. **The answer is A.** The passage clearly states, "*I Know Why the Caged Bird Sings* was popular among white audiences because it did not have

an openly hostile attitude or hold grudges about the effects of slavery." Answers to the questions posed in choices B, C, D, and E are not supported by information in the passage, because they are beyond the scope of the passage.

25. **The answer is C.** The author discusses how high horizontal winds and vertical turbulence/convective updrafts affect long distance seed dispersal. Answer choice A might have appeared to be correct. Although the passage does mention that scientists studied some characteristics of the plant, the main purpose of the passage is to discuss weather conditions that affect long distance seed dispersal. Answer choices B, D, and E are not supported by details in the passage.

26. **The answer is B.** The passage suggests that for some plants, the ability to disperse seeds across long distances contributes to the continuance of the species. "Seed dispersal is crucial for the survival of many species of plants. Long distance dispersal of seeds affects many ecological and evolutionary processes." Answer choice D might have appeared to be correct. However, the passage states that the dandelion is one of the *best* examples of plants that rely on long distance wind dispersal not that it is one of the *only* examples of such a plant. Likewise, answer choices A, C, and E are not supported by the passage.

27. **The answer is C.** To "postulate" means to "make a claim, or assert the truth of." "Instigate" means to "urge on"; "deplore" means to "condemn"; "subsume" means to "contain or include"; "transpose" means to "change the order or arrangement of." None of these words fit within the context of the sentence, so answer choices A, B, D, and E are incorrect.

28. **The answer is C.** "Irascible" is an adjective that means "easily angered." "Tolerant" is an adjective that means "respectful and forgiving under provocation." "Choleric" means "bad tempered," which is a synonym of "irascible," so answer choice B is incorrect. "Adroit" means "skillful or adept," which is not an antonym of "irascible," so answer choice E is incorrect. Likewise, answer choices A and D are incorrect because neither "serious" nor "finicky" are antonyms of "irascible."

29. **The answer is B.** To "vilify" means to "make vicious statements about" someone or something. To "eulogize" means to "praise highly," which is most nearly opposite in meaning to "vilify." "Censure" means to "criticize or disapprove of"; "incinerate" means to "burn completely"; "parse" means to "break or separate into components"; "squelch"

means to "crush or squash." None of these word are antonyms of "vil-ify," so answer choices A, C, D, and E are incorrect.

30. **The answer is E.** A "scale" represents an orderly progression or range of "notes." Likewise, a "spectrum" represents an orderly progression or range of "colors." Answer choices A, B, C, and D contain related word pairs, but none have the same relationship as "scale" and "notes." A "song" is not an orderly progression of "singers," nor is a "family" an orderly progression of "children," for example.

Quantitative

1. **The answer is B.** To solve this problem, you must determine the value of the quantity in each column. Factors are all of the numbers that will divide evenly into one number. The greatest odd factor of 360 is 45 ($45 \times 8 = 360$); the greatest even factor of 360 less than 90 is 72 ($72 \times 5 = 360$). The quantity in Column B (72) is greater than the quantity in Column A (45).

2. **The answer is D.** To solve this problem, select values for x and y. The quantity in Column A is greater when x and y are between 0 and 1; the quantity in Column B is greater when x and y are both greater than 1. Because it is not specified what the values of x and y are, you cannot determine a relationship between the quantities.

3. **The answer is A.** The problem states that $a > c$ and that both a and c are greater than 0 (they are positive numbers). This means that $ca > c^2$. Pick numbers to verify:

   ➤ When $a = 2$ and $c = 1$, $ca = 2$ and $c^2 = 1$.

   ➤ When $a = 4$ and $c = 3$, $ca = 12$ and $c^2 = 9$, and so on.

   Therefore, the quantity in Column A has a larger numerator than does the quantity in Column B. Because, based on information in the problem, $a > b$, the quantity in Column A has a smaller denominator than does the quantity in Column B. Because the quantity in Column A has a larger numerator and smaller denominator than the quantity in Column B, the quantity in Column A is greater than the quantity in Column B.

4. **The answer is A.** The easiest way to solve this problem is to first rec-ognize that $\sqrt{3}$ is between 1.5 and 2. Substitute both 1.5 and 2 for $\sqrt{3}$ in each quantity as follows:

➤ $3 + 7(1.5) = 13.5$

➤ $7 + 3(1.5) = 11.5$

The quantity in Column A is greater than the quantity in Column B.

➤ $3 + 7(2) = 17$

➤ $7 + 3(2) = 13$

The quantity in Column A is still greater than the quantity in Column B. Therefore, you can conclude that if you performed the calculations shown, the quantity in Column A would be greater than the quantity in Column B.

5. **The answer is B.** To solve this problem, set the values in the numerators equal to each other and the values in the denominators equal to each other as follows:

➤ If $\dfrac{4x}{3y} = \dfrac{8}{6}$, then $4x = 8$ and $3y = 6$.

Now you can solve for x and y.

➤ $4x = 8$, so $x = 2$

➤ $3y = 6$, so $y = 2$.

Substitute 2 for x and 2 for y into $\dfrac{9x}{12y}$ to get $\dfrac{(9 \times 2)}{(12 \times 2)}$, or $\dfrac{18}{24}$. Reduce this fraction by dividing both the numerator and the denominator by 6 to get $\dfrac{3}{4}$.

6. **The answer is B.** According to the figure, t is the supplement of the 30 degree angle. The sum of supplemental angles is 180°. Therefore, $t = 180 - 30$, or 150°. Because s is the supplement to t, $s = 180 - 150$, or 30°. The figure shows that p is the complement of s. Complementary angles total 90°. Therefore, $p = 90 - 30$, or 60°. Calculate $2p + 3s - t$ as follows:

➤ $2(60) + 3(30) - 150 =$

➤ $120 + 90 - 150 = 60$.

7. **The answer is B.** The easiest way to solve this problem is to recognize that $3{,}200 \div 80$ is 40. Therefore, $3{,}200 \div 79$ will be slightly larger than 40, but it will still be less than 45. The quantity in Column B is greater than the quantity in Column A.

8. **The answer is B.** To solve this problem, first recognize that $\frac{6}{12} = \frac{1}{2}$, and $\frac{15}{30} = \frac{1}{2}$. Because the numerator in Column A is greater than 12, $\frac{6}{13}$ must be less than $\frac{1}{2}$. Because the numerator in Column B is less than 30, $\frac{15}{28}$ must be greater than $\frac{1}{2}$.

9. **The answer is A.** To solve this problem, simply calculate the values in each column, as follows:

➤ The decimal equivalent of 80 percent is 0.8; $(0.8)(40) = 32$

➤ The decimal equivalent of 60 percent is 0.6; $(0.6)(50) = 30$

Therefore, the quantity in Column A (32) is greater than the quantity in Column B (30).

10. **The answer is A.** This problem tests your knowledge of absolute values $|4 - 3x| = 5$ can be written as $4 - 3x = 5$. Solve for x as follows:

➤ $4 - 3x = 5$

➤ $-3x = 1$

➤ $-x = \frac{1}{3}$

Therefore, $x - \frac{1}{3}$.

11. **The answer is C.** The first step in solving this problem is to solve the equation for x, as follows:

➤ $\frac{3}{4}x + 7 = 28$; subtract 7 from both sides.

➤ $\frac{3}{4}x = 21$; multiply both sides by $\frac{4}{3}$.

➤ $x = 28$

Therefore, the quantity in Column A is equal to the quantity in Column B.

12. **The answer is B.** This problem takes two steps. The question states, "two positive integers whose product is 18," which means your choices are:

➤ $1 \times 18 = 18$

➤ $2 \times 9 = 18$

➤ $3 \times 6 = 18$

Now that you have completed the first step, you have three potential solutions for the second step. You are looking for the sum of two positive integers that must coordinate with the first step and be one of the answer choices. The second step of the problem indicates that you should add the integers in each of the first steps, as follows:

➤ $1 + 18 = 19$, which is not one of the answer choices.

➤ $2 + 9 = 11$, which is answer choice B.

➤ $3 + 6 = 9$, which is not one of the answer choices.

13. **The answer is C.** The best way to solve this problem is to set up two equations, as follows:

➤ Equation 1: Seniors = 5 + 2(Sophomores)

➤ Equation 2: Seniors + Sophomores = 20. You know this because, according to the problem, $\frac{1}{5}$ of the class are neither Seniors nor Sophomores. $\frac{1}{5}$ of 25 is 5, so 25 – 5, or 20 students are either Sophomores or Seniors.

Rearrange Equation 2, as follows:

➤ Seniors = 20 – Sophomores. Now substitute this value into Equation 1 and solve for the number of Sophomores.

➤ 20 – Sophomores = 5 + 2(Sophomores). Solve for the number of Sophomores:

➤ 15 = 2 Sophomores + 1 Sophomore; there are 5 Sophomores.

If there are 5 Sophomores, there must be 15 Seniors. Therefore, the quantity in Column A is equal to the quantity in Column B.

14. **The answer is E.** According to the pie chart, hydroelectricity is included in the "Other" category. Because the chart does not indicate what part of the "Other" category is composed of hydroelectricity, you do not have enough information to calculate the percentage of hydro-electricity.

15. **The answer is C.** According to the pie chart, nuclear energy com-prises 7% of the primary energy sources, and coal comprises 11% of the primary energy sources. Therefore, the ratio of nuclear power to coal is $\frac{7}{11}$. Answer choice A might have appealed to you, but it is incorrect because it indicates the fraction equivalent of 7%, not the ratio of nuclear power to coal.

16. **The answer is D.** Column B asks for the number of parts produced *after* the second shift's first break. Because there was no information provided regarding what occurred after the first break, you cannot determine a relationship between the quantities in Column A and Column B.

17. **The answer is B.** To solve this problem, set the radius of the base equal to x. The height will then be equivalent to $5x$. The formula for the circumference of a circle is $2\pi r$, so the circumference if the base of K is $2\pi x$. You know that $2\pi x$ will be greater than $5x$ because 2π is approximately equal to 2(3.14), or 6.28. Therefore, the quantity in Column B is greater than the quantity in Column A.

18. **The answer is B.** The figure shown is a regular hexagon. To find the sum of the measures of the interior angles of an n-sided polygon, use the formula $180° \, (n - 2)$, where n is the number of sides. The sum of the measures of the interior angles of a hexagon is $180° \, (6 - 2)$, or $720°$. Because the angles are congruent, each angle is $\frac{720°}{6}$, or $120°$. Therefore, $x = 180° - 120°$, or $60°$.

19. **The answer is E.** This problem has three steps. Before you begin, remember that "7^3 divided by 9" is another way of saying $(7 \times 7 \times 7) \div 9$. The first step is calculating $7 \times 7 \times 7$. You should recognize that $7 \times 7 = 49$. Simply multiply 49×7 to get 343. An easier calculation might be to multiply 7 by 50 to get 350, and then subtract 7 from 350 to get 343. Now, you need solve the second step, which is $\frac{343}{9}$. Use long division to solve, as follows:

➤ 9 goes into 34 three times $(9 \times 3 = 27)$

➤ 34 minus 27 = 7; bring the 3 down from the ones place in 343

➤ 9 goes into 73 eight times $(9 \times 8 = 72)$

➤ $73 - 72 = 1$

So, 343 divided by 9 equals 38, remainder of 1.

20. **The answer is D.** According to the chart shown, the recommended daily dietary intake of sodium is less than 2,400 milligrams for both 2,000 and 2,500 calorie diets. You can eliminate answer choice A, because it does not include Roman numeral II. The chart also indicates that the recommended daily dietary intake of potassium is 3,500 milligrams for both 2,000 and 2,500 calorie diets. Therefore, both Roman numeral II and Roman numeral IV correctly answer the question, but neither Roman numeral I nor Roman numeral III do.

21. **The answer is E.** According to the chart shown, if you eat a total of 2,000 calories per day, the recommended daily dietary intake of fat is less than 65 grams. Therefore, an appropriate amount of fat to consume would be 60 grams.

22. **The answer is C.** The easiest way to solve this problem is to pick numbers for the variables that work within the equations given. Start with the first equation, as follows:

➤ $a + c = 17$

If a is 15 and c is 2, the equation works.

Replace c with 2 in the second equation and solve for b.

➤ $b - 2 = 2$, so b must be 4.

Now, because a is 15 and b is 4, $a + b$ must equal 19.

As long as you pick two numbers that solve the first equation, and use those numbers in the subsequent equations, you will always arrive at 19 as a solution.

23. **The answer is D.** The formula for the circumference of a circle is $2\pi r$. The measure of the radii of both circles must be provided to determine which circumference is larger. Because those measures are not given, you cannot determine the relationship between the quantities in Column A and Column B.

24. **The answer is B.** A point located on the circumference of a circle always travels farther than a point located within the circumference of the circle. Therefore, because 6 inches from the center of the wheel is still within the circle (remember, the radius is 9 inches), the quantity in Column B is greater than the quantity in Column A.

25. **The answer is D.** The measures of the angles are not given, so you cannot determine the relationship between the quantities in Column A and Column B.

26. **The answer is D.** To solve this problem, apply the distance formula, which says that distance = rate × time. You know that the rate is equal to x and the time is $\frac{y}{60}$ because the problem states the time in minutes. Thus, the number of miles that the car traveled in the last y minutes would be $x \times \frac{y}{60}$, or $\frac{xy}{60}$.

27. **The answer is C.** The first step in solving this problem is to perform the mathematical operations in the correct order. Because you should perform the operations inside the parentheses first, your first step should result in the following:

➤ $(37 - 9) = 28$

➤ $(13 + 15) = 28$

You now have (28)(28), or 28^2, under the square root. The next step in solving this problem is to recognize that squaring any number and then taking the resulting product's square root leads to the original number. In this case, that number is 28. Remember that you will not be required to perform any complicated calculations on this test; most questions that seem difficult can often be solved easily through the application of a little logic.

28. **The answer is C.** This problem requires you to move the decimal point the appropriate number of places. The first step in solving this problem is to recognize that $81.24 \times \frac{1}{100}$ is equivalent to $\frac{81.24}{100}$. Because you are dividing 81.24 by 100, you must move the decimal place to the left two places (there are two zeros in 100).

➤ $\frac{81.24}{100} = 0.8124$

GRE Vocabulary List

The following words have been selected by experienced GRE instructors as representative of the vocabulary level that is expected on the GRE. Many of the words have appeared on actual GRE tests numerous times.

A

abate—To reduce or lessen.

aberration—A deviation or departure from the norm.

abeyance—A temporary inactivity or suspension.

abjure—To forswear or abstain from; to give up.

abrade—To wear down or erode.

abrogate—To end or do away with something.

abridge—To shorten or reduce.

abscond—To withdraw and hide, typically to avoid arrest.

absurd—Extremely ridiculous or completely lacking reason.

abysmal—Very profound or deep; very bad.

accretion—A gradual increase in the amount or size of something.

acquisitive—Characterized by a strong desire to gain or retain information.

acrid—Harsh or bitter taste or smell.

acute—Sharp; quick and precise; intense.

adhere—To stick fast; to remain in support of.

adjacent—In the nearest position; next to.

adroit—Showing skill and experience.

aesthete—One with an excessive sensibility to beauty.

aesthetic—Appeals to the senses because it is beautiful.

affinity—Natural attraction; inherent similarity.

aggrandize—To extend or exaggerate.

alienate—To isolate oneself from others or another person from oneself.

amalgamate—To merge or combine into a single thing.

ambiguous—Unclear or capable of having more than one meaning.

ambivalent—Characterized by uncertainty; unable to decide between opposites.

ameliorate—To enhance or improve something.

amenable—Responsive to suggestion; willing.

amiable—Friendly and pleasant.

amortize—To reduce gradually over a period of time.

anachronistic—Out of order; chronologically misplaced.

annotate—To provide with extra notes or comments.

anodize—To coat or protect a metal surface with oxide.

anomaly—Something that is different from the norm.

antibody—A protein normally present in the body that neutralizes an antigen, thereby producing immunity to the antigen.

apathy—A lack of any emotion or concern.

arabesque—An intricate and elaborate design or composition.

arbitration—The process of resolving a dispute by presenting it to a third party.

arboreal—Relating to trees.

ardor—Intense feelings; passion.

aristocracy—The upper class.

aristocrat—A member of the elite, ruling class.

articulate—*v.* To clearly explain; *adj.* the quality of being able to speak clearly.

ascribe—To attribute to a specific source; to assign a characteristic.

asperity—Roughness or severity.

assay—*n.* An analysis or examination. *v.* to subject to analysis; to examine.

assertion—A declaration or affirmation.

assimilate—To incorporate into; to make similar.

assuage—To lessen or ease.

assiduous—Characteristic of careful and persistent effort.

assumption—Something believed to be true without proof, unsupported evidence.

aver—To declare as true; to maintain.

aversion—Strong dislike.

B

banish—To force to leave; to exile.

beneficent—Characterized by acts of kindness; beneficial.

benevolence—An inclination to be kind or charitable.

benign—Kind, mild.

bequest—*v.* The act of passing on; *n.* something that is passed on.

bereft—Being deprived of or losing something.

blithe—Carefree or joyous; casual.

bolster—*n.* A narrow cushion. *v.* to support or strengthen.

bourgeoisie—Middle class.

brazen—Bold or shameless; insolent.

buoyant—Tending to float; lighthearted.

burgeoning—Thriving or growing rapidly.

C

cadge—To beg.

capricious—Impulsive.

castigate—To punish or criticize severely.

catalyst—Something that causes something else to happen, usually without being directly involved in or changed by the process.

celestial—Of or relating to the heavens; supremely good or divine.

censure—A formal criticism or intense disapproval.

chronicle—A detailed narrative.

churlish—Vulgar or surly; difficult to work with.

circumscribe—To enclose or define limits.

circumspect—Mindful of potential consequences; prudent.

cite—To quote as an example or proof.

cleave—To split or tear apart; also, to cling to.

coagulate—To transform into a soft, solid mass.

coalesce—To unite or come together.

coerce—To force or threaten someone into thinking a certain way; to compel.

cogent—Convincing and reasonable.

cognitive—Relating to conscious intellectual activity, such as thinking, reasoning, and learning.

coherent—Sticking together; orderly and logical.

coincidental—Occurring by chance.

commensurate—Corresponding in size, degree, or duration.

commingle—To blend or mix together.

complaisant—Showing a willingness to please; obliging.

comprise—To consist of; to include.

concede—To admit or reluctantly yield; to surrender.

concoct—To prepare by mixing ingredients together; devise a plan.

congruent—Corresponding; equal, as in length.

consternation—Alarm or fear.

conducive—Contributive; favorable.

contradict—To assert the opposite.

converge—To meet or come together at a common point.

convivial—Festive and sociable.

cordial—Sincere; courteous.

correlate—To have corresponding characteristics.

corroborate—To confirm, to substantiate with evidence.

countenance—Facial features or expression.

craven—Cowardly; fearful.

credulous—Easily deceived; believes too readily.

cryptic—Mystifying; hidden or concealed meaning.

culmination—Completion or climax.

culpable—Deserving of blame; guilty.

curmudgeon—An ill-tempered, stubborn person.

D

debilitate—To weaken or impair.

decimate—To destroy large numbers of; to inflict great damage upon.

decry—To denounce or criticize.

defamation—A malicious or abusive attack on one's character.

delve—To deeply search through.

demagogue—A leader or speaker who appeals to the emotions or prejudices of the people.

demise—The end of existence; death.

demur—To express opposition.

denigrate—To speak ill of; to belittle.

depict—To represent or describe.

deplore—To condemn; disapprove of or regret.

deposition—Testimony given under oath.

derision—Contempt or scorn.

derivative—*adj.* Copied or adapted. *n.* something derived.

desiccant—A substance used as a drying agent.

desiccated—Dried up from a lack of moisture.

desultory—Inconsistent and irregular, aimless.

deterrence—A negative emotional influence.

dexterity—Skill and ease of movement, especially of the hands; cleverness.

diatribe—An abusive, insulting verbal attack.

didactic—Intended for the purposes of teaching or instructing.

dilate—To make larger; expand.

diligent—Continuously putting in great effort.

disabuse—To free someone of believing something that is untrue.

discern—To differentiate or distinguish; to perceive.

disconcerting—Unsettling.

disinter—To bring up into view.

dislodge—To remove from a former position.

disparity—The state of being different or unequal.

disperse—To scatter or spread out.

dissemble—To disguise or conceal.

dissident—*adj.* Disagreeable. *n.* one who disagrees.

dissipate—To drive away; scatter.

dissonance—Lack of harmony; discord.

diverge—To move apart, or extend in different directions; to differ in opinion.

divest—To get rid of.

docile—Easy to train or teach.

doctrinaire—A stubbornly persistent or impractical person, particularly with regard to a specific theory.

dogmatic—Characterized by a strong belief in a certain unproven doctrine or opinion.

dubious—Unsure, skeptical.

E

eccentric—*adj.* Departing from convention. *n.* one who deviates from the norm.

eclectic—Combining elements from many different sources or styles.

effrontery—Characterized by insolent and presumptuous behavior.

egalitarian—*adj.* Favorable or equal standards for all. *n.* one who believes in equality of all people.

egregious—Noticeably bad or offensive.

elegy—A mournful poem or song.

eloquent—Very clear and precise; quality of being skilled in clear and precise speech.

elucidate—To clarify.

emaciated—Undernourished and characterized by thinness.

emancipation—The act of freeing or liberating.

emollient—*adj.* Softening or soothing. *n.* a softening agent.

empirical—Based on or can be proven by observation and experiment.

emulate—To follow an admirable example; imitate.

encomium—Warm praise; a tribute.

endorse—To support or sign.

enervate—To weaken or deprive of strength.

engender—To give rise to; originate.

enigmatic—Unexplainable, puzzling.

entity—A discrete unit or being.

enumerate—To state things in a list.

ephemeral—Temporary; fleeting.

epicure—A person with refined taste.

equivocal—Uncertain or ambiguous.

erosion—The process or wearing away; weathering.

erudite—Learned; having great knowledge.

esoteric—Understood by few people; mysterious.

espouse—To choose to follow or support something.

estimable—Admirable; deserving of esteem.

ethical—In line with the principles of right and wrong.

eulogy—High praise; a speech often given in praise of someone who has died.

euphemism—An inoffensive expression substituted for one that is deemed offensive.

exacerbate—To intensify bitterness or violence.

exceptional—Having uncommonly great qualities.

excoriate—To chafe; to denounce.

exculpate—To remove blame; acquit.

exhort—To urge or provoke.

exigent—Demanding immediate attention; urgent.

explicate—To explain or make comprehensible.

expunge—To get rid of or erase.

extant—Currently existing.

extenuating—Partially justifiable.

extol—To praise or glorify.

extrovert—A person characterized by concern with things outside of himself or herself.

extricable—Capable of being freed.

exultant—Gleeful because of success.

F

faction—A quarrelsome group, usually formed within a larger group, whose members generally disagree with the consensus of the larger group.

fallacy—An error in reasoning.

familial—Relating to the family.

fathomable—Capable of being understood.

fatuous—Foolish or delusive.

feckless—Lacking in purpose; careless.

feign—To fabricate or deceive.

feint—*n*. A deceptive, diversionary action. *v*. to make a deceptive show of.

fidelity—Faithfulness or allegiance.

florid—Flushed with color; ornate.

fluxes—A continued flow.

foil—*v*. To prevent from being successful. *n*. a setback.

foment—To incite or agitate.

forage—To hunt around or search for food.

formidable—Awe-inspiring, capable of causing fear.

fortuitous—Happening by accident or chance.

forum—A public meeting place; a medium for open discussion.

fracas—A noisy fight; a brawl.

G

gainsay—To deny or contradict.

garrison—A military post; the troops stationed at a military post.

garrulous—Very talkative.

gaudy—Tastelessly flashy.

genre—A type, class, or category.

gist—Main idea.

glib—Doing something with ease and slickness, but lacking sincerity.

gratuitous—For no reason and at no cost.

gregarious—Sociable; enjoying the company of others.

grievous—Causing grief or pain; serious.

guile—Cunning; shrewdness.

H

hackneyed—Unoriginal, overused.

harrow—To torment or cause suffering and agony.

hierarchical—Classified according to various criteria into successive levels.

herbaceous—Characteristic of a nonwoody plant.

heterogeneous—Comprised of dissimilar elements; not homogeneous.

hew—To cut or shape with an ax.

hitherto—Until this time.

hypothesis—A tentative explanation that can be tested by further investigation and experimentation.

I

iconoclast—One who seeks to destroy traditional or popular ideas and beliefs.

idiosyncrasy—A peculiar characteristic.

idolatrous—Having an excessive adoration of someone or something.

idyll—A literary work, poem, or experience that's carefree and simple.

immutable—Not subject to change.

impending—Threatening to occur.

imperturbable—Hard to excite or upset; very calm.

impetuous—Characterized by sudden emotion; impulsive.

implosion—A violent, inward collapse.

inadvertent—Unintentional, often related to carelessness.

inchoate—In the beginning stages.

incinerate—To set fire to and burn until reduced to ashes.

incongruous—Inconsistent; lacking in harmony.

incorrigible—Impossible to change or reform.

indigenous—Native; innate.

inevitable—Impossible to avoid; predictable.

infer—To conclude from evidence.

ingenuity—Cleverness or imagination.

inherent—Naturally occurring, permanent element or attribute.

inimical—Harmful or unfriendly.

innate—Possessed at birth; a natural characteristic.

inscrutable—Difficult to understand; having an obscure nature.

insinuate—To subtly imply.

insipid—Dull; lacking in flavor or zest.

insular—Isolated; narrow-minded.

integral—Essential or necessary.

intemperate—Excessive; subject to extremes.

intercede—To mediate, or plead on another's behalf.

interpolate—To insert or introduce between.

intractable—Difficult to manage; stubborn.

inundate—To quickly overwhelm or exceed capacity.

inure—To cause to accept; habituate.

invariable—Not subject to question or change; constant.

irascible—Easily angered.

isotope—One of two or more atoms with the same atomic number but with different numbers of neutrons.

J

jovial—Full of joy and happiness.

judicious—Sensible; having good judgment.

juxtapose—To place things next to each other to compare or contrast.

K

keen—Quick-witted; sharp.

kudos—Compliments for achievements.

L

labyrinthine—Highly intricate and complex.

lambaste—To beat or scold sharply.

laudable—Deserving praise; favorable.

languish—To become weak; to become disenchanted.

latter—The second of two things mentioned; nearer the end.

lavish—*adj*. Elaborate and luxurious. *v*. to freely and boundlessly bestow.

lenient—Easy-going; tolerant.

lethargic—Deficient in alertness; lacking energy.

listless—Characterized by a lack of energy.

liturgy—A prescribed set of forms for public religious worship.

loathsome—Offensive; disgusting.

loquacious—Very talkative or rambling.

lucid—Easily understood; clear.

ludicrous—Laughable or foolish.

M

magistrate—A civil or judicial official vested with limited power.

magnanimous—Courageous or generous.

maladroit—Inept or incompetent person.

malevolent—Purposefully wishing harm on others.

malinger—To pretend or exaggerate illness to escape work.

manifest—*adj*. Clearly recognizable. *v*. to make clear. *n*. a list of transported goods or passengers used for record keeping.

mar—To inflict damage; to impair.

melancholy—Glumness; deep contemplative thought.

melodramatic—Overly emotional or sentimental.

mercurial—Prone to sudden, unpredictable change; volatile.

metamorphosis—A transformation or change.

meticulous—Very careful and precise.

mettle—Courage.

minuscule—Extremely small; unimportant.

miscreant—Villain; evildoer.

mitigate—To reduce the severity of something.

mollify—To calm down or alleviate.

munificence—The act of liberally giving.

mutation—An alteration or change.

N

nadir—The lowest point.

nascent—Just beginning to exist.

negligent—Having a habit of behaving carelessly.

negligible—Meaningless and insignificant.

noisome—Offensive or disgusting; harmful.

nostalgia—A bittersweet longing for the past.

noxious—Unwholesome or harmful.

O

obdurate—Firm, stubborn.

obscurity—The condition of being unknown.

obsolete—No longer in use; outmoded.

obtuse—Lacking intellectual clarity; blunt, or slow-witted.

obviate—To render unnecessary.

occult—Supernatural or kept secret.

odium—Hatred.

oligarchy—A political system governed by a few people.

onerous—Very troublesome.

opaque—Impenetrable by light; not clear.

opprobrium—Infamy, disgrace, or contempt.

ossify—To become bony.

ostracize—To eliminate from a group.

P

paean—A joyful expression or exultation.

paradox—A statement that seems contradictory but is actually true.

paragon—An example of excellence.

parse—To break down into components.

penchant—A tendency or fondness.

pedantic—Characterized by a narrow concern for formality.

perceive—To become aware of something, usually through the senses.

percolate—To slowly pass through.

peripatetic—*adj.* Walking from place to place. *n.* one who walks from place to place.

peripheral—Located in or near a boundary.

perjury—Knowingly lying under oath.

perpetuate—To prolong the existence or idea of; to make everlasting.

pertinent—Relevant or appropriate.

peruse—To examine with great care.

pervasive—Spread throughout.

phenomenon—An unusual or significant occurrence.

philistine—*adj.* Indifferent. *n.* one who lacks knowledge in a specific area.

pith—Significant; essential.

placate—To calm.

placid—Calm or quiet.

plagiarize—To copy another's work and pretend that it is original.

platitudinous—Making a claim of importance; pretentious.

plausible—Reasonable; likely.

plethora—Excess or overabundance.

poignant—Profoundly moving; incisive.

polarity—The possession of two opposing attributes or ideas.

postulate—To put forth or assert.

pragmatic—Concerned with facts; practical.

precarious—Unsure of oneself; insecure.

precedent—An example or event that is used to justify similar occurrences at a later time.

precipitate—To cause something to happen very suddenly or prematurely.

precept—A guiding rule or principle.

preclude—To prevent or make impossible.

precursor—One that precedes or suggests another.

presage—An omen or other warning sign.

prescience—Foresight; the power to see the future.

presumably—By reasonable assumption.

prevaricate—To lie.

primordial—Happening first or very early.

probity—Integrity and uprightness.

prodigal—Wasteful; extravagant.

profuse—Plentiful or abundant.

progeny—Offspring or product.

prognosis—Forecast or prediction.

proletariat—The poorest class of working people.

proliferate—To grow or increase rapidly.

prolixity—Wordiness; boring verboseness.

promulgate—To publicize.

propagate—To cause to multiply or spread.

prototype—An original form of something.

protract—To lengthen or prolong.

prowess—Great skill or ability in something.

proximate—Very near; closely related.

prudish—Exaggeratedly proper; righteous.

Q

quaff—To drink heartily.

querulous—Characterized by constant complaining or whining.

quixotic—Unpredictable and impractical.

quotidian—Ordinary; occurring daily.

R

rancor—Bitter resentment.

rarefy—To thin out.

recondite—Not easily understood; ambiguous.

rhetoric—Effective use of language; a style of speaking or writing.

recalcitrant—Stubbornly resistant; defiant.

recluse—Withdrawn from society.

recompense—Payment or compensation in return for something.

reconciliation—The reestablishing of cordial relations.

recondite—Difficult to understand.

refute—To prove to be false; to deny the truth of.

relegate—To refer or assign to a particular place or category.

renunciation—A rejection.

rent—The past tense of rend; to rip apart.

reparation—Compensation given to make amends.

reproachful—Expressing disapproval.

repudiate—To reject or refuse as valid.

resolute—Definite; determined.

resplendent—Dazzling or brilliant in appearance.

resonant—Strong and deep; lasting.

resurrect—To bring back to life.

rigor—Strictness or severity.

rumination—Meditation.

S

sacrilege—To misuse something that is considered sacred.

sage—One revered for experience and wisdom.

salutary—Promoting physical well-being.

sanctimonious—Hypocritical; feigning righteaousness.

sanction—*n*. Authoritative permission. *v*. to give official approval to.

satirize—To insult using witty language.

sedulous—Persevering; industrious.

sidereal—Relating to the stars.

skepticism—An attitude of doubt or disbelief.

solace—Comfort; safety.

solicitous—Concerned; thoughtful.

specious—Appearing to be reasonable but is actually deceptive.

speculate—To theorize on the basis of inconclusive evidence.

spontaneous—Arising without apparent external cause; unrestrained.

squelch—To crush or silence.

stanch—To stop or check the flow of.

static—Fixed or stationary.

stint—A length of time spent in a particular way.

stoic—Indifferent or unaffected.

stratagem—A clever scheme.

subjective—Depending on a person's attitudes or opinions.

substantiation—The act of validating or supporting.

subsume—To contain or include.

subvert—To undermine, ruin, or overthrow.

supine—Laying down on the back; indifferent.

surfeit—An overabundance or excessiveness.

susceptible—Easily influenced or likely to be affected.

synchronized—Occurring at the same time and at the same rate.

syntax—Systematic arrangement of words in sentences.

T

tacit—An expression that uses no words.

tangential—Slightly connected; superficially relevant.

temperance—Moderation and self-restraint.

tenuous—Very thin or consisting of little substance.

terrestrial—Relating to dry land as opposed to water; relating to the Earth as opposed to other planets.

torpor—State of sluggishness.

tout—To promote or solicit.

tractable—Easy to control or work with.

transmutation—A change or transformation.

transcend—To go above and beyond; to rise above.

transgress—To exceed or violate.

transpose—To reverse the order of; interchange.

tyro—A beginner; a novice.

U

unalloyed—Pure; complete.

unilaterally—Performed in a one-sided manner.

unstinting—Very generous.

unprecedented—Having no previous example.

urbanity—Refinement and elegance.

usury—A high rate of interest charged on borrowed money.

utilitarian—Useful or practical.

utopian—Ideal; visionary.

V

vacillate—To swing or waver.

variegated—Having a variety of colors or marks.

vehement—Forceful; extreme intensity of emotions.

venal—Corrupt easily; to pay off.

venerable—Worthy of respect and honor.

veracity—Truthfulness.

verbose—Wordy; long-winded.

verisimilitude—The quality of appearing to be true or real.

veritable—Genuine or authentic.

versatile—Having many uses or a variety of abilities.

vilify—To make negative statements about; to malign.

vindication—The act of clearing someone or something from blame.

virtually—In almost all instances; simulated as by a computer.

viscid—Very sticky.

vituperate—To criticize in an abusive way.

voluminous—Large in volume or bulk.

voracious—Excessively greedy.

W

wane—To gradually decrease.

wary—Cautious and untrusting.

whet—To sharpen or stimulate.

wily—Very sly; deceptive.

X

xenophobe—One who fears strangers or foreign peoples.

Z

zealous—Very passionate or enthusiastic.

zenith—The peak point.

Math Reference

It is assumed that most GRE test-takers will have a basic understanding of certain mathematical concepts and skills. The following reference information should serve as a review of the concepts tested on the GRE General Test.

Arithmetic

These questions can involve basic arithmetic operations, operations on radical expressions, and operations involving exponents, factoring, absolute value, prime numbers, percents, ratios, and number lines.

The Properties of Integers

The following are properties of integers that are often tested on the GRE.

➤ Integers include both positive and negative whole numbers.

➤ Zero is considered an integer.

➤ Consecutive integers follow one another and differ by 1.

➤ The value of a number does not change when multiplied by 1.

➤ Multiplication by 0 always results in 0.

➤ Division by 0 cannot be defined.

➤ Multiplication or division of two integers with different signs (+ or –) yields a negative result.

➤ Multiplication or division of two negative integers yields a positive result.

Order of Operations (PEMDAS)

Following is a description of the correct order in which to perform mathematical operations. The abbreviation PEMDAS stands for Parentheses, Exponents, Multiplication, Division, Addition, Subtraction. It should help you to remember to do the operations in the correct order, as follows:

➤ **P**—First, do the operations within the *parentheses*, if any.

➤ **E**—Next, do the *exponents*, if any.

➤ **M**—Next, do the *multiplication*, in order from left to right.

➤ **D**—Next, do the *division*, in order from left to right.

➤ **A**—Next, do the *addition*, in order from left to right.

➤ **S**—Finally, do the *subtraction*, in order from left to right.

Fractions

The following are properties of fractions and rational numbers that are often tested on the GRE.

➤ The reciprocal of any number, n, is expressed as 1 over n, or $\frac{1}{n}$. The product (multiplication) of a number and its reciprocal is always 1.

➤ To change any fraction to a decimal, divide the numerator by the denominator. For example, $\frac{3}{4} = 3 \div 4$, or .75.

➤ Multiplying and dividing both the numerator and the denominator of a fraction by the same nonzero number results in an equivalent fraction. So, $\frac{2}{7} \times \frac{2}{2} = \frac{4}{14}$, which can be reduced to $\frac{2}{7}$.

➤ When adding and subtracting like fractions, add or subtract the numerators and write the sum or difference over the denominator. So, $\frac{1}{8} + \frac{2}{8} = \frac{3}{8}$, and $\frac{4}{7} - \frac{2}{7} = \frac{2}{7}$.

➤ When multiplying fractions, multiply the numerators to get the numerator of the product, and multiply the denominators to get the denominator of the product. For example, $\frac{3}{5} \times \frac{7}{8} = \frac{21}{40}$.

➤ To divide fractions, multiply the first fraction by the reciprocal of the second fraction. For example, $\frac{1}{3} \div \frac{1}{4} = \frac{1}{3} \times \frac{4}{1}$, which equals $\frac{4}{3}$.

➤ A mixed fraction consists of a whole number and a fraction. For example, $3\frac{5}{6}$ means $3 + \frac{5}{6}$.

Decimals

The following are properties of decimals that are often tested on the GRE.

➤ Place value refers to the value of a digit in a number relative to its position. Starting from the left of the decimal point, the values of the digits are ones, tens, hundreds, and so on. Starting to the right of the decimal point, the values of the digits are tenths, hundredths, thousandths, and so on.

➤ When adding and subtracting decimals, be sure to line up the decimal points. For example:

$$
\begin{array}{r}
236.78 \\
+\ 113.21 \\
\hline
349.99
\end{array}
\qquad \text{and} \qquad
\begin{array}{r}
78.90 \\
-\ 23.42 \\
\hline
55.48
\end{array}
$$

➤ When multiplying decimals, it is not necessary to line up the decimal points. Simply multiply the numbers, then count the total number of places to the right of the decimal points in the decimals being multiplied to determine placement of the decimal point in the product.
For example:

$$
\begin{array}{r}
173.248 \\
\times\quad\ .35 \\
\hline
60.63680
\end{array}
$$

➤ When dividing decimals, first move the decimal point in the divisor to the right until the divisor becomes an integer. Then move the decimal point in the dividend the same number of places. For example, $58.345 \div 3.21 = 5834.5 \div 321$. You can then perform the long division with the decimal point in the correct place in the quotient.

Ratio, Proportion, and Percent

The following are properties of ratios, proportions, and percents that are often tested on the GRE.

➤ A ratio expresses a mathematical comparison between two quantities. A ratio of 1 to 5, for example, is written as either $\frac{1}{5}$ or 1:5.

➤ A proportion indicates that one ratio is equal to another ratio.

➤ When working with ratios, be sure to differentiate between part-part and part-whole ratios. If two components of a recipe are being compared to each other, for example, this is a part-part ratio (2 cups of flour:1 cup of sugar). If one group of students is being compared to the entire class, for example, this is a part-whole ratio (13 girls:27 students).

➤ The term percent means per one hundred. So, $52\% = \frac{52}{100} = .52$.

➤ To calculate the percent that one number is of another number, set up a proportion:

➤ What percent of 40 is 5?

➤ 5 is to 40 as x is to 100

➤ $\frac{5}{40} = \frac{x}{100}$

➤ Cross multiply and solve for x:

➤ $40x = 500$

➤ $x = \frac{500}{40} = 12.5$

➤ 5 is 12.5% of 40

Squares and Square Roots

The following are properties of squares and square roots that are often tested on the GRE.

➤ Squaring a negative number yields a positive result.

➤ The square root of a number, n, is written as $\sqrt{n}$, or the nonnegative value a that fulfills the expression $a^2 = n$.

➤ A number is considered a perfect square when the square root of that number is a whole number. For example, 25 is a perfect square because $5^2 = 25$, and 5 is a whole number.

Arithmetic and Geometric Sequences

The following are properties of arithmetic and geometric sequences that are often tested on the GRE.

➤ An arithmetic sequence is one in which the difference between one term and the next is the same. To find the nth term, use the formula:

$a_n = a_1 + (n-1)d$, where d is the common difference

➤ A geometric sequence is one in which the ratio between two terms is constant. For example, $\frac{1}{2}$, 1, 2, 4, 8..., is a geometric sequence where 2 is the constant ratio. To find the nth term, use the formula $a_n = a_1(r)^{n-1}$, where r is the constant ratio.

The Number Line

The set of all real numbers (including integers, fractions, square roots, and so on) has a natural order, which can be represented by a number line. Every real number corresponds to a point on the line.

Factors and Multiples

The following are properties of factors and multiples that are often tested on the GRE.

➤ A prime number is any number that can only be divided by itself and 1.

➤ Factors are all the numbers that will divide evenly into one number. For example, 1, 2, 4, and 8 are all factors of 8.

➤ Common factors include all the factors that two or more numbers share. For example, 1, 2, 4, and 8 are all factors of 8, and 1, 2, 3, and 6 are all factors of 6. Therefore, 8 and 6 have common factors of 1 and 2.

➤ The greatest common factor (GCF) is the largest number that will divide evenly into any two or more numbers. For example, 1, 2, 4, and 8 are all factors of 8, and 1, 2, 3, and 6 are all factors of 6. Therefore, the greatest common factor of 8 and 6 is 2.

➤ A number is a multiple of another number if it can be expressed as the product of that number and a second number. For example, $2 \times 3 = 6$, so 6 is a multiple of both 2 and 3.

➤ Common multiples include all of the multiples that two or more numbers share. For example, $3 \times 4 = 12$; $3 \times 8 = 24$; $3 \times 12 = 36$.

In addition, $4 \times 3 = 12$; $4 \times 6 = 24$; $4 \times 9 = 36$

12, 24, and 36 are all common multiples of both 3 and 4.

➤ The least common multiple (LCM) is the smallest number that any two or more numbers will divide evenly into. For example, the smallest number that 3, 4, and 5 divide into evenly is 60 ($3 \times 4 \times 5$).

➤ The arithmetic mean is equivalent to the average of a series of numbers. Calculate the average by dividing the sum of all of the numbers in the series by the total count of numbers in the series. For example, a student received scores of 80%, 85%, and 90% on three math tests. The average score received by the student on those tests is 80 + 85 + 90 divided by 3, or $\frac{255}{3}$, which is 85%.

➤ The median is the middle value of a series of numbers. In the series (2, 4, 6, 8, 10), the median is 6.

➤ The mode is the number that appears most frequently in a series of numbers. In the series (2, 3, 3, 4, 5, 6, 7), the mode is 3.

➤ The commutative property of multiplication is expressed as $a \times b = b \times a$, or $ab = ba$. For example, $2 \times 3 = 3 \times 2$.

➤ The Distributive property of multiplication is expressed as $a(b + c) = ab + ac$. For example, $x(x + 3) = x^2 + 3x$.

Absolute Value

Absolute value describes the distance of a number on the number line from 0, without considering which direction from 0 the number lies. Therefore, absolute value will always be positive.

Algebra and Functions

These questions can involve rules of exponents, factoring, solving equations and inequalities, solving linear and quadratic equations, setting up equations to solve word problems, coordinate geometry (slope, y-intercept, x-intercept, graphs), and functions.

Factoring

The following are properties of factoring that are often tested on the GRE.

➤ The standard form of a simple quadratic expression is $ax^2 + bx + c$, where a, b, and c are whole numbers. $2x^2 + 4x + 4$ is a simple quadratic equation.

➤ To add or subtract polynomials, simply combine like terms. For example, $(2x^2 + 4x + 4) + (3x^2 + 5x + 16) = 5x^2 + 9x + 20$.

➤ To multiply polynomials, use the distributive property, expressed as $a(b + c) = ab + ac$. Also remember the *FOIL* method: Multiply the *F*irst terms, then the *O*utside terms, then the *I*nside terms, then the *L*ast terms. For example,

$2x(4x + 4) = 8x^2 + 8x$; and $(x + 2)(x - 2) = x^2 - 2x + 2x - 4$, or $x^2 - 4$.

➤ You might be required to find the factors or solution sets of certain simple quadratic expressions. A factor or solution set takes the form $(x \pm$ some number$)$. Simple quadratic expressions will usually have two of these factors or solution sets. For example, the solution sets of $x^2 - 4$ are $(x + 2)$ and $(x - 2)$.

➤ To find the common factor, simply look for the element that two expressions have in common. For example, $x^2 + 3x = x(x + 3)$.

➤ You might have to find the difference of two squares. For example, $a^2 - b^2 = (a+b)(a-b)$.

Exponents

The following are properties of exponents that are often tested on the GRE.

➤ $a^m \times a^n = a^{(m+n)}$

➤ $(a^m)^n = a^{mn}$

➤ $(ab)^m = a^m \times b^m$

➤ $\left[\dfrac{a}{b}\right]^m = \dfrac{a^m}{b^m}$

➤ $a^0 = 1$, when $a \neq 0$

➤ $a^{-m} = 1/a^m$, when $a \neq 0$

➤ $a/b^{-m} = ab^m$, when $b \neq 0$

Inequalities

The following are properties of inequalities that are often tested on the GRE.

➤ Greater than is expressed with this symbol: >

➤ Greater than or equal to is expressed with this symbol: ≥

➤ Less than is expressed with this symbol: <

➤ Less than or equal to is expressed with this symbol: ≤

➤ Inequalities can usually be worked with in the same way equations are worked with.

➤ When an inequality is multiplied by a negative number, you must switch the sign. For example, follow these steps to solve for x in the inequality $-2x + 2 < 6$:

  ➤ $-2x + 2 < 6$

  ➤ $-2x < 4$

  ➤ $-x < 2$

  ➤ $x > -2$

Word Problems

When solving word problems, translate the verbal statements into algebraic expressions. For example:

➤ Greater than, more than, and sum of means addition (+)

➤ Less than, fewer than, and difference means subtraction (−)

➤ Of and by means multiplication (×)

➤ Per means division (÷, or /)

Functions

The following are properties of functions that are often tested on the GRE.

➤ A function is a set of ordered pairs in which no two of the ordered pairs has the same x-value. In a function, each input (x-value) has exactly one output (y-value). For example, $f(x) = 2x + 3$. If $x = 3$, then $f(x) = 9$. For every x, there is only one $f(x)$, or y.

➤ The *domain* of a function refers to the *x*-values, whereas the *range* of a function refers to the *y*-values.

Coordinate Geometry

The following are properties of coordinate geometry that are often tested on the GRE.

➤ The (*x*,*y*) coordinate plane is defined by two axes at right angles to each other. The horizontal axis is the *x*-axis, and the vertical axis is the *y*-axis.

➤ The origin is the point (0,0), where the two axes intersect, as shown in Figure B.1.

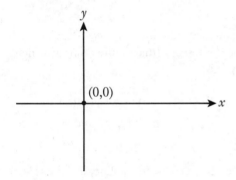

Figure B.1 The origin.

➤The slope of a line is calculated by taking the change in *y*-coordinates divided by the change in *x*-coordinates from two given points on a line. The formula for slope is $m = (y_2 - y_1) / (x_2 - x_1)$, where (x_1, y_1) and (x_2, y_2) are the two given points. For example, the slope of a line that contains the points (3,6) and (2,5) is equivalent to (6–5)/(3–2), or $\frac{1}{1}$, which equals 1.

➤ A positive slope means the graph of the line goes up and to the right. A negative slope means the graph of the line goes down and to the right. A horizontal line has slope 0, whereas a vertical line has an undefined slope, as shown in Figure B.2

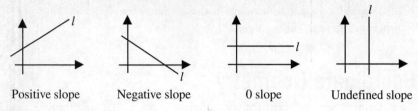

| Positive slope | Negative slope | 0 slope | Undefined slope |

Figure B.2 Slope direction.

➤ Two lines are parallel if and only if they have the same slope.

➤ Two lines are perpendicular if and only if the slope of one of the lines is the negative reciprocal of the slope of the other line. In other words, if line a has a slope of 2, and line b has a slope of $-\frac{1}{2}$, the two lines are perpendicular.

➤ The slope-intercept form of the equation of a line is $y = mx + b$, where m is the slope of the line and b is the y-intercept (that is, the point at which the graph of the line crosses the y-axis).

➤ To find the distance between two points in the (x,y) coordinate plane, use the following formula $\sqrt{([x_2-x_1]^2+[y_2-y_1]^2)}$, where (x_1, y_1) and (x_2, y_2) are the two given points.

➤ To find the midpoint of a line given two points on the line, use the following formula:

$$\left(\frac{[x_1 + x_2]}{2}, \ \frac{[y_1 + y_2]}{2}\right)$$

➤ A translation slides an object in the coordinate plane to the left or right, or up or down. The object retains its shape and size, and faces in the same direction.

➤ A reflection flips an object in the coordinate plane over either the x-axis or the y-axis. When a reflection occurs across the x-axis, the x-coordinate remains the same, but the y-coordinate is transformed into its opposite. When a reflection occurs across the y-axis, the y-coordinate remains the same, but the x-coordinate is transformed into its opposite. The object retains its shape and size.

Geometry

These questions can involve parallel and perpendicular lines, circles, triangles, rectangles, and other polygons, as well as area, perimeter, volume, and angle measure in degrees.

Quadrilaterals, Lines, Angles

The following are properties of quadrilaterals, lines, and angles that are often tested on the GRE.

➤ A line is generally understood to be a straight line.

➤ A line segment is the part of a line that lies between two points on the line.

➤ Two distinct lines are said to be parallel if they lie in the same plane and do not intersect.

➤ Two distinct lines are said to be perpendicular if their intersection creates right angles.

➤ In a parallelogram, the opposite sides are of equal length, and the opposite angels are equal.

➤ The area of a parallelogram is A = (base)(height).

➤ A rectangle is a polygon with four sides (two sets of congruent, or equal sides) and four right angles. All rectangles are parallelograms.

➤ The sum of the angles in a rectangle is always 360 degrees.

➤ The perimeter of both a parallelogram and a rectangle is P = $2l + 2w$, where l is the length and w is the width.

➤ The area of a rectangle is A = lw.

➤ The lengths of the diagonals of a rectangle are congruent, or equal.

➤ A square is a special rectangle where all four sides are of equal length. All squares are rectangles.

➤ When two parallel lines are cut by a transversal, each parallel line has four angles surrounding the intersection, that are matched in measure and position with a counterpart at the other parallel line. The vertical (opposite) angles are congruent, and the adjacent angles are supplementary (they total 180°), as shown in Figure B.3.

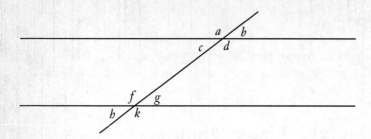

Figure B.3 Parallel lines cut by a transversal.

As you just saw in Figure B.4, the following calculations hold true:

➤ a = d = f = k

➤ b = c = g = h

➤ a + b = 180°

➤ c + d = 180°

➤ f + g = 180°

➤ *h* + *k* = 180°

➤ An acute angle is any angle that is less than 90°.

➤ An obtuse angle is any angle that is greater than 90° and less than 180°.

➤ A right angle is an angle that measures exactly 90°.

Triangles

The following are properties of triangles that are often tested on the GRE.

➤ In an equilateral triangle, all three sides have the same length.

➤ In an isosceles triangle, two sides have the same length.

➤ The sides of a 3-4-5 right triangle have the ratio 3:4:5.

➤ The sum of the interior angles in a triangle is always 180°.

➤ The perimeter of a triangle is the sum of the lengths of the sides.

➤ The area of a triangle is A = $\frac{1}{2}$ (base)(height).

➤ The Pythagorean Theorem states that $c^2 = a^2 + b^2$, where *c* is the hypotenuse of the triangle and *a* and *b* are two sides of the triangle.

➤ Figure B.4 demonstrates angle measures and side lengths for special right triangles.

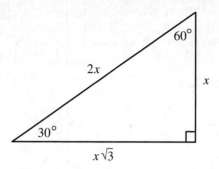

Figure B.4   Special right triangle.

Circles

The following are properties of circles that are often tested on the GRE.

➤ The radius (r) of a circle is the distance from the center of the circle to any point on the circle.

➤ The diameter (d) of a circle is twice the radius.

➤ The area of a circle is $A = \pi r^2$.

➤ The circumference of a circle is $C = 2\pi r$, or $C = \pi d$.

➤ The equation of a circle centered at the point (h,k) is $(x - h)^2 + (y - k)^2 = r^2$, where r is the radius of the circle.

➤ The complete arc of a circle has 360°.

➤ A tangent to a circle is a line that touches the circle at exactly one point.

Other Polygons

The following are properties of other polygons that are often tested on the GRE.

➤ A pentagon is a five-sided figure, as shown in Figure B.5.

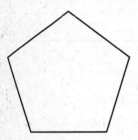

Figure B.5 Pentagon

➤ The sum of the interior angles of a pentagon is (5 – 2)(180°), or 540°.

➤ A hexagon is a six-sided figure, as shown in Figure B.6.

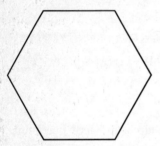

Figure B.6 Hexagon

➤ The sum of the interior angles of a hexagon is (6 – 2)(180°), or 720°.

➤ An octagon is an eight-sided figure, as shown in Figure B.7.

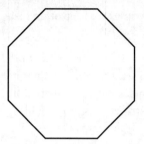

Figure B.7   Octagon

➤ The sum of the interior angles of a hexagon is $(8 - 2)(180°)$, or $1,080°$.

Three-Dimensional Figures

The following are properties of three-dimensional figures that are often tested on the GRE.

➤ The formula for the volume of a rectangular solid is $V = lwh$, where l = length, w = width, and h = height.

➤ The surface area of a rectangular solid is the sum of the area of the six faces of the solid. The formula for the surface area of a rectangular solid is $A = 2(wl + lh + wh)$, where l = length, w = width, and h = height.

Data Analysis

These questions can involve elementary probability, statistics (mean, median, mode, percentiles), and interpretation of line graphs, bar graphs, circle graphs, and tables.

➤ Carefully read the labels on the tables, charts, or graphs.

➤ Make sure that you understand the relationships between the data represented in the graphs.

Probability and Outcomes

The following are properties of probability and outcomes that are often tested on the GRE.

➤ Probability refers to the likelihood that an event will occur. For example, Jeff has three striped and four solid ties in his closet; therefore, he has a total of seven ties in his closet. He has three chances to grab a striped tie out of the seven total ties, because he has three striped ties. So, the likelihood of Jeff grabbing a striped tie is 3 out of 7, which can also be expressed as 3:7, or $\frac{3}{7}$.

➤ Two specific events are considered independent if the outcome of one event has no effect on the outcome of the other event. For example, if you toss a coin, there is a 1 in 2, or $\frac{1}{2}$ chance that it will land on either heads or tails. If you toss the coin again, the outcome will be the same. To find the probability of two or more independent events occurring together, multiply the outcomes of the individual events. For example, the probability that both coin-tosses will result in heads, is $\frac{1}{2} \times \frac{1}{2}$, or $\frac{1}{4}$.

Need to Know More

The purpose of this book is to help you prepare for the GRE. Although this book provides you with helpful information about the test and realistic practice materials to get you ready for the real thing, the following additional resources might also be useful in your preparation:

➤ The official GRE website at http://www.gre.org offers a wealth of up-to-date information about the GRE. After you get to the "Test Takers" section of the website, you can find out about test locations and fees, register for the test, learn about your score report, order additional score reports, and more.

➤ *Practicing to Take the General Test, 10th Edition* (ISBN 0886852129), published by the Educational Testing Service, is a great source of practice material for the GRE. This book is usually available at all the major bookstores. Pick one up as a great complement to *GRE Exam Cram*. Or, you can order it online at http://www.study-smart.com/gradschool.htm.

➤ Advantage Education offers many programs for students planning to go to graduate school, including programs that prepare students for the GRE and GMAT, as well as Admissions Counseling. To learn about individual tutoring, workshops, courses, and other programs, visit http://www.study-smart.com.

➤ High school and college textbooks are extremely valuable resources. The content areas tested on the GRE Quantitative Section are the same content areas that you studied in high school, and perhaps college. Hence, textbooks cover many of the relevant skills and subjects you will need for success on the GRE. If you do not have your textbooks, your school library should have copies that you can use.

➤ Don't forget to talk to professors and students who have some experience with the GRE. They might be able to shed some additional light on getting ready for the test. It is in your best interest to be as well prepared as possible on test day.

Index

How can we make this index more useful? Email us at indexes@quepublishing.com

J – K – L

kind/type (analogy relationships), 36

LCM (least common multiple), 87
linear equalities with one variable, 100-101
linear equations with one variable, 95-96
lines, 235
  equations, 104
  segments, 106
logic, applying (quantitative comparison question answer strategies), 82

M

main idea/primary purpose questions (Reading Comprehension questions), answer strategies, 71
main ideas, determining (Reading Comprehension questions), 66-68
math references
  algebra and functions
    coordinate geometry, 233-234
    exponents, 231
    factors, 231
    functions, 232
    inequalities, 232
    word problems, 232
  arithmetic
    absolute values, 230
    arithmetic sequences, 229
    decimals, 227
    factors, 229-230
    fractions, 226-227
    geometric sequences, 229
    integers, 225-226
    multiples, 229-230
    number lines, 229

order of operations (PEDMAS), 226
    percents, 228
    proportions, 228
    rational numbers, 226-227
    ratios, 228
    square roots, 228
    squares, 228
  data analysis, 239-240
  geometry
    angles, 235
    circles, 237
    hexagons, 238
    lines, 235
    octagons, 239
    pentagons, 238
    quadrilaterals, 235
    rectangular solids, 239
    triangles, 236
mean, 95
median, 95
midpoint formulas (geometry), 106-107
mixed numbers, converting to improper fraction, 89
mode, 95
multi-step questions, answering (quantitative comparison question answer strategies), 82
multiple choice questions, Quantitative sections, 80
multiples, 87, 229-230
multiplication
  Associative Property of Multiplication, 86
  Commutative Property of Multiplication, 86
  Distributive Property of Multiplication, 86
  fractions, 88
  polynomials, 98

R